G

THE
PLATEAU TONGA

THE
PLATEAU TONGA
OF NORTHERN RHODESIA (ZAMBIA)

Social and Religious Studies

by

ELIZABETH COLSON

Professor of Anthropology
University of California, Berkeley
Sometime Director of the
Rhodes-Livingstone Institute

Published on behalf of
THE INSTITUTE FOR SOCIAL RESEARCH
UNIVERSITY OF ZAMBIA
by
MANCHESTER UNIVERSITY PRESS

© E. COLSON 1962
Published by the University of Manchester
at the UNIVERSITY PRESS
316–324 Oxford Road, Manchester, M13 9NR

Distributed in the U.S.A. by
HUMANITIES PRESS, INC.
303 Park Avenue South, New York, N.Y. 10010

First published 1962
Reprinted 1970

GB SBN 7190 1011 X

Printed in Great Britain by Butler & Tanner Ltd., Frome and London

FOREWORD

DR. ELIZABETH COLSON ended her first spell of field research for the Rhodes–Livingstone Institute among the Plateau Tonga of Northern Rhodesia in September 1947: four months later, in January 1948, she read the first paper analysing her data to a meeting of the Royal Anthropological Institute, the paper on 'Rain-shrines' reproduced here. Her fascinated audience immediately realized that they were listening to one of the greatest anthropologists of the post-war generation, for this first paper showed that Dr. Colson had an original insight, a vivid and intuitive analytical ability, and great skill as a field worker. These gifts are demonstrated throughout this series of essays: for example, the essay on rain-shrines grasps magnificently the manner in which ephemeral shrines, serving hundreds of small communities, slow the drift of people through thousands of apparently formless moves, while the essays on the linkages set up by loans of cattle and by residential moves of people exhibit the meticulous and comprehensive data which underly her analytic vision.

Before Dr. Colson came to work in Africa, she had carried out a year's study of *The Makah Indians*[1] of Washington; and her book reporting this study confirmed the reputation established by her early papers on the Tonga. It analyses how a small community of Red Indians continues to maintain its identity, and preserve something of its cultural heritage, despite external pressures and internal schisms. Many passages in it—I consider particularly the section on scandal and gossip and slander—opened quite new lines of interpretation in anthropology. When she published a general account of the Tonga in *Seven Tribes of British Central Africa*,[2] and papers on several aspects of Tonga political life, we realized that through her analyses we were learning about a quite

---

[1] Manchester University Press, 1953.
[2] Ed. Colson and Gluckman, Oxford University Press for the Rhodes–Livingstone Institute, 1951; Manchester University Press, 1960 and 1961.

new type of society. For the Tonga, as she says,

> might be defined as culturally a have-not group. They have never had
> an organized state. They were unwarlike and had neither regimental
> organization nor armies. They were and are equally lacking in an age-
> grade set-up, secret societies, and social stratification of all kinds. The
> Tonga would not even attract those fascinated by the intricate rules of
> lineage organization, for while they have clans and smaller matrilineal
> kin-groups, they have them in a characteristically unorganized fashion
> which leaves the investigator baffled, and with a frustrated desire to
> reorganize their social structure into some more ordered system. It is
> only in the rain-rituals and their associated shrines that the Tonga show
> a half-hearted groping towards the establishment of a larger com-
> munity than that which existed in the village or in the ties of kinship . . .
> ('Rain-shrines').

These essays trace the significance of a series of ties and linkages
to show that in its very formlessness Tonga society has a structure
which exerts some control over its individualistic members. This
society exhibits, through Dr. Colson's analysis, better than any
other I know, how a criss-cross of allegiances and conflicts, a multiple 'web of group affiliations' (Simmel), maintains considerable
order in the absence of a governmental hierarchy of authority:

> Tonga society, despite its lack of political organization and political
> unity, is a well-integrated entity, knit together by the spread of kinship
> ties within any one locality. It obtains its integration and its power to
> control its members and the different groups in which they are aligned,
> by the integration of each individual into a number of different
> systems of relationships which overlap. When a man seeks to act in
> terms of his obligation to one set of relationships, he is faced by the
> counterclaims upon him of other groups with which he must also
> interact. This entanglement of claims leads to attempts to seek an
> equitable settlement in the interests of the public peace which alone
> enables the groups to perform their obligations to one another and a
> Tonga to live as a full member of his society ('Social Control and
> Vengeance').

In this essay Dr. Colson analyses how pressures to resolve a dispute operate after a murder, by presenting a specific case and
tracing the influence of various kinds of social relations on the injured and injuring parties: I know of no equivalent treatment of
an African 'stateless' society. And she goes on, in my opinion

rightly, to point out that the same sorts of processes are probably effective 'in societies organized on the lineage principle, and that a further analysis of the data would show that these societies obtain their stability not because their groups are lineally organized, but because of the presence within each local group of people with a diverse set of ties linking them to those in other areas' (*ibid.*). This essay has stimulated much modern research and interpretation,[1] though its stimulus has not always been acknowledged.

I have been urging Dr. Colson to try to find time to weave together these several analyses of Tonga political life, ever since she published her detailed and penetrating study of *Marriage and the Family among the Plateau Tonga of Northern Rhodesia*.[2] I urged her thus because I felt that in the process of bringing them together, she would be able to bring out even more clearly her main points and show their mutual interdependence, while she would have more space to compare the Tonga with other societies and thus add more emphatically to our general theory. Particularly, I thought she should take space to compare her own analysis of joking-relationships between clans with others' analyses of this Central African institution, in the background of Radcliffe-Brown's theoretical treatment of joking. But secondly, I wanted her analysis of Tonga political organization to be available in an easily accessible form for teaching purposes. I consider that one of our first tasks as teachers about society is to get students to understand the multiple means by which values and customs attach individuals to different groups or to other individuals, and the effect of this 'conflict' of allegiances in social life. Dr. Colson writes so clearly and concisely, that even though her essays can inspire old practitioners to new research they are also intelligible on the surface to the neophyte. For years therefore we at Manchester have been distributing to our students cyclostyled copies of some of these articles.

I had hopes of succeeding in persuading Dr. Colson, despite her

---

[1] E.g. my own re-analysis of the Nuer, in Chapter 1 of *Custom and Conflict in Africa*, Blackwell, 1955.

[2] Manchester University Press for the Rhodes–Livingstone Institute, 1958.

own modest evaluation of her work, to carry out this rewriting, when she was invited to undertake a new piece of research in Africa. The Federal Government of the Rhodesias and Nyasaland was planning to dam the Zambezi at the Kariba Gorge, and this would drown the homeland of the Gwembe Valley Tonga (or We) cousins of the Plateau Tonga. Dr. Colson was invited by the Rhodes–Livingstone Institute to study these Valley Tonga, before they were moved out of their homelands, and then to do a follow-up study of them when they were settled in their new homes. She had to go to Rhodesia for a year, write her report,[1] then return for another field-trip and write another report. Clearly it would be many years before she could tackle the Plateau Tonga again, though her study of subtle and marked variations between them and the Valley people[2] has already enriched both pieces of work. I was therefore delighted when Mr. C. M. N. White, Acting Director of the Rhodes–Livingstone Institute, proposed that these essays be collected and re-published; and I was even more delighted when Dr. Colson asked me to write a 'Foreword' to the collection. *Faute de mieux*, this is better than leaving the essays scattered; indeed, collecting them is a very good second-best, to be commended to students of man in all disciplines and at all levels.

I hope still that this collection will not make Dr. Colson feel estopped from the major rewriting of her analysis of Plateau Tonga political organization, but that she will one day do it in comparison with their Valley cousins. I am sure that when she does this, even more will emerge. This is inevitable, and reflects in no way on the essays as they stand. Dr. Colson did not have space in these essays to consider fully and in detail the mutual interdependence of the various institutions she discusses—such as the connection between the very unusual rule for Africa that milk from a woman's marriage-cattle threatens ill to her uterine siblings, and the absence of segmentation and fixed genealogical positioning of individuals within the matrilineal kin-group, and

---

[1] See her *Social Organization of the Gwembe Tonga*, Manchester University Press for the Rhodes–Livingstone Institute, 1960.

[2] *Vide ibid.*

the relation of these facts to the absence of fixed positioning of ancestral spirits—incidentally, hers is the only report on an 'ancestral' system of this type. These points are all dealt with in their interconnections: but it is possible that a further working over would highlight them somewhat differently. I say this, even though I can only add to the extant analyses by suggesting one point I consider Dr. Colson might have weighted more. The Tonga are highly mobile: they move to settle with many different kinds of kin, or with mere clan-fellows, or even with strangers. The village headman has little if any authority. When before 1918 the British tried to set up chiefs, they recognized 116 leaders, for a population which by 1945, despite rapid increase, lay between 70,000 and 110,000. This shows graphically how little instituted authority there was. Only the small rain-shrine community marked the prototype of some organized political system, by imposing on neighbouring villages a few days of ritual peace and establishing a few ritual offences against the shrines. Dr. Colson states that these shrines were ephemeral, new ones arising and old ones becoming forgotten as new leaders emerge to replace older leaders in terms of new concatenations of alignments in neighbourhoods. Rain-shrines mostly served only a few square miles and perhaps four or five villages, though one or two had wider reputations. The shrines were approached to secure rain, good crops, freedom from epidemics and pestilences, all community goods affecting those who lived together. They did not affect the welfare or ill-faring of individuals. Their spirits, known as *basangu*, made themselves known by possessing individuals; but some of these *basangu* spirits might in another set of relationships be *mizimu* spirits, acting as guardians to their kinsfolk or afflicting these with ills to get their dues. The *basangu* spirits, and the good things sought from them, are related to the lives of men and women on particular areas of land. *Mizimu* spirits, unattached to locality, follow their kinsfolk where these go, and affect them differently.

For the kinship system, and especially the twelve dispersed, exogamous, matrilineal clans, embody another set of good things. This emerges in the essay on clan joking-relationships. Dr. Colson

seems to vary in her judgment on these clans. For example, in her
essay here on 'Social Control and Vengeance' she writes that these
clans

are dispersed groups without leaders or a corporate life to impress upon
their members the obligations of clanship. Clanship does not imply
common responsibility, though it mitigates hostility between fellow
clansmen. Effective organization is dependent upon much smaller
groups composed of those who consider themselves to be descended
by matrilineal links from a common ancestress, who recognize their
common obligations and rights, and who join in common action.
This is the group which should undertake the work of vengeance if
just claims are not satisfied.

But in her general account of the Tonga in *Seven Tribes of British
Central Africa*[1] she states that the Tonga think of clans as the most
important thing they have, though she qualifies this statement in
her essay on clan-joking: 'The clan is much less integrated than
the matrilineal group, and its functions are not as clearly defined.
True, the Tonga, even today, will argue that the clan system is
of the greatest importance in their lives, but this is because they
are usually thinking of the matrilineal group which is only
situationally distinguished from the clan of which it forms part.'
But she goes on immediately to stress the clans' importance: 'Still,
though the clan is widely dispersed and owns no property, has no
shrines, no common rites, no occasions on which all its members
gather for some common purpose, the clan is the single unit
in Tonga social life which has more than ephemeral existence.'
Villages and neighbourhoods break up, people move, matrilineal
groups are disrupted. Membership of the clans is attained at birth
and persists, save for the enslaved, and the clans persist: Tonga
regard it as 'an invariable human institution . . . find it practically
impossible to conceive of any society in which people are not
divided into clans'. I suggest that in the light of this perduring
character of the clans, an analysis of the duties of clan-joking
partners can be pushed a little further than Dr. Colson has
taken it.

---

[1] *Op. cit.*

In brief, clan-jokers, known by a term whose root is 'sister's child', are privileged to upbraid their fellows in the following situations. They shame a man or woman who has so misbehaved as to incur community disapproval, which his matrilineal kin cannot express since these kin are required to help one another. Clan-jokers also chide those who waste their kin's property, who commit incest, who try to commit suicide. They deal with the ill omen of a collapsed granary. They bury suicides and lepers. They clown at funerals to cheer up the survivors and to tell them to end mourning, alleging that the survivors killed the deceased by sorcery. Finally, they can in emergency in a ceremony stand for any kinsman who is not available. Surveying these duties, we see that the clan-jokers are concerned with morality, with care for property, with food, with maintaining the rules of exogamy that spin the network of kinship ties, with symbolizing all kinship, with preserving life, with burial of the ill-omened dead and urging life despite death. In Tonga society the observation of these rules cannot be urged by kinsmen lest they be suspected of denying their will to assist, or asserting a wish that the delinquent die in order that they take his property: 'strangers' undertake this duty, and they do so through a joking-relationship which proclaims a social interest in what a person does, while it emphasizes that they are not directly involved in his property relations: thus the institution fits Radcliffe-Brown's theory of joking-relationships.[1] The social interest in life, in property, in morality, in kinship, and in intermarriage of 'enemies', is thus attached to the only enduring groups of Tonga society. Hence the clans stand for an ultimate social morality, through the system which interlinks many clans as clan-jokers; and one set of values of social life are embodied in the only enduring groups, as other values are represented through rain-shrines.

In putting forward this suggestion I can only draw attention to the clan-jokers of the Tallensi, those who are friends of one's friends and friends of one's enemies; and to the fact that beyond

---

[1] See his essay in *Structure and Function in Primitive Society*, Cohen & West, 1952.

them lie the clans which exercise moral coercion on people, so that they can plead with him who is abandoning hope and he must heed them.[1] Again, I draw attention to the manner in which V. W. Turner analyses the Ndembu as a society whose values of unity are embodied in the cults of affliction.[2] The ultimate values of a 'society' tend to be attached to the most permanent groups of large-scale organization, or to the most authoritative persons, as Fortes and Evans-Pritchard pointed out in their discussion of why mystical values are attached to political office.[3] But since (as they also showed) conflicts ensue between those who are closely associated in pursuing these values, the task of symbolizing those values may be shifted on to 'strangers'—and the Tonga institution of clan-joking is a notable example of this rule.

I must not take more on myself than I have been invited to do. I hope my brief hint of the type of enquiry which arises from Dr. Colson's essays, will show that the inspiration of her work extends even beyond her own achievement—and that achievement in itself, is sufficient warranty of the value of this book.

Max Gluckman

Department of Social Anthropology
University of Manchester
October 1961

---

[1] M. Fortes, *Dynamics of Clanship among the Tallensi*, Oxford University Press for the International African Institute, 1945, pp. 91 f.

[2] *Schism and Continuity in an African Society*, Manchester University Press for the Rhodes–Livingstone Institute, 1957.

[3] Introduction to *African Political Systems*, Oxford University Press for the International African Institute, 1940, p. 16.

CONTENTS

TABLES

DIAGRAMS

MAP

PREFACE

THE seven articles which are now being published together under a single cover are the result of field work carried out among the Plateau Tonga under the auspices of the Rhodes-Livingstone Institute. The work was financed by a grant from the Colonial Development and Welfare Fund. The sections on rain-shrines and on modern political organization were written after I had worked among the Plateau Tonga for one year, 1946–7. The other parts were written after the completion of my work and incorporate information obtained also in 1948–50. All appear here as originally published with one exception. When I wrote of the system of clan joking-relationships, I ventured to generalize for the Gwembe Tonga as well as for the Plateau Tonga although at that time I had spent only one month in the Gwembe Valley. Subsequent field work, in 1956–7, led to the discovery that a portion of the Gwembe people do not have clan-joking. I have therefore made a few minor corrections (in square brackets) in the original article.

My thanks are due to the editors of *Africa*, *The Rhodes-Livingstone Journal*, the *Kroeber Anthropological Society Publications*, *The International Archives for Ethnography*, and *African Studies* for permission to republish material which originally appeared in these journals. Full details about where the chapters in this book first appeared are given at the end of the bibliography.

I wish to acknowledge also the assistance of my Tonga informants, of Government officials, of my clerk and interpreter, Mr. Benjamin Sipopa, of Mr. Mathias M. Chona, who verified a number of points for me after I had left the field, and of Professor M. Gluckman and Dr. I. G. Cunnison for their help and criticism of the original manuscript. Finally I must thank Professor M. Gluckman for graciously consenting to write a foreword to the collection.

E. C.

PREFACE TO THE SECOND EDITION

IT is now twenty-two years since the first of the essays included in this volume was written. In the intervening years the colonial Northern Rhodesia to which they refer has become the independent country of Zambia. Children who were growing up in the villages where I lived in the nineteen forties have been to university and some are now playing important roles in world events. Mazabuka District has been divided into Mazabuka and Choma Districts. The very landscape has changed as the old compact villages have scattered out into discreet homesteads. I have paid brief visits to old friends in the area on various occasions since I finished my concentrated research among the Plateau Tonga in 1950, and realize something of the enormous changes which have taken place in the last two decades. At the same time it seems inappropriate to attempt to rewrite these essays written at a time when I was immersed in the life of the area and knew much more about it than I do today. They must stand therefore as a record of a particular era in the life of a people who have seen many changes in the thousand years or so that they have been occupying this particular part of Zambia. I would call the reader's attention to the existence of one additional article which supplements and updates material included here. This is the article written by myself and Mark Chona, 'Marketing of cattle among Plateau Tonga', which appeared in *Human Problems in Central Africa*, No. 37, pp. 42–50, 1965.

CHAPTER I

ANCESTRAL SPIRITS AND SOCIAL STRUCTURE AMONG THE PLATEAU TONGA

IN this chapter, I am going to describe beliefs held by the Plateau Tonga about the activities of a particular type of spirits, the *mizimu*, and attempt to show how these reflect the ideal organization of Tonga social structure. The term *mizimu* (*muzimu* in the singular) is usually translated by anthropologists as 'ancestral spirits', but I shall use the native term since this translation does not cover the various ways in which the Tonga use the term and I can find no adequate English equivalent.

I have already published a sketch of Tonga social organization.[1] I need only say here in introduction that the Plateau Tonga are a Bantu-speaking people inhabiting Mazabuka District in the Southern Province of Northern Rhodesia. Their number today has been variously estimated as between 80,000 and 120,000 people. Until British Administration introduced a Native Authority system, they had no large-scale political organization of their own. The basis of their own system was twofold: an organization into a large number of small dispersed groups of matrilineal kinsmen, and an organization into local neighbourhoods composed of a few villages with a common rain shrine and cult. Although the rain shrines no longer hold the allegiance of many Tonga, the local neighbourhoods continue. To most Tonga they are of greater importance than the chiefdoms or the Plateau Tonga

---

[1] See Colson, 1951. Most of the time I was collecting material for this chapter I lived in villages in the area east of the Northern Rhodesian railway, and my account is therefore most reliable for the eastern people and may not apply to all Tonga. However, I worked in two chiefdoms in the west during my first tour and attempted to check my material with informants drawn from the whole of Tonga country. In 1949, I spent a month in the Gwembe District among the Tonga of the Zambezi Valley. They are closely related to the people on the Plateau. In the course of this chapter, I have noted variations in their customs from those described for the Plateau.

Native Authority which have been imposed upon the old structure. The matrilineal groups are still important units, although
their functions have been curtailed with the outlawing of self-help
and the institution of courts. They have also been affected by the
diminished importance of the cult of the *mizimu* which is an
integral element in the organization of such groups.

In this chapter, I shall write as though all the Tonga still held to
the old beliefs about the *mizimu*. This, of course, is not true.
Missions have worked in the area since 1905. Many Tonga are
Christians, of eight different sects. Others are sceptics who deny
the old beliefs without accepting those introduced by the missionaries. Many claim that they have forgotten the *mizimu*, and
that these no longer affect them in any way. There are whole
villages where no one makes offerings to the *mizimu* or considers
them in any way. On the other hand, there are many Tonga to
whom the *mizimu* are a vital part of life. They would claim, along
with the old man who heard a woman suggest that the *mizimu*
had disappeared since people stopped believing in them: 'No, the
mizimu can never die. They will always be there affecting us.'

Little specific information has been published about the Tonga
beliefs in the *mizimu*, though many have referred to the cult. I
have not attempted to draw this scattered material together and
evaluate it. Much of it is contradictory, and from it no coherent
picture emerges.[1]

THE 'MIZIMU' AND THEIR CULT

The Tonga are constantly making offerings to the *mizimu*.
There are the regular offerings made by all adult men and women
whether they are involved in any misfortune or not. They have
been taught that on certain occasions offerings must be made, and
they have learned the names of the *mizimu* which they must call.
Changes in the location of a household must be announced to the
mizimu, by offerings made before leaving the old dwelling and
soon after entering into the new one. Changes in status must be

---

[1] Myers, 1927, and Hopgood, 1950, are the most lengthy accounts. The latter
discusses the *mizimu* with reference to beliefs in God.

announced, as when a household is instituted for the first time, when a man first builds his own cattle kraal, when a man obtains a new gun or plough or other major item of equipment such as a large iron pot. The initiation of some activity and its successful completion—a hunt, a fishing expedition, a journey to work in white country—call for offerings to the *mizimu*. So do the beginning and end of the agricultural year. At planting time, each local community carries out rites to ask for rain and good crops, and these are community rites in which the *mizimu* are not involved. But each family though it contributes beer for the general rite also privately asks its own *mizimu* for assistance. At harvest time, when the community again gathers to offer thanks for the harvest, each family also privately thanks its *mizimu* for help in making the crop. Finally, from time to time, a household should make beer especially for the *mizimu* though there is no special reason for doing so: 'Even if everything is going well with me, I should still make an offering for the *mizimu* to tell them that I am all right and that I want to continue to be all right and that they should help me just as they have been doing.' Even though beer is brewed primarily for sale, or for gaiety, it is also considered to be made for the *mizimu*, at least among conservative people.

These offerings are concerned with a single household, though large numbers may come to the beer drink which follows later in the day. On two other occasions, large numbers of people gather for offerings to the *mizimu* of their line, and these occasions are not the primary concern of a single household. Offerings to the ancestors form part of the ritual of a girl's puberty ceremony and also of the ritual of the final mourning after a death. But these too are set occasions, when the offerings are made because it is customary to do so.

The *mizimu* are also important in another sphere, as causal explanations evoked to account for illness or other misfortune which has befallen some individual. *Mizimu* are not the only spirit agency which may be involved, and it is necessary to consult a diviner to have the cause of the misfortune identified. If the diviner indicates that the *mizimu* are involved, he will also name some particular *muzimu* and announce that it is angry because it has been neglected. Either it has not been called when offerings have been made, or the offender has been dilatory in making offerings. The remedy is a special offering at which the offended *muzimu* is invoked by name and assured that it will henceforth be remembered.

Besides the *mizimu* and the High God, known as Leza,[1] the Tonga distinguish three other types of spirits which have the power to affect living people. These are the *basangu*, which are effective in affairs of general community interest and which make their demands known through people whom they possess;[2] the *masabe*, which are described as the spirits of animals or of foreigners and which cause illness to those whom they possess until these learn the dances appropriate to the possessing spirit;[3] the *zelo* (*celo* in the singular), which we may call the ghosts of dead people.

If the Tonga are asked to describe these spirits and the *mizimu* and to explain how they differ from one another, they describe each group in terms of its actions. They are not concerned to analyse the nature of the spirits or their ultimate origin, nor are they concerned if the spirits are sometimes said to act in ways which are contrary to the general dogma which relates them to human beings. 'We call them all wind (*luwo*) because they are invisible. We do not know what they look like. We know which is affecting us by the way in which it acts.' In the great majority of situations where the Tonga are concerned with spirits, it is either on a set occasion for an offering, in which they know the particular spirit involved because this is defined by the situation itself, or because they must deal with an effect which is disturbing to their lives. To remove the effect, they must first identify the causal agency, and this is generally done through the diviner. The identification of the agency defines in broad terms the appropriate

---

[1] See Hopgood, 1950, pp. 61–7, for an excellent description of Tonga concepts of Leza, who is regarded as the creator and the ultimate cause of all that happens.

[2] For a further discussion, see below, pp. 92–100.

[3] The *masabe* cult was introduced about 1906, apparently from the Karanga. See Casset, 1918, p. 104.

actions for dealing with the effects. If the action appears to be successful, this demonstrates that they have also been successful in identifying the agent. This ends their interest in the matter for the time being, and they do not feel that it is relevant to their purpose to enter further into the nature of the spirit agency. Since in general they are concerned with the spirits in moments of personal crisis, they have little reason to see how the belief in the spirits is embedded in their social system nor are they troubled by inconsistencies or contradictions in what they believe. The anthropologist, however, is concerned with the social rather than the personal implications of the beliefs, and it is largely with this aspect that I shall deal in this chapter. Radcliffe-Brown has written: 'In my own experience it is in ancestor-worship that we can most easily discover and demonstrate the social function of a religious cult.' [1] Certainly among the Tonga, social structure and the cult of the *mizimu* are so intertwined that a study of one leads inevitably to the other.

The Nature of the 'Mizimu'

Mizimu and ghosts (*zelo*) are both thought to be the spirits of former living people, but the two are distinct. A few Tonga have told me that *mizimu* and ghosts are one and the same thing. Others have argued that the ghost exists only for the period between a death and the time when the kinsmen assemble for the final mourning rite and that this transforms the ghost into the *muzimu*. But most maintain that the two are completely different entities, and a study of their actions on different occasions is consistent with this interpretation and not with any identification of ghost and *muzimu*.

When a person dies, therefore, two spirits remain, one the *muzimu* and one the ghost. The ghost is always a newly created spirit, some saying that it originates in the dying breath. Not all people produce a new *muzimu* when they die, and I have never been able to get a clear statement as to how the *muzimu* originates.

---

[1] Radcliffe-Brown, 1952, p. 163.

Indeed, various people have told me: 'I have never been able to understand this myself, and I don't think anyone else does either.' There is general agreement, however, that only those who have achieved a certain status during their lifetime give rise to a new *muzimu* after death, while others leave behind them only the already existing *muzimu* associated with them since their naming. Once created, moreover, the *mizimu* are not immortal like the ghosts who are independent of the devotion of living people for their continued existence. When the living cease to remember the *mizimu* and no longer call upon them by name, they become nameless spirits wandering at large, who now work only for evil. 'They have become like ghosts.' Over these the living have no control, for in forgetting the names they have lost the means of summoning or propitiating the spirits.

Over ghosts, the living have no direct control, unless they are sorcerers, and ghosts are presumed to be only evil. They may act against the living of their own volition, or they may be agents of sorcerers who have pressed them into service. A sudden dangerous or mortal illness is therefore usually attributed to ghosts. The *muzimu* is not actively evil in the same way. It may cause injury to the living, but this is not its primary purpose, nor is it free like the ghost to cause injury to anyone with whom it comes in contact. The *muzimu* is dependent upon the living for its own continued existence, and it causes injury to keep its memory alive in the living so that they may provide the offerings on which it depends. If the living refuse to listen to its demands, then it is thought to enlist the aid of the ghosts to inflict more drastic punishment. Some Tonga say that the *muzimu* travels always with the ghost which originated with it on a person's death and which acts as its intermediary with other ghosts.

The *muzimu* has its own ghost with it when it comes to ask for beer. If it receives nothing, then it becomes angry and says, "What can we do, my ghost? We alone cannot kill this man or make him very ill. We must go to the other ghosts." Then the ghost goes to invite all the ghosts to come and kill the person, and it accompanies them when they come with a rush to kill the man. The *muzimu* does not come that time, but it stands off and waits until the man is dead. Also the ghosts who actually kill are never those who come from your own kinsmen.[1] Never since we have been born have we known our own ghosts to kill us. It is always strange ghosts we find who have killed.

Here we are already faced with a contradiction in Tonga belief, for the Tonga hold that one type of sorcery is made effective by the owner using it to kill some relative whose ghost then works with him. While it helps its master to obtain fortune and success, it is nevertheless angry at having been killed and it demands the sacrifice of still further relatives in revenge.

Nevertheless, the distinction between ghosts and *mizimu* remains clear, and the *mizimu* are absolved by the Tonga of being the immediate cause of the death of their living kinsmen. Some indeed deny that *mizimu* ever kill. 'Long ago perhaps some people died because of the *mizimu*, but today they die only from sorcery, for envy and hatred are very great today.'

The *mizimu* are thought to be concerned that they should not be forgotten, and so they send sickness and other misfortune to the living as a reminder that beer and other offerings must be provided. They are anxious that the living should maintain the customs that they practised when they were alive, and therefore they punish departures from custom. In return they offer to the living some protection against other spirits and against sorcery. They should also assist the living to obtain the good things of life—children, good harvests, herds of cattle, and an orderly existence. These in turn permit the living to procure grain for beer, to marry wives who will brew the beer for offerings, and to perpetuate the names of the *mizimu* through the children whom they beget and who, to some extent, are regarded as the living representatives of the *mizimu*. The living propitiate the spirits to ensure for themselves the good things which they desire; the spirits assist the living to these goods so that they in turn may continue to exist. Each is dependent upon the other, and there is partnership

---

[1] I am using *kinsmen* to mean relatives of the matrilineal group, and therefore as an exact translation of the Tonga term, *basimukowa*. Paternal kinsmen will refer to members of the father's matrilineal group, the *bashanaushi*. This usage differs from the standard one, but it is more convenient than the long 'kinsmen of the matrilineal group' and 'kinsmen of the father's matrilineal group'.

between the living and the *mizimu* in achieving their common ends.

But the *mizimu* are not concerned with all the living, and the living are not concerned with all the *mizimu*. The relationships between them are a projection of those which exist between living persons organized in the kinship system. *Mizimu* and living members of a kinship group are parts of a single whole, and the ties between them transcend the bounds of time and space. Or rather, since the Tonga kinship system is not given a local focus, nor does an ordered genealogical framework or any scheme of historical incidents create a time scale into which the living and the *mizimu* can be fitted, the system exists outside time and space in a perpetual present.

INDIVIDUALS AND THEIR 'MIZIMU'

The Tonga maintain that the *mizimu* which are concerned with them, and therefore with which they are concerned, are the spirits of former members of the matrilineal kinship groups of their mothers and fathers, though they also say that the spirits of the matrilineal groups of their two grandfathers may occasionally intervene in their affairs. Nevertheless, it is the affiliation with the two parental groups which is primarily stressed in relation to the *mizimu*, as it is throughout social life. Some of these *mizimu*, however, are of more importance to an individual than are others. When a Tonga speaks of his *mizimu*, or refers to the *mizimu* of someone else, he may be using the term very broadly to include all those spirits which are concerned with him, or more narrowly to refer to particular *mizimu* who stand in a special relationship to him. His meaning is usually clear from the context. For analysis, however, it is necessary to distinguish the different uses of the term, and I shall therefore use the following classification in writing about the role of the *mizimu* in any one individual's life.

1. *Mizimu* as a general term includes all the spirits of former members of the lines of the father and mother, and may even be used still more generally for all the spirits of former

members of any group with which a person feels a kinship relationship. If I write of the *mizimu* of a matrilineal group, however, it refers only to the spirits of former members of this group.

2. Guardian *Mizimu* are those associated with the names which each person receives soon after birth. They act as his special guardians throughout life, and from them he is thought to derive his personality.

3. House *Mizimu* are the particular spirits which an adult person installs as the guardians of his household.

4. Inherited *Mizimu* are those which are associated with a person because he has been given the name of someone recently deceased as part of the funeral rites.

5. Own *Muzimu*. This is the new *muzimu* which comes into existence only after a person's death. No living person has his own *muzimu*.

The guardian *mizimu* have a special significance in each person's life. They can be regarded as symbolic representations of the overwhelming importance of the paternal and maternal matrilineal groups in determining the original social status of any individual, and of their responsibility for his wellbeing throughout life. Names are identified with *mizimu*, and the giving of a name implies assumption of social responsibility for a child. A man who begets a child by an unmarried woman may obtain the right to name his child, which is then affiliated to his matrilineal group and comes under the power of its *mizimu* in the same fashion as any child born in wedlock. A man who begets an adulterine child by a married woman has no such right. The woman's husband is the legal father. He names the child, thus bestowing upon it a guardian *muzimu*, and it comes under the protection of the *mizimu* of his line quite as much as do children he has begotten. The names which thus recognize the existence of the child and give it its initial place in society are bestowed some months after birth. The first name is given by the father or his relatives, and it is a name belonging to a former member of this line. The second is given by the mother's relatives and is the name of a former member of her line. Each name is associated with a *muzimu*. The Tonga say that the *mizimu* themselves may decide which of their living kin shall receive their names, and thus become their special charges. When a woman is in labour, the midwives call the names of various *mizimu*, saying, 'Nangoma, come forth! Mavwali, come forth! Nankambula, come forth! Cimuka, come forth!' The child should be born when they call the appropriate name, and they then know that it is this *muzimu* which has chosen to give its name to the child. They may have no such indication, and may later learn the appropriate name through divination. If the child becomes ill, the diviner may attribute the illness to the desire of a particular *muzimu* to give its name to the child. Even if the child's name has been decided at its birth, the name may still be changed since the guardian *muzimu* has failed in its duty by permitting the illness, or the relatives may decide that henceforth the child shall bear both names and both *mizimu* will be regarded as its guardians and as concerned with its fate. In addition, it will have a name and a guardian *muzimu* from the other parent's side. Occasionally the name is chosen by the relatives without any form of divination. However a name is chosen, it is not identified with the child until the time of the formal naming rite.

The Tonga deny that the guardian *mizimu* associated with its names are incarnate in the child,[1] and at any one time there may be many people who bear the name of the same *muzimu*. One informant said: 'We never say that a person has a *muzimu* (*ulamuzimu*) or that he is entered [*wanjilwa*] by a *muzimu*. We say that the *muzimu* looks after him (*wamulela*) or that it herds him (*wamwembela*).' Some have also told me: 'No person while he is living has a *muzimu* which is part of himself. He only becomes a *muzimu* after he dies.' Nevertheless, I have heard Tonga speak of a person as having a *muzimu* in the sense of a part of consciousness or personality. Thus, if a man dreams of another, it is said that their two *mizimu* have wandered forth in sleep and met. Some have also said that perhaps animals have *mizimu* because one some-

---

[1] Among the neighbouring Ila, according to Smith and Dale, *mizimu* are reincarnated in the living who bear their names. Cf. Smith and Dale, 1920, Vol. II, pp. 152–3.

times dreams of animals, but that perhaps it is only the ghost (*zelo*) of animals that one sees in dreams. When they are asked to explain the contradictions inherent in this use of the word *muzimu* when they have denied that a living person has a *muzimu* of his own, they do not see that it is a point worth discussing and are willing to permit both statements to stand without attempting to adjust them. They remain positive, however, that guardian *mizimu* are not reincarnated in their ward.

Despite this, a person is closely identified with the two guardian *mizimu* whose names he bears. He may be honoured by being addressed by the clan name of the father of either of these *mizimu* just as he is honoured by being addressed by the clan name of his own father. The two guardian *mizimu* are thought to determine his character and interests. They react to affairs that concern him as though the incidents were directed against themselves. If a man delays in his marriage payments, the diviner may find that the cause of his wife's barrenness, or the death or illness of her child, is due to the anger of either of her guardian *mizimu*. As one Tonga explained it: 'I gave my mother's name to my daughter. Now if my daughter's husband fails to pay his bridewealth, then the *muzimu* will become angry and say, "Why has this man married me without paying bridewealth? It is not a real marriage at all." And the *muzimu* will stop her from bearing a child, or if she does bear a child it will always be ill because the *muzimu* is angry.'

A person's evil deeds may be attributed to his guardian *mizimu*, as well as any particular skills or abilities or interests which mark him off from others. A man known as a troublemaker killed another during a beer drink. When his maternal relatives were discussing the matter, they said: 'Perhaps from his father's side he received a *muzimu* which has caused him to do this. What could he do? A man must work with the *mizimu* that belong to him.' Another explained once: 'If you name your child after a *muzimu* which is bad, the child will be bad. If you name it after someone who was fierce, the child will be fierce. Now X has killed a man. If X's *muzimu* is given to a child, that child too will grow to kill someone.' However, the Tonga might not be prepared to carry this argument to its ultimate conclusion in predestination. As one put it: 'Perhaps the *muzimu* whose name they gave to X makes him like that. We think his heart is not all right. Even among you Europeans there are people who are bad, who like to fight, who cannot understand what other people tell them. Such a person has only his own mind and cannot understand what others tell him. That is why we say sometimes that it is due to the *mizimu*. But we don't really know why a person should be like that.' Nevertheless, to most Tonga the obvious answer to any type of personal deviance is a reference to the guardian *mizimu*. In one area there was a persistent rumour that an immigrant from the Gwembe District was actually a woman, though 'she' dressed as a man, worked at men's occupations, and grew furious at any reference to 'her' sex. When I queried why 'she' should behave in this fashion, people shrugged their shoulders, expressed disgust, and then remarked that probably the *muzimu* after whom 'she' was named had behaved the same way when alive. It makes no difference to this argument that *mizimu* are vague abstractions, save for those who have died so recently that they were known personally to the living, or that the same name is borne by people of varying personalities. The Tonga do not argue that because one who bears a name has a certain nature that all of that name have that nature; nor do they say that the *muzimu* has a certain nature, and therefore those who bear its name will have this nature. They say only that the person's nature is such and therefore the guardian *muzimu* as a person was such.

If a person shows particular aptitudes, these may be attributed to the guardian *mizimu*, or other *mizimu* of the same lines may be thought to have given him the capacity to perform certain skills which they practised in their lifetime. The particular *muzimu* responsible may be identified through a dream or through divination. The Tonga recognize that even small children show different interests, and they think that these interests persist throughout life. By watching a small boy at play, you can tell whether as a man he will love cattle and acquire wealth, or whether he will be content to be a fisherman or hunter without much chance of growing rich. But it is hopeless to seek to change him, for his interests are determined by the *mizimu*. Diviners, hunters, blacksmiths, craftsmen who make wooden drums or mortars, basket-makers, and potters, all are thought to practise their skills under the direction of a *muzimu* which as a living person had had that skill.[1] Success in attaining a prominent position may be attributed to one's guardian *mizimu*, though others may whisper that it is due to sorcery. One man who through his own efforts had acquired wealth and importance as the headman of a large village spoke of his success as due to the guardian *muzimu* whose name be bore: 'Ndaba was an important man with many followers. Before I was born, his *muzimu* came and said that I should be called by his name. Now it is easy to see that I am indeed Ndaba, for I too have become an important man with many people who depend upon me.' There is no expectation that a *muzimu* will pass on its skills to all who bear its name—it may choose one or pass over all its namesakes to endow a person of another name with its skill. The Tonga do not seek to ensure the character and attributes of their children by the names which they bestow upon them, but as they observe character and attributes unfolding they turn to the *mizimu* as convenient explanations.

As an extension of this belief, a man's successes and failures are not his alone, but belong to the groups which have supplied him with a guardian *muzimu* and share with him a ritual attachment to it. When he dies, the two groups will take the property which he has accumulated. Members of his own matrilineal group will receive the larger portion, but a share is also due to the matrilineal group of his father.[2] While he lives, the two groups share responsibility for his actions. They should help him to pay damages for such offences as he commits. Both should defend him against the vengeance of others. Both should contribute to the marriage payments for his first wife. Responsibility is accepted the more easily because of the belief that the individual, at least to some extent, is merely the vehicle through which a *muzimu* continues to act— and the *muzimu* is common to them all.

The guardian *mizimu* may thus be viewed as symbols of the identification of a person with his kinship groups. But when as

---

[1] Cf. Colson, 1949, pp. 15–16.
[2] Cf. Colson, 1950.

an adult, he establishes his own independent household, he acquires a new social position. His household is one of the units in the local community, and he takes his place within the community as its head. Within the household are joined not only the interests of his own paternal and maternal matrilineal kinship groups, but also of the matrilineal groups of his wife. The importance of his new position is ritually recognized, for he now for the first time becomes capable of making offerings to the *mizimu*. At the same time, the new household is also given a ritual recognition, by the installation of one or more of the husband's *mizimu* as special guardians of the house. Significantly enough, these are rarely the husband's guardian *mizimu*, which stress his identification with his paternal and maternal kinship groups. These remain as his individual guardians, but henceforth his house *mizimu* will hold a dominant position in all that concerns him as his interests are centred in the well-being of his household.

The fact that he has achieved a position of his own is further recognized, for when he dies he himself will become a *muzimu*. Those who die before they set up a household leave behind them only the guardian *mizimu* of their names. I argue that this is because their social personality is still derived from attachment to their matrilineal groups, and their death is of concern only to these two groups. The head of a household is of importance to others besides his own paternal and maternal kinsmen, and his importance to his kinsmen is now at least partially a reflection of the position which he occupies in the community. This is given recognition by attributing to him a *muzimu* of his own when he dies.

At the same time, the primary affiliation of each person to his matrilineal kinsmen is stressed, for the new *muzimu* which he has created bears the name of his guardian *muzimu* from his maternal line, and it has power to affect only those of this line and their offspring. His death breaks the tie which has been created between his own matrilineal group and that of his father by their common interest in him. His father's group have no concern with his own *muzimu*, and it cannot affect them. Part of the funeral rite emphasizes the finality of the break with the father's line in contrast to the continuity with the maternal line. This is embodied in every funeral, whether or not a new *muzimu* is thought to be involved. For, although not every person becomes a *muzimu*, each person once named is associated with his guardian *mizimu*. Formerly, when a child died before it was named, there was no mourning, for no *mizimu* were involved. Even today, the old women will tell the mother to hush her wailing, saying that this is only a ghost (*celo*) or only a person (*muntu*), and the mourning is usually curtailed. But if a person dies after being named, someone must be chosen to inherit the *muzimu* (*kwanga muzimu*). This is the deceased's guardian *muzimu* from his maternal line in the case of one who dies before establishing a household; it is his own *muzimu* otherwise. The father's group come to the mourning, and they are said to take away with them the name which they gave to their child and with it the associated guardian *muzimu*. The name from the maternal side is perpetuated in another member of the group. The person chosen is anointed with oil at the nape of the neck, given tobacco, and as beads are placed about his neck he is told: 'Your name is now such and such.' This rite is thought to continue the attachment of the now inherited *muzimu* to the group to which it belongs. If it is a newly created *muzimu*, however, a further rite is performed some months after the death, when the people gather for the final mourning. In the interim, though the *muzimu* has been inherited, it is thought to be wandering disconsolately in the bush. At the final rite, an offering is poured in its name, and it is told to take its place among the other *mizimu* of the line with the assurance that the living will not forget it while it remembers them. Henceforth, it may appear in many different roles—it may be installed as the guardian of a household, its name may be given to any number of children to whom it will be thought to act as guardian, or it may only be invoked occasionally by a diviner who attributes illness to its anger at being neglected. Its importance will reflect the importance which the person attained in life. Those of little importance to their kinsmen are usually soon forgotten.

The new *muzimu* is a creation of the living, and not an automatic emanation of the dead man. The Tonga believe that the matrilineal group has the right to decide whether or not a dead man's own *muzimu* shall come into existence. They may refuse to mourn for a man or to inherit his *muzimu* if he dies as a leper or if he has been killed as a sorcerer. They may also refuse to inherit the *muzimu* of a suicide. This is in line with their belief that a *muzimu* once in existence can demand the right to act as guardian for new members of the group who would thus be endowed with the unfortunate characteristics of the dead person. They maintain that if no one inherits the spirit, and if no rite is performed to call it to join the other *mizimu*, then the *muzimu* does not exist and therefore it cannot affect them. Its powers and potentialities for evil have been dammed at the source. This happened to E15, shown on the genealogy given below. He was a leper, and when he died no one inherited his *muzimu*. His kinsmen say that he has never affected them in any way: 'He is now only a ghost wandering in ths bush.' In this belief, again, they are not completely consistent. A diviner may diagnose an illness as due to the anger of a *muzimu* because its mourning rites have not been performed. In 1950, we found the people of a village mourning because the diviner had announced that a man had died while at work in the Union of South Africa and his *muzimu* was sending illness to his kinsmen to announce his death and to ask that the mourning be performed. His relatives had heard nothing from him since he went away to work, and they had had no report of his death. That he should have a *muzimu* which could affect them is contrary to the dogma that only a *muzimu* already recognized by the group has effective power over it, and this is not the only case that belies the dogma. Nevertheless, it is consistent with my interpretation of the own *muzimu* as a recognition by the community of the place that the dead held in their lives. If for some reason he was so disturbing to them that they wish only to forget him, then they deny to him a *muzimu*. If they are prepared to remember him, then he has a *muzimu* whether or not the rites which are said to establish the new *muzimu* have been performed and these can be performed at some later date.

The one who inherits a *muzimu* does not assume the social personality of the dead, as we shall see below in the discussion on succession. He does, however, stand in a special relation to his inherited *muzimu*. This is true whether he has inherited the guardian *muzimu* of a youth or a dead adult's own *muzimu*. When he makes offerings, he ought to include the inherited *muzimu* among those he calls. He may also be laid under special restrictions which do not apply to those who have never inherited a *muzimu*. Thus, if a girl has inherited a *muzimu*, a special rite should be performed the first time she has sexual intercourse, lest the inherited *muzimu* be angry and send sickness to her, prevent her from bearing children, or harm such children as are born to her. I am told that among the Tonga in the Gwembe Valley, the same rite used to be performed for a boy who had inherited a *muzimu*, but the people of the Plateau deny that they ever had the rite for boys.

It may be of importance that this is one of the few rites involving a *muzimu* that calls for the participation of a large number of matrilineal kinsmen. Usually when a *muzimu* of the matrilineal line is to be propitiated only the person involved, or his guardian if he is still immature, need take part in the rite. Other members of the matrilineal group need not attend. I would argue that the difference is due to the manner in which a person obtains an inherited *muzimu*. The choice of names, and therefore of guardian *mizimu*, for a child is a matter for the immediate relatives, and is not a subject of general discussion among his kinsmen. If a man installs a *muzimu* of his matrilineal line as a house guardian, he himself decides which *muzimu* it shall be. In either case, the choice may be guided by divination, which is thought to establish that a particular *muzimu* itself has chosen to concern itself in the matter. Other *mizimu* are propitiated when a diviner has announced that they are demanding offerings, and again it is not a matter of general discussion among a group of kinsmen. But the choice of the inheritor of a *muzimu* is made by the assembled group during the funeral without recourse to divination. Moreover, since they are all witnesses to the inheritance of the *muzimu*, they must take part in the rite which propitiates it.

The person who inherits a *muzimu* thus has a recognized obligation in respect to it, but at the same time he retains his own identity, and his guardian *mizimu* continue to be involved in his

C

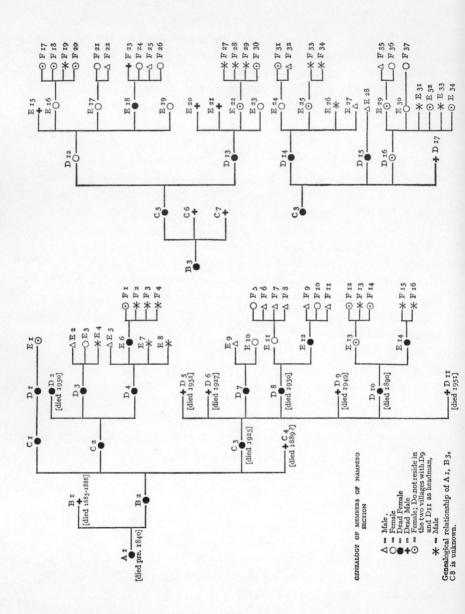

GENEALOGY OF MEMBERS OF NAMPEYO SECTION

△ = Male.

○ = Female.

● = Dead Female.

+ = Dead Male.

⊙ = Female; Do not reside in the two villages with D9 and D11 as headman.

✱ = Male

Genealogical relationship of A1, B3, C8 is unknown.

destiny and are not superseded by the inherited *muzimu*. When he dies, his matrilineal group will have to find someone to take his *muzimu*, which will bear the name given by them at his naming. If his inherited *muzimu* was that of an important man, they will also try to find someone to reinherit it. But so short is the memory of the Tonga for their predecessors that I could not find an instance of a *muzimu* having been inherited more than twice. Most are inherited only once. Nevertheless the people do not feel that a *muzimu* is lost to them when the one who has inherited dies in his turn, for by that time they have given the name to new children and it thus remains within the group.

A *muzimu* in the role of guardian *muzimu* may be inherited as often as those who bear its name die before they have reached social maturity when they can produce their own *mizimu*; for when the immature die it is the guardian *muzimu* which is inherited. If ten children receive the name Mwene and all die before establishing a household, someone will be chosen to inherit the name at each funeral though this implies the inheritance over and over again of the same guardian *muzimu*. This seems anomalous in terms of the structure of Tonga belief about the nature of the *mizimu* and their relationship to the matrilineal group, but again it is consistent with our interpretation of the guardian *muzimu* as an acknowledgment of the person's position within the kinship group. Even if he dies before he has achieved a position of his own, his kinsmen recognize their loss and appoint someone to inherit the *muzimu* identified with him.

In summary of the above analysis, each person receives his initial position within society as a member of his own matrilineal group and as a child of his father's matrilineal group. The two groups indicate their acceptance of responsibility for him by giving him a name which is associated with a guardian *muzimu*. During childhood and youth, the person is equally dependent upon his two groups, and their role in his life is roughly similar. The two guardian *mizimu*, one from each side, are of equal importance, and both are thought to determine his personality. As an adult, the person acquires a new position of his own as the head of a household. At the same time, he also becomes a responsible member of his matrilineal group upon whom others depend for assistance. Thereafter when he dies his own *muzimu* is thought to come into existence. With this his guardian *muzimu* from the matrilineal group has become merged. The matrilineal group signify their recognition of the position of the person within the group by appointing someone to inherit the *muzimu*. Since the person is not fully identified with his father's group, the guardian *muzimu* from this side does not become identified with his own *muzimu* which represents the position which he has occupied in the community. When he dies, his father's group have no further claims upon the position he has occupied, and they signify that their rights and obligations are at an end by the withdrawal of the guardian *muzimu* with which they have provided him. This is not inherited as it represents an interest for the one lifetime only.

The 'Mizimu' and the Matrilineal Group

So far this analysis of the cult of the *mizimu* has been concerned with the way in which it reflects the identification of the individual with the kinsmen of his father and mother. In this section, I shall analyse the way in which the cult reflects the relationships which exist between kinsmen within a matrilineal group. Each such group claims that it is a united body, in relationship to the *mizimu* of its line, and indeed the members are likely to describe the common tie that binds them together as due to the fact that all of them are affected by the same *mizimu*.

The matrilineal group is the basic kinship unit of Tonga society. It is a group of kinsmen who claim a putative descent through females from a common ancestress, though they are not concerned to trace their descent and are frequently ignorant of their exact relationship to each other. The duties of members of the group involve the obligation of visiting each other when ill, of mourning the deaths of members of each other's families, of helping to provide bridewealth for the males of the group, of assisting each other to pay fines and damages, of purifying the spouses of those who die, and of finding people to inherit the positions and *mizimu* of their dead. In case of need, they should assist each other with food and other gifts. In former days they formed a vengeance group to uphold each other's rights against outsiders, and were held jointly responsible by outsiders for each other's actions. They also have certain joint rights. They should share in the bridewealth given for the women of the group and they share the estates of their deceased members.

The group does not form a land-holding unit, and its members need not live together in a single locality. In the absence of an organized political structure with instituted positions of authority, kinsmen lacked the incentive for remaining together that the possibility of succession to official titles vesting in the group could provide. Today hereditary chiefdoms instituted by the Administration have provided this incentive for a few groups. Custodianship of local rain-shrines has also been hereditary within the matrilineal group of the founder and the groups in which this right vests have therefore had a tenuous focus. The position of village headman again tends to be hereditary in the matrilineal line, though an outsider may succeed if no suitable successor is available from within the group. But villages need not necessarily remain within one area. In pre-European days there was no barrier to the formation of new villages, and even today it is not difficult for the man who can command sufficient followers to found his own village and thus emerge as a village headman. Leadership within the group itself is largely based on seniority, personal qualities, and wealth, and thus changes over a period of years, as now one man, then another, emerges as a leader while the successors of earlier leaders prove unable to maintain a dominant position in the community and sink back into obscurity. In the past probably matrilineal groups were held together by the knowledge that a man's chief protection against the aggression of others lay in the possession of a strong body of kinsmen who would maintain his rights. Today when the need for protection has passed, groups are held together by their common rights of inheritance in the estates of fellow kinsmen and by the expectation of material assistance in emergencies. Groups therefore find their focus, not in a territory, but in a strong or wealthy man who is able to assist them. Today if a man is wealthy, with many cattle or with a large cash income from the sale of maize or other produce, other men and women see some point in stressing their kinship with him and so with each other, and the matrilineal group is slower to disintegrate (and is therefore larger) than where there is no important person to act as a focus for their kinship.

Since people can demand assistance and exercise the right to inherit whether or not they live together, there is no need for members of a matrilineal group to reside in a single locality. Usually they are dispersed through a number of different neighbourhoods, and assemble only for funerals, puberty ceremonies, and other ritual occasions which require joint action. Marriage is usually virilocal, but a man's choice of residence is a matter for his personal decision. He may settle with paternal relatives, with maternal relatives, with affines, or with strangers.[1] Uterine siblings may live miles apart. Matrilineal kinsmen in everyday association, living in the same village or in the same small neighbourhood, may not be able to trace how they are related to each other.

The Tonga dogma in regard to the matrilineal group is that it is an undifferentiated whole, that all of its members wherever they are living and however they are related to each other have the same status in the group. This formulation represents an ideal, but it also has some relation to the real facts of social life.

Perhaps it is the dispersed nature of the group that leads the Tonga to insist upon its unity and to deny that degree of relationship is important. Members of a matrilineal group who do live close together are also in constant association with people who belong to other groups—indeed, the majority of their associates will be outsiders. This can be illustrated by referring to the genealogy on page 18. In 1950, D11 who was still alive was head of a village containing 28 men, of whom only 6 (including D11) belonged to D11's matrilineal group. Of the 35 women in the village, only 8 belonged to this group. The other 28 men in the village were members of 13 different matrilineal groups; the other 27 women were members of 18 different matrilineal groups. The

---

[1] Cf. below, pp. 180–83.

neighbouring village was under the headmanship of D9, who died in 1949. There, 10 of the 27 men in the village belonged to this matrilineal group, while the other 17 belonged to 9 other groups. Seven of the 32 women of this village belonged to the matrilineal group of the headman; the other 25 belonged to 9 other groups. Other members of D11's matrilineal group lived in nearby village under headmen of other matrilines, or they were living outside the neighbourhood. Some lived miles away. Since people are surrounded by outsiders, amongst whom they live and with whom they co-operate in ordinary activities, membership within the matrilineal group as a whole is the overwhelming fact that they stress. The relationships which they have with outsiders are different in kind from those which they have with each other, and the differences in degree that may mark their own relationships sink into unimportance and are barely recognized in the dogma of the group. This is the more true since members of a matrilineal group act alone on very few occasions. Their corporate activity takes place within situations where outsiders are also present. At a funeral, and in subsequent mourning ceremonies, all those living in one neighbourhood should participate. All attend, but the members of the matrilineal group concerned have special roles in the ceremony. Girls' puberty ceremonies are occasions for general neighbourhood gatherings, but again the matrilineal group involved has a special role to play. Formerly when they gathered to protect a member, or to seek vengeance for some offence against him, they were posed as a united group against a similarly mobilized unit. People see themselves therefore in general as members of an undifferentiated body of matrilineal kinsmen, in contrast to the outsiders who are also present.

The matrilineal group does in fact lack a formal internal segmentation differentiating one set of collaterals from another. Nevertheless, the Tonga are aware that uterine siblings and their immediate descendants may have an emotional bond which overrides membership in the larger group and that such people may see themselves as a unit in contrast to the rest of their maternal kinsmen. This unit is called a 'womb' (*ida*), and is usually referred to by the name of some living member rather than by the name of the woman from whom descent is traced.[1] It may be applied to groups composed of a varying number of generations from the founder, depending upon context, but since a 'womb' is based on family affection rather than on a recognized ordering of hierarchical units, in practice it rarely refers to any save a group of siblings, or the descendants of a common grandmother. The distinction, moreover, is usually made only in situations where the unity of the whole matrilineal group is being stressed along with the obligations of all its members, whatever their descent, to participate in the affairs of the group. All members are held to have the right to receive a share of the estate when someone dies. If the estate contains only a few cattle, one may be assigned to a representative of each womb with the proviso that he must share the increase with other members of the womb. When a group is seeking a suitable successor for a deceased kinsman, the available candidates are canvassed. The descendants of a particular woman may then be told, 'It is the turn of your womb now to take the place. Our womb did it the last time.' Whenever it is necessary to choose a successor, the Tonga stress this obligation of those from other wombs to take the place of the dead. If a woman dies, someone other than her uterine sister should be chosen for the rite in which her husband is purified. If a man dies, it is considered inappropriate for his uterine brother to perform the purification of the widow or to succeed to his position. A sister's son or a sister's daughter's son (who ranks as brother) is a suitable choice, but the most desirable is a classificatory brother or a classificatory sister's son from another womb, for such a succession strengthens the links between the different members of the group and hinders a splitting into independent segments based on womb membership. If a womb is repeatedly forced to provide its own successors, its members will feel that they have been rejected by the rest of the

---

[1] The Tonga of the Gwembe Valley refer to the founding ancestress of any line as the *nacanzo*, and her name is frequently remembered. Among the people of the Plateau the word is known in this sense only to those who have close links with the Valley, and the Plateau people have no comparable term. Hopgood records the word *Nacanzo* as another name for God and derives it from the verb *anza*, 'to create', 'to originate'. See Hopgood, 1950, p. 66.

matrilineal group. Today with the developing emphasis upon property rights and the diminishing importance of having the support of a large body of kinsmen to secure life and property, the old rule is no longer always observed. Nevertheless, the Tonga still phrase succession in terms of the duty of a body of kinsmen to assist each other.

The Tonga are thus concerned to maintain the integrity of the group as a whole and see the possibility of fission along genealogical lines as a threat to this integrity. Such incipient segmentation as does occur is distrusted as being contrary to the dogma that all have equal rights and responsibilities whatever the relationship. Sometimes a disgruntled person grumbles that only a real brother or a real mother's brother will recognize his obligation to help and that other members of the group discriminate in favour of their own close kin. But usually nothing annoys a Tonga more than a suggestion that such a distinction might be right and natural. The force with which they repudiate the suggestion is probably an indication of the difficulty they find in making principle square with practice.

The following conversation with Ezra, one of my best informants, bears on this point. We were speaking of Nathan who belongs to Ezra's matrilineal group and lives in his village. I asked Ezra about Nathan's grandmother, and how she and his own mother were related.

He said: 'My mother called her sister.'

I said: 'But they didn't have the same mother or the same grandmother, so the relationship is really remote.'

Ezra retorted: 'It is a close relationship! We Tonga don't try to follow out and say which relative is closer than another.'

I asked: 'Well, which do you feel is closer to you, Rueben who is the son of your own sister or Nathan?'

Ezra replied: 'I don't make any difference between them; they are equally close because they are both of my matrilineal group (*mukowa*).[1] Nathan mourns that he was born alone because he has no brothers or sisters born of his mother, but we think he is

---

[1] The same word is used for 'clan'.

foolish. No man is born alone even if he is the only one from his womb, for all have *mukowa* and they are as close as those of one womb.'

I said: 'This is very hard for us Europeans to understand because we distinguish degrees of relationship.'

Ezra said: 'That just proves that you Europeans have no *mukowa*. We Tonga don't make any difference like that within the *mukowa*.'

I argued: 'But you do make a difference, for you say that those born of the same womb should not succeed each other.'

'Yes, that is true. My brother born of the same womb cannot take my place. When I die, they cannot chose my real brother to take my place. They must chose someone else. But that is the reason why we can't say that those who come from different wombs in the *mukowa* are farther apart than those who come from one womb. If we chose the brother to succeed, then we might have made a difference. But as it is, when a man dies, they bring another man from somewhere else to take his place, and so there is always a mixing of those born from different wombs.'

When I asked him why they disliked the succession following within the same womb, he said: 'If those of the same womb must take the place, they will be angry and ask if they alone share *mizimu*. They will feel that the others reject them.'

If we examine what actually happens, however, it is obvious that the rights and obligations of matrilineal kinship are affected by both genealogical and spatial separation, though the two may offset each other. Uterine siblings wherever they may live will probably assist each other, share bridewealth, and accept the other rights and duties of their kinship. So may those descended from a common grandmother. In effect, this means all those who consider themselves to be of one womb. Equally, kinsmen who live together in one neighbourhood will often ignore genealogical distance, and though some may not know how they are related, they will accept their common obligations and privileges, denying that genealogical factors are of importance. Someone similarly related who is living in another locality may decide that he is too far away to be bothered to concern himself in their affairs and he

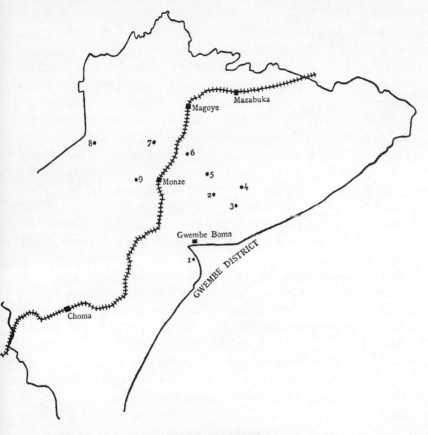

MAZABUKA DISTRICT

Scale = 1 : 1,000, 000

+++++ Railway

1 -- Siamaundu Section
2 -- Nampeyo
3 -- Escarpment of Chona Chieftancy
4 -- Nadongo
5 -- Njola

6 -- Kataba
7 -- Choongo Section
8 -- Bwengwa
9 -- Fufwa

may appear only at important funerals. Eventually, there may come to be several sections of the group, each gathered around a wealthy man, living some distance apart. The entire group will then co-operate only on occasions involving senior members, and ordinary deaths will not be reported to members of the other sections. Nevertheless, so long as the tradition of their common kinship persists, the people will claim that they belong to a single matrilineal group and that all have equal rights of inheritance, etc. If pressed, they will admit that they do not exercise these rights in fact, and do not honour their obligations. Nevertheless, they argue: 'If they came, we would give to them. If we went there, we could inherit or take their places. We are still one group, for we name with the same names and have the same *mizimu.*' They say this despite the fact that they may have no knowledge of what names actually are being bestowed upon members of the other sections, and it is very unlikely that they concern themselves with the same *mizimu.*

The genealogy on page 18 refers to a portion of such a dispersed matrilineal group, which now has a number of sections which unite only at important funerals. They claim to have come originally from the Shamaundu country in the south-eastern portion of Tonga country on the edge of the Zambezi escarpment. Some members of the group still live in that area. About 1840, B1 and his sister B2, with other matrilineal relative whose links have been forgotten, moved north into Nampeyo country in what is now Chona chiefdom east of the town of Monze. There some members have remained. The Nampeyo section is today composed of descendants of B2 and some additional members whose links to A1 have been forgotten. Other members of the group moved from Shamaundu into the Fufwa area west of Monze, and still others moved further west into the Bwengwa area in Simuyobe chiefdom. I have no further details on the dispersion from Shamaundu, Fufwa, and Bwengwa centres, but the Nampeyo one provided further offshoots. Some members moved a few miles north into Nadongo area about 1880; others moved further north to Njola, in what is now Mwansa chiefdom. Others moved into the escarpment hills in the eastern portion of Chona chiefdom. These were all people whose relationship to B1 has now been forgotten. Two brothers who had married remote kinswomen of B1 formed their own village near his in Nampeyo and then about 1900 moved with their families and other followers north to Kataba area in Sianjalika chiefdom. In the 1920s, when the land on which they were settled was alienated for European development, these people were dispossessed and moved west into Chongo chiefdom. These different groups may now be considered to be different sections of the one matrilineal group. However, they still claim kinship with each other, though ordinarily they have little contact. In 1950, I visited a village in Fufwa with the leader of the Nampeyo section. He and the headman knew of each other's existence and greeted each other enthusiastically as kinsmen, claimed that they could succeed each other, had reciprocal rights of inheritance, ought to aid each other as though they were brothers born of the same womb. In actual fact, I could not discover that the Fufwa man had ever attended a funeral or any other kinship occasion in the Nampeyo area, nor had the Nampeyo man ever attended a funeral in the Fufwa group. For all practical purposes, their kinship was in abeyance. Other sections are in slightly closer contact, and some members still attend important funerals, and occasional visits are exchanged for other purposes.

Nevertheless, there is movement from one local section to another, and once a member of one section settles with those of another they stress the fact of their common membership in one group and ignore the fact that they cannot trace their relationship and that they have been settled apart previously. When D10 died about 1890 in Nampeyo country, her relatives there sent to the Shamaundu section to ask for a kinswoman to provide the husband with a replacement, and a girl (D15) was sent to them for this purpose. A number of women (e.g. D16 and E24) have come from Shamaundu country to live with their kinsmen at Nampeyo and they have married in that neighbourhood. When their daughters married, the portion of the bridewealth taken by the maternal relatives has gone to descendants of A1 in preference to the claims of their immediate maternal relatives who live at a distance. Men and women from the Nadongo section have come to live at Nampeyo in preference to living with their close relatives at Nadongo. Such movement still continues. In 1950, a woman appeared without warning at Nampeyo and said that henceforth she planned to live in this neighbourhood with her matrilineal kinsmen. She said that her mother had told her before she died: 'My kinsmen are at Nampeyo. Go there and tell them my name and they will accept you because they will know that you belong to their matrilineal group.' Now she was following her mother's instructions. None of the people at Nampeyo knew much about her, as she and her mother had never lived in the neighbourhood. She belonged to a branch which had moved from Shamaundu some generations earlier and had lived isolated from the rest of the group. But the older people at Nampeyo did remember having been told that her mother was their kinswoman. Therefore they were prepared to accept her and her children as full members of their group.

Differentiation by descent into 'wombs' and by locality into 'sections' therefore are facts, but the Tonga seek to deny their importance. The differentiation within the group which they recognize and stress is based on generation differences. Kinship terms reflect this division and govern it. On the genealogical chart on page 18, all members of D generation call each other sibling, and males call all members of E 'sister's child', while females call all members of E 'child'. The reciprocal terms used by members of generation E to generation D are 'mother's brother' and 'mother'. Members of D call all members of F generation 'sibling', though females of D may also call them 'grandchild' and in turn be called 'grandmother'. Members of generation G will again be called either 'sister's child' or 'child', depending on the sex of the speaker. Alternate generations are thus equated. The terms are applied long after any memory of the actual relationships involved has disappeared. Within the matrilineal group, therefore, only two types of relationship are thought to exist between males. For women the situation is slightly more complex. But males are either 'brothers', or they are 'mother's brother' and 'sister's son' respectively. The one is an easy relationship, the other demands respect and restraint. 'Brothers' call each others' children 'my child', and in turn they are addressed as 'father'. This classification is of some importance in determining the actions of members of the matrilineal group in particular instances. Men may receive bridewealth for their daughters and for the daughters of their siblings. 'Sisters' sons' are forbidden to take bridewealth for the daughters of their 'mother's brothers', for these women are their cross-cousins and potential wives. Equally, they are forbidden to take bridewealth for their 'sisters' in whose matrimonial affairs they should not concern themselves. Men of generation D, therefore, take bridewealth for women of generation E, and are forbidden to hold bridewealth for women of their own generation or for those of F, for these again rank as 'sisters'. Men of generation E take bridewealth for women of generation F, and are concerned in arranging the marriages of these women. When men of generation E receive bridewealth for their daughters, they do not share with men of D.

Generation is also of some importance in determining succession. I propose in the following paragraphs to examine some instances of succession and the inheritance of the *muzimu* to show the part played by descent and generation.

Succession or taking the place (*kulya izina*, 'to eat the name') is not the same as the inheritance of the *muzimu* of the dead. In this the Tonga differ from some of the other peoples of Northern Rhodesia where the heir receives both the spirit and the personal position of the dead.[1] Only married men who are the heads of households are succeeded, and usually only if their wives agree to be inherited. Many times when I asked who had taken the place of a particular person, I was told: 'His wife was already dead so nobody took the place', or, 'His wife refused to be inherited, so nobody took the place.' As we shall see later, the most significant

---

[1] Among the Bemba, at every death someone must be appointed to assume the name, the status, the social obligations, and the guardian spirit. The identification of the successor with the dead appears to be complete. See Richards, 1934, p. 269. Dr. Cunnison informs me that the peoples of the Luapula Valley have a similar custom. For the Ila, there is no information on whether or not the heir also takes the spirit of the deceased.

feature of a man's personality is his position as head of a household, and this is dependent upon the possession of a wife or wives. If he dies without a wife, by definition he has no household, and no one can take the place which is non-existent. Women are rarely succeeded. I have recorded perhaps five or six instances in all. In their case, succession only occurs if the matrilineal group is willing to offer the widower a new wife in her place, and this it has no obligation to do. The successor of a man is said to take his name and his place within the household of which he formed the centre. If the dead man was a village headman, the successor may also replace him in this role, but the villagers may insist on finding another headman and he then has only the dead man's position in his own household. The wife and children call the successor by the kinship terms they used for the dead man, instead of by those previously used. The successor's position in relation to other members of his group is not altered. They continue to use the same kinship terms as before. They may or may not address him and refer to him by the name of the dead man. Most commonly they continue to use the name under which he has been known previously, which is usually a nickname rather than a name from his guardian *mizimu*. If he wishes, he may move to the dead man's homestead, in which case he is more likely to be called by the dead man's name, as others continue to speak of going to such-and-such a place, using the locative form of the name of the head of the homestead. But he is not obliged to move. If, as sometimes happens, he already has a homestead of his own, he is likely to remove the inherited wife or wives to his own place. There he builds for them huts which are usually dedicated to the *muzimu* of the dead husband, who thus continues to guard the interests of his wives and the young children who remain in the household. In either event, the successor is now head of the homestead. It is *his* paternal ancestors who are ritually of most importance, and the paternal *mizimu* of the former head no longer guard its interests. In any case, the successor is not identified with the *muzimu* of the dead man, for this has been given to the one who inherits the *muzimu*. When the successor dies in his turn, his relatives seek to find someone to take his place. They are not concerned to differentiate the position which he has inherited from that which he has achieved for himself. These are now one and the same thing. Sometimes, the responsibilities of the dead man are split up among a number of heirs. It may then be difficult to decide just which one is the successor to the position. This happens when there are a number of wives who are taken by different members of the group. If one heir takes over one or more wives and occupies the homestead of the dead man, he will be considered to have taken the place, whether or not other wives have fallen to the lot of other men. But if each man removes his inherited wife to his own place, and the homestead dies, people may say that there has been only the inheritance of wives and no succession.

In choosing a successor, the relatives seek to find someone who will be able to care for the wives and children, which involves finding someone who will be acceptable to the wives and their relatives. If the dead man was a headman or the head of a large homestead, they will also wish to find someone who can look after people properly—a man of peaceful disposition, of sound, judgment, able to give good advice, unlikely to squander the property of his predecessor lightly on his own concerns. Therefore only an adult man will be chosen to succeed since only an adult can perform the functions inherent in the position. The people will also try to choose a man whose succession will upset existing relationships as little as possible. The most suitable person is therefore a 'brother'. 'Sisters' sons' encounter a number of obstacles to their succession. If a man of generation E has married the daughter of a man of generation D, an approved form of marriage, he may not be considered a suitable successor, for the wives of D rank as 'mother' to his wife, and it is wrong for 'mother' and 'daughter' to be the wives of one man. When a successor was sought for D9, it was argued that E2 and E5 were disqualified because they had married daughters of D5, and the objection to them was as strong as it was to E9 who had married a daughter of D9. When D11 died, people again used this same argument to bar them from succession, although one of them was eventually permitted to inherit one of the widows. The Tonga also feel that the privileged joking which exists between cross-cousins who are potential spouses

D

makes the succession of the sister's son unduly difficult, for he then becomes 'father' to his cross-cousins and must be treated with respect. The rule that men should not hold bridewealth for women of their own generation also acts as a barrier to succession. The heir takes over his predecessor's obligations with respect to the bridewealth cattle he has been holding for the women of his group, and if the 'sister's son' succeeds he is likely to find himself holding bridewealth cattle for his 'sisters'. On the whole, therefore, the Tonga prefer to find a successor among the 'brothers'—which includes sister's daughter's sons—of the dead man, although they frequently decide to overlook all objections and take a 'sister's son'. If all else fails, they may even choose a successor from a generation senior to that of the dead man, but this is considered a last resort.

Choice is also influenced by the desire to find a successor in another womb. When D6 died in 1927, the people tried to persuade either E2 or E9 to take the place. Both men refused, and finally D11 succeeded, though F9 was persuaded to inherit one of the wives. When D9 died in 1949, D11 attempted to find a successor to purify the wives and take the place. He considered some men from other sections who are not shown on the chart, as well as most of those who are. He was urgent that some man descended from C2 should succeed. He argued: 'I took the place when my brother D6 died. Our womb has done enough. It is now the turn of your womb. If you refuse to take the place, then we will be separate, and we of our womb will refuse to succeed when one of you dies.' All those descended from C2 refused on various grounds. D11, considerably disgruntled, finally managed to persuade F15, a descendant of his own sister, to take the place. In 1951, D11 himself died, and again the group had to find a successor. They finally chose F13, although F15 argued that someone else ought to be chosen because their womb (from D10) had done enough in succeeding D9. F11 who had been approached declined on the grounds that his brother (F9) had inherited one of the wives of D6 'and therefore our womb has done enough'. In all three cases, the succession remained in the womb of C3, but in the last instance members of other wombs were brought to share some of the responsibility. One of the widows of D11 was inherited by E5, from the womb of C2, and another was inherited by a man belonging to the Chongo section whose relationship with D11 is quite unknown. When D5 died in 1952, E28 succeeded, although again no one knows how the two men were related.

Succession, and the right to succeed, plays a disproportionate part in Tonga thinking about the nature of the matrilineal group, for actually succe_____ In a census of 17 villages, I asked 266 men o_____ h_d ever succeeded to a place _____ the men were possib _____ hers were debarred b _____ tians who refuse to fo _____ es on polygyny gives _____ this involves the inh_ _____ the 266 men there were _____ no had never succeeded _____ rvative and progressive _____ ion fall into the follow _____ other's brother'; fifteen, _____

The inheritance of the *muzimu* take_ _____ atly. It is a way of ensuring that the dead is not forgotten, but the one who inherits the *muzimu* is not identified with the dead man nor does he take his social position. It is said that he, like the successor, receives the name of the dead and may be addressed by kinship terms appropriate to the dead man. If this is true, I failed to observe it. I have also been told that a woman would not marry the one who had inherited her father's spirit because he would now be her 'father'. I failed to check this information sufficiently to be sure that it is reliable. On the whole, one could argue that the inheritor

---

[1] The 17 villages are from Chona, Ufwenuka, and Mwansa chiefdoms east of the railway line. The Chona villages are under Roman Catholic influence, but most of the people are conservatives who respect the old customs. The Ufwenuka and Mwansa villages are under Seventh Day Adventist influence. They have a larger proportion of progressive people who reject the old customs. Nevertheless, succession still occurs in all three areas, and the distribution of instances in my sample is roughly similar for the three chiefdoms.

of the *muzimu* has no obligations to the living, but only to the dead. Since this is so, a child may be chosen to inherit the *muzimu*. When the deceased is an adult, a child almost invariably is chosen, presumably because this prevents any clash between the inheritor of the *muzimu* and the successor. When a small child dies, a mother or grandmother or some other woman of the line usually inherits its guardian *muzimu*. While successors must be of the same sex as the deceased, this is not true of inheritors of the *muzimu*. Males usually inherit the *muzimu* only of other males, but females may be chosen to inherit the *muzimu* of either males or females, especially if the deceased is a child and only the guardian *muzimu* is involved.

Here as in succession, the dogma is that since all are members of the matrilineal group any one of them may be chosen. If possible, however, they choose someone of another womb. When B1 died, his *muzimu* was inherited by a man who cannot be linked to him, and who is not shown on the chart. When this man died in turn, B1's *muzimu* was reinherited by E28. When D6 died, his *muzimu* was inherited by F3, then a small boy. When D9 died, his *muzimu* was inherited by F25. The relationship between the two cannot be traced. When D11 died, his *muzimu* was inherited by F32, a boy of about fourteen. Again the relationship cannot be traced. F32's mother is one of the immigrants from the Shamaundu section, though she has lived in the Nampeyo area since the time of her puberty seclusion. Here again, as with succession, one finds the emphasis upon the general responsibility of the group, which counteracts the tendency for those who come from the same womb to feel themselves set apart from those of other wombs. Since the inheritor of the *muzimu* does not become the guardian of the position or the property of the dead, it is easier here to insist upon the identification of the group than it is in the case of succession where ambition complicates the issue. But since the *muzimu* of an adult is usually inherited by a child, the choice is thereby limited to those in the immediate locality, possibly even in the same village, for young children after weaning do not accompany their elders to funerals.

Unfortunately, it is impossible to gather data on a quantitative basis to show how widely, in a genealogical sense, the inheritance of the *muzimu* is distributed. Even in groups one knows well, it is often impossible to trace relationships. To attempt to gather the information from other people is even more hopeless. I have therefore had to be content to classify my data on the taking of the spirit only into generations and types of relationship, with the full realization that usually a classificatory relationship is involved. Even the generation label is not absolute, for 'brother' is used by a man to refer to men of generation +2 and generation −2 as well as to men of his own generation. To determine in each case exactly which generation was referred to was impossible in the time available. (See Table 1, p. 38.)

The quantitative information, poor as it is, indicates that with respect both to succession and inheritance of the *muzimu*, the preference for succession in the 'sibling' generation is not overwhelming. Nevertheless, it operates frequently enough, linked as it is with the prejudice against succession and inheritance by the uterine sibling, for it to be a counterforce to the familial sentiment which finds its expression in the concept of the 'womb'. The classification together of alternate generations delays the splitting into 'wombs' for a further generation, and by another generation 'the womb' from which a particular line has sprung has already lost its significance, for the feeling of close personal ties upon which is is based has vanished with the death of the uterine siblings who formed its core.

The belief in the unity of the matrilineal group is reflected in the belief that they are all one before their *mizimu*. In defining membership within the group, the Tonga are apt to say: 'We name with the same names. Therefore we are one matrilineal group.' Now the names and the *mizimu* are identified, and it is for this reason that the names are considered important. Today in the Native Authority courts when the assessors find it necessary to consider how those involved in a case are related they will ask: 'Can you name for the same *mizimu*? If one of you dies can the other inherit your *muzimu*?' If the answer is 'yes', the fact of relationship is established, and they need question no further to discover the degree of relationship. This is usually irrelevant to the decision. It may be necessary to determine the generations to which the disputants belong, but this is a different matter.

The unofficial status of the 'womb' is reflected in the fact that it does not have a set of *mizimu* of its own. The names and the

TABLE I

Inheritance of the *Muzimu**

Generation	Type Relationship of Deceased to Inheritor	Male Informants	Female Informants
	MATRILINEAL GROUP		
+3	MMMB	2	—
	MMM	—	1
+2	MMB	4	—
	MM	—	19
+1	MB	27	4
	M	—	4
	MZ	—	3
Own	B	14	4
	Z	—	6
	MZD	—	1
−1	C	—	31
	ZC	1	10
−2	DC	—	8
	ZDC	—	1
Unspecified		3	3
	IRREGULAR		
+2	MF	1	—
−1	S	1	—
−2	SD	—	1
TOTAL		53	96

* M = Mother; F = Father; B = Brother; Z = Sister; C = Child; S = Son; D = Daughter.

The information is drawn from inhabitants of the same 17 villages used for data about succession, and covers those over the apparent age of fourteen. 50 males were not asked about taking the spirit, 253 denied having taken one. 120 females were not asked for information, 210 denied having taken a spirit. The more progressive people in the Mwansa and Ufwenuka villages frequently claimed to have abandoned the custom as contrary to Christian practice or because they were trying to follow the ways of the Europeans. But even in this area, older people may insist on the rite despite the protests of younger men and women.

mizimu are the spiritual estate of all members of the matrilineal group. The Tonga would reject any suggestion that only those descended from a particular person, or from his or her uterine sibling, has a claim upon his *muzimu* and his name, or that a *muzimu* is concerned only with these descendants. Members of different wombs do not segregate ritually for offerings to a particular set of *mizimu* to whose service they, and they alone, are dedicated. The cult of the *mizimu* unites the whole group and the undifferentiated nature of the cult reflects the undifferentiated nature of the matrilineal group.

Since neither rights and obligations nor ritual dependence upon the *mizimu* are dependent upon descent, people are not concerned to remember the names of their ascendants or the siblings of these people. People rarely know the name of a great-grandmother. If asked, they are likely to retort, 'I don't know. The old people never bothered to explain this to me'. Unless they have grown up in the same area with their mother's mother, they may not be able to recall her name, though usually they can. One woman (E32) said that her mother's mother had been C3. I had already talked with her mother (D14) and with the son of C3, and they were certain that they had neither the same mother nor even the same great-grandmother. When I argued the matter with E32, she shrugged her shoulders and said: 'Well, what does it matter? You can ask my mother. Maybe she knows. I just thought they had the same mother.' And for all practical purposes it does not matter.

Since ancestors are not remembered, what then are the *mizimu*? Apart from the belief in their ritual powers, they are a set of names, which refer either to known members of the group who have died so recently that they are still remembered or they refer to a few people of a generation or so earlier who were sufficiently striking in some way so that tales about them are still current in the community. And lastly, of course, they are the names current among known members of the matrilineal group, for every name bestowed is assumed to represent a guardian *muzimu*. The theory is that each matrilineal group has its own names which are bestowed upon its members generation after generation. In actual fact, most people are known by their nicknames, and in many cases these are the names passed on to the next generation. Sections of matrilineal groups which have been apart for several generations, therefore, are quite unlikely to share the same set of names. Important people become known to other sections, and their names may be current in more than one area, but the general stock of names will probably vary from one section to another. Where the names are the same, they probably refer to quite different *mizimu*, at least in those cases where the name is referred to some former known member of the group. The Tonga say of the different sections: 'We are members of the same group because we share the same *mizimu*.' The truth is that they think they share the same *mizimu* because they know that they have a tradition that they are related.

Among those members of a matrilineal group who form a section, there is more substance to the assertion that they have the same *mizimu*. In actual fact, of course, the few men and women who have sufficiently powerful personalities so that they dominate their kinsmen and spread the fame of their names throughout the neighbourhood become the *mizimu* which are most often invoked as causal explanations and to which offerings are most frequently made. But in death, as in life, their domination affects their distant kinsmen as well as members of their own immediate womb. The *mizimu* of less important men and women are forgotten, or they coalesce with more famous *mizimu* of the same name just as do the *mizimu* from earlier generations. Thus E24 bears the same name as C4, and if she personifies her guardian *muzimu* it is as C4. She was born in a different area, and her name probably originally referred to someone who had lived in that area. She has named her daughters after A1 and C3. One of her sons is named after B1. Her daughter's daughter bears the name of C3. If there is illness in her family, the diviner may find that it is due to the *muzimu* of any one of these and is unlikely to attribute the illness to a *muzimu* in her own direct line. She has as much right to make offerings to these *mizimu* as do members of the womb in which they were once included.

Although the Tonga see the matrilineal group as a unit held together by a mystical relationship involving a common set of *mizimu*, the *mizimu* are seldom invoked to enforce the obligations of kinship. The *mizimu* are thought to send illness because they want offerings, and not because they wish to punish internal dissensions within the group, or to uphold a more general morality. In part this may be due to the fact that the Tonga do not conceive the *mizimu* as having a more moral nature than they themselves. We have already seen that they attribute a man's evil deeds to the working of his guardian *mizimu*. The *mizimu* which are endowed with personality are those of people who have died so recently that their delinquencies as well as their good actions are remembered. In dying and becoming *mizimu*, they have not been transformed into saintly spirits, but they are expected to work for the general good of their living kinsmen. I have never heard Tonga comment on behaviour of which they disapprove that the *mizimu* will punish the evil-doer. I have heard them say, 'He is wrong to do this. God (*Leza*) will mock him.' This ethical note is rarely struck in relation to the *mizimu*. Instead, they are conceived to act rather like important men among the living, who attempt to attract followers from amongst their kinsmen without regard to their degree of relationship and in return give them some measure of support. The *mizimu* too are described as concerned with building up as large a following as possible among their living kinsmen, and they do this through their demands for offerings, for the right to give a name to a child, for the right to become a house guardian. They are expected to assist their followers, who will otherwise abandon them to concentrate their offerings on other *mizimu* of the line, but they do not discriminate amongst them, and therefore are neutral in disputes between kinsmen.

I suggest that this indifference can be related to the diffused nature of the obligations of kinship arising from the dogma that the group is undifferentiated. The Tonga insist that all members have equal rights and obligations. This comes perilously near to the formula that what is everybody's business is nobody's business. Where everyone has a general obligation, no one has a specific one, and a person may have to approach kinsman after kinsman and argue the case before his needs are met. He cannot claim that close kinsmen have any greater obligation than distant kinsmen. He cannot base his claim on any specific relationship set up through the bridewealth institution. It is said that formerly women were not told which of their relatives held their bridewealth. They knew only it had been received and divided between their matrilineal group and their father's group. They and their children therefore, could not base a demand for help against a particular person on the ground that he had taken the bridewealth. Though today women usually know who holds their bridewealth, it is still considered bad manners for them or their children to base a demand for help upon this knowledge. I heard one case before a Native Authority court in which a man was suing a kinsman for the return of his mother's bridewealth on the ground that his kinsman had refused to help him and his siblings. The court lectured the elder man on his moral obligation to assist his kinsman, but held that the younger man had no case since the acceptance of bridewealth did not create a specific obligation to render assistance to the woman and her children. In practice, of course, a man first approaches the kinsmen he knows best. These will be members of his womb, or more distant kinsmen who are living in the same small neighbourhood. The Tonga also agree that a youth ought to be assisted by the man for whom he has worked as cattleherd during boyhood. If these kinsmen refuse to help him, he cannot count upon mobilizing a section within the matrilineal group to enforce his claim. Today he might appeal to the courts, but he rarely does so unless a specific charge such as theft or assault is involved. The courts could hardly intervene since this would involve converting a general right into a specific one against a particular person. Before the British introduced courts and a hierarchy of authority, there was no neutral body to which a man could submit a claim. Then, as to a large extent today, a man was dependent upon the willingness of his individual kinsmen to recognize their obligations to him. If they refused, he might sever all relations with them and take refuge among strangers; he might take what he wanted secure in the knowledge that he could not be punished as a thief; or he might convert his quarrel with them into a quarrel between his own group and some other matrilineal group by committing an offence against a member of another group. Thus a man might elope with a girl, and her relatives then presented their demand for compensation. If their demand was not met, they might sieze the property of any member of the offender's group. For the group is seen as a unity not only by its members, but also by outsiders.

In these circumstances, it is not surprising that *mizimu* are not invoked to enforce claims against kinsmen. I recorded only one instance of a man citing a *muzimu* as authorizing his request, and this involved an inherited *muzimu*. F3 had inherited the *muzimu* of D6. One day he came to D11, the successor of D6, saying that he had dreamed that D6's *muzimu* had told him to go to the successor and ask for a spear and a beast as his share in the estate of D6. He was given a spear, but no cattle. D11 argued: 'When my brother D6 died, he left spears, but he had no cattle. I can give F3 a spear. That is all right. But how can the *muzimu* of D6 say that I must give him cattle when he had no cattle!' Later when I tried to discuss the matter with D11, he sniffed: 'F3 is just saying this about the *muzimu* of D6 because he himself wants cattle.' On the whole, the Tonga see no reason why the *mizimu* should concern themselves in these affairs between living kinsmen. The division of an estate is made without reference to the dictates of the *mizimu*. When I asked Tonga informants if the *mizimu* would be angry and punish a man who refused to help his kinsman with bridewealth, they laughed and said that it had nothing to do with the *mizimu*, that they had never heard of a *muzimu* sending illness or other misfortune for this reason: 'It's up to me if I want to give to him. Nothing will happen if I don't.' Again I asked a man what would happen if he refused to go when called to make the offerings to the paternal *mizimu* for his brother's son. He promptly replied: 'My brother would be angry and say that I had no love for his son.' I asked: 'But what of your *mizimu* to whom the offerings would be made?' He denied that they would take any action against him. Informants also doubted that the *mizimu* would do anything if two members of the group quarrelled. On the whole they thought that the *mizimu* would not intervene to restore harmony.

Quarrels and certain other actions may give rise to a mystical retribution, which may fall upon the offender, the person he offends, or some other member of the group. This is referred to as *malweza*. But this is usually represented as a more or less automatic response to the offence, and not as a punishment sent by the *mizimu*. If a man strikes his sister, one of his parents, one of their

siblings, or any member of a generation older than his own, it is
malweza. Subsequent misfortune to either the offender or his
victim may be attributed to the *malweza* unless there has been a
ritual reconciliation. D5 quarrelled with his father and they eventually came to blows. A year or so later, the father died. The
diviner found that it was a case of *malweza*. Those who told me of
the incident said that it was *malweza* and not the *mizimu* which had
acted. Incest is also classed as *malweza*. The retribution may fall
upon either of the offenders or on any member of their matrilineal
group. If the offenders are paternal parallel cousins, then the
retribution may fall on members of either of their matrilineal
groups or on members of the paternal group which they have in
common. Again most Tonga with whom I discussed the matter
considered this to be a matter in which the *mizimu* were not
concerned. A few, however, said that the *malweza* retribution is
due to the anger of the *mizimu*. When they were asked how this
interpretation could be squared with the dogma that *mizimu* affect
only members of their matrilineal group or the offspring of this
group, they argued that while this was true nevertheless where
paternal parallel cousins were involved it was still possible for some
other member of their matrilineal groups to be affected. For, they
said, the *mizimu* of the paternal group would be angry, and would
call together the *mizimu* of the offender's matrilineal groups. The
paternal *mizimu* would point out: 'Look how your people have
brought filth into our group.' The *mizimu* of the two matrilineal
groups would then grow angry, and send misfortune to some
member of their groups. But most Tonga with whom I talked
saw no necessary connection between the *mizimu* and *malweza*,
and those who have abandoned belief in the *mizimu* may still
carry out rites to ward off the effects of *malweza*.[1]

On the whole, therefore, it can be argued that the *mizimu* are
neutral in respect to the internal affairs of the group to which
they act as guardians. They leave men free to settle their own

---

[1] *Malweza* also occurs in other contexts where kinship is irrelevant. If a man
breaks one of the taboos connected with a rain-shrine, it is *malweza*. The spirits
connected with the rain cults are known as *basangu*, and the *mizimu* are not
involved.

affairs, hampered from intervention by the dogma that they are equally attached to all members of the group rather than to smaller units within it.

However, if a man feels himself neglected during his lifetime, his own *muzimu* may be accused of sending illness to his kinsmen after his death; or it may do so if the funeral rites are not carried out properly. Mourning rites are the one occasion when it is incumbent on every member of the group to be present. Each one has a specific responsibility to take part in the rite—therefore misfortune to any one of them may be interpreted as due to the anger of the *muzimu* of the deceased. The knowledge that all adults are potential *mizimu* who may after death retaliate against the living for neglect may give force to the obligations of kinship. So may the fact that if a man repeatedly scandalizes his kinsmen they may abandon him as a sorcerer and refuse to perform the funeral rites which recognize the existence of his own *muzimu*, though this threat is rarely realized today. On the whole, however, the Tonga are not inclined to stress what may happen. They consider what has happened, and find an explanation for it. So, if they are asked: 'Aren't you afraid that if you treat a man like this that his own *muzimu* after his death will attack you?', they will reply: 'But we don't know that anything will happen. When something happens, then we will go to the diviner and he will discover perhaps that it is due to the anger of the *muzimu* and then we will know that this is the result. But how can you know in advance? Perhaps nothing will happen.' With this common-sense approach, men are able to live together and adjust their response to the demands of various kinsmen against what they see as practicable possibility without a pervading fear of ultimate consequences.

Though the *mizimu* are not invoked in the daily give-and-take between members of a matrilineal group, they can be used as a lever to enforce claims against other groups. A *muzimu* may send sickness to a woman or her children to extract bridewealth from her husband. If either maternal or paternal relatives monopolize the bridewealth to the detriment of the claims of the other group, the *mizimu* of the offended group may send sickness to the woman or her children. If a murder has been committed, and the compensation has not been forthcoming, the *mizimu* of the victim's group may be held responsible for the sickness or death of someone who is an offspring of both their group and the offender's. Here the *mizimu* act within a specific relationship to enforce a recognized specific obligation, and the misfortune falls upon the person who is the nexus for the relationships of the two groups involved.

The cult of the *mizimu* reflects other characteristics of the matrilineal group, such as the lack of formal leadership. Rank and position within the group are not ritually buttressed, nor do the *mizimu* play any part in supporting the pretensions that a man or woman may have for pre-eminence over kinsmen. There is no cult centre upon which all members of the group are dependent. No one plays the part of priest to make offerings to the *mizimu* on behalf of the group as a whole, or for any unit within it. Every person, once recognized as an adult, may approach the *mizimu* of his line on his own behalf, though he frequently invites some other member of the group to attend and pour the offering.

The dispersed nature of the group is reflected in the limitation of the field within which the *mizimu* are thought to act. Where kinship and community are conterminous, interests which pertain to the community can be expressed in ritual framed in terms of kinship and an ancestral cult. But among the Tonga, the local group is not a descent group with a common body of ancestors. Members of the same matrilineal group live scattered in different localities and different communities. Under these circumstances, it is only too obvious that the *mizimu* do not control the harvest, for as far as his crops are concerned a man has a common fate with others of his local community. This may be very different from that of his kinsmen who live in other localities more or less favoured with rains, insect plagues, etc., than his own. The ancestors are therefore of minor importance in crop rituals, and community spirits of another type come to the fore, for those who share a common fate are members of many different matrilineal groups with different *mizimu*. Former leaders may appear in both cults, but in one they appear in the guise of *mizimu* concerned only with their own kinsmen and the offspring of these people. In the other, they appear as *basangu*, concerned with all those who dwell within the local community.[1]

Like their living kinsmen, *mizimu* are not tied to a given area. They are thought to follow their kinsmen in their wanderings. A person cannot escape from his *mizimu* by moving to another area, or even by leaving Tonga country altogether. Wherever their kinsmen are, there they are present, though this implies that they are present in many different places at the same time. This has already been implied by the belief that members of different sections have the same *mizimu*.

Nevertheless, a man or woman ought to die in his or her own homestead wherever this may be, or at least within the neighbourhood community of which the homestead forms a part. If he dies elsewhere, his kinsmen must bring a beast known as *ingolomokwa* which is slaughtered in a rite to send his *muzimu* back to his own neighbourhood. This is the neighbourhood where he has built his huts and cultivated a field, even though he has only lived within it for a year or so before his death. He has a right to die there though he has no kinsmen within the community. Elsewhere, he is a stranger, and even though he dies in the homestead of a kinsman, in a community surrounded by other kinsmen, his *muzimu* must be sent back to its home. This seems to contradict the accepted dogma that *mizimu* are attached to kinsmen and not to a given locality, but it recognizes the important fact that people are members of local communities as well as of matrilineal groups, and that they take their place within a community as a member of a household or homestead.

The Household and the Cult of the 'Mizimu'

For a further understanding of the cult, one must turn from a consideration of the matrilineal group to the household, the basic local unit of Tonga society. We have already said that a man may settle where he will, and usually takes his wife to live with him.

---

[1] See below, pp. 93–5. *Basangu* is the term used among the Tonga east of the railway line. Tonga in the western chiefdoms speak of these spirits as *baami ba imvula*, 'lords of the rain'.

In the unsettled days before European administration outlawed self-help and the resort to vengeance, a man was sometimes required to settle with his wife's relatives for the first few years of married life, until he had proved himself a worthy husband to whom she could be entrusted, and only then might he remove her to his home. Even today, if the man comes from some distance and is now well known to the woman's guardians, he may be required to live uxorilocally for a short period before he is permitted to remove his wife. In most marriages, residence is virilocal from the beginning. Nevertheless, this does not mean that a man may build a homestead apart from other people. Instead, for the first year or longer, he is required to build with an established family, and he and his wife are spoken of as being *kulelwa* ('cared for') during this period. They have their own field, their own granary, and their own hut. But the wife works with other women of the family, and the young couple eat with those who are caring for them. Though the young wife may do most of the cooking for the homestead, she is said not to 'cook' by herself during this period. She has no hearth. No fire should be built inside their hut. People do not gather there to eat and sing and talk. And most important of all, she may not brew beer at her house. If she makes beer, it must be at the house of some older woman who has already been permitted to brew. The young husband should not be called upon to decant the beer at beer drinks although he may attend and drink beer, for he is still only a boy. Throughout this period, the couple are dependent, as they were throughout childhood, upon the ritual offices of others to propitiate the *mizimu* and to make offerings on their behalf. Their house is not a shrine for the *mizimu*, who are not aware that a new family has been established. Indeed, at the time of the marriage, only the *mizimu* of the girl's father's line are informed of the event, when a representative of the line pours an offering and announces, 'I now throw away my daughter. She has gone to be married to so-and-so'. The *mizimu* of her matrilineal line are not informed nor are the *mizimu* of her husband. The existence of the new household is acknowledged only after the final marriage payment has been made. This is the *ciko*, which today usually consists of four head of cattle. This is generally given only after a number of years of marriage and sometimes after one or more children have been born. It can be thought of as the payment which transfers permanent rights in the woman to the husband's matrilineal group, for it gives them the right to appoint a successor if the husband dies, and thus to continue the household which he has founded. Today women may refuse to be inherited, and probably they always had some voice in the matter, but the payment of *ciko* is an important step in establishing a permanent union.[1] After the receipt of this final payment, the wife's relatives take the initiative in the rite that establishes the household. Representatives of her father's group and of her own matrilineal group come to place grain to sprout for beer, and later return to help her brew. Representatives of the husband's two groups are also expected to assist. On the day when the beer is ready, relatives of husband and wife gather at the house to drink, dance and sing. But before this is done, offerings are made to the *mizimu* of the husband, and the house is placed under their care.

One particular *muzimu* is usually recognized as the guardian of the house with the responsibility of protecting all who live within its doors or who are attached to it. Only rarely will this be one of the two guardian *mizimu* of the husband, whose names he has borne since infancy. These are still important to him and should receive offerings from time to time, but henceforth the *muzimu* which guards his house will be of primary importance in his life. A man usually dedicates his house to the *muzimu* of his father, if his father is already dead, but he may dedicate it to a *muzimu* of his matrilineal line, or perhaps to the *muzimu* of his father's father under whose protection he himself grew up in his father's household. He is free to choose any *muzimu* from his matrilineal line, although the choice may be dictated by the diviner. However, a man dedicates his house only to the *muzimu* of a man. As a woman

---

[1] Torrend, 1931, p. 199, gives *ciko* as a word meaning family, 'literally a fire-place, also the cattle or money given by a wooer to the parents of his betrothed'. My informants maintained that *ciko* meaning 'fire-place' and *ciko* meaning 'bridewealth' were two words, differentiated apparently by tone, and they did not recognize the use of *ciko* as a word for family.

E

can never be the legal head of a household in which she is also a wife, so the *muzimu* of a woman cannot be house guardian for a household centred on a man.   The husband is the priest of the household. In making offerings to the *mizimu*, he himself may pour the offerings to the *mizimu* of his matrilineal line, at the left-hand side of the door. He should call a member of his father's group to make the offerings on the right side of the door to the *muzimu* of his father and to other *mizimu* of that line, for *mizimu* are thought to heed only members of their own line. He is a child of their line, and not a member.[1]

The husband is dependent upon his wife for the approach to his *mizimu*, for the offering should consist of beer brewed by the wife who lives in the house. She may be assisted by other women in the brewing, but the beer must be brewed at least ostensibly by her. Purchased beer is useless as an offering. If a woman cannot brew, because of a shortage of grain, illness, or some equally good reason, the husband may make an offering with water or meal, but at the same time he must announce to the *mizimu* that his wife will brew for them as soon as possible.

The wife and her *mizimu* have an inferior role in the ritual of the household though they are essential to it. The *mizimu* of the wife may send sickness to the wife or her children, to announce their desire for beer, and she will then brew for them. But offerings are made most often in the name of the husband's *mizimu*. Even if the wife has brewed for her own *mizimu*, her husband should first pour an offering to his *mizimu*, who are the primary guardians of the household. Moreover, the wife does not make offerings at the doorway. In some areas, she pours her offering at the bed post. In others, she makes her offering at the centre pole of the hut. Only if a woman who is divorced or widowed occupies a house by herself may she install a *muzimu* of her own line as the guardian of the house and make offerings to the *mizimu* at the door, for she is then the owner of the house. In that case, she may dedicate her house to the *muzimu* of either a man or a woman. If she remarries, and her husband comes to live in her house, he must make her a

---

[1] Compare the Ila ritual. See Smith and Dale, 1920, Vol. II, p. 166.

token payment, which gives him rights in her house, field and granary, and thereafter he may install his *mizimu* as primary guardians of the house. The wife's *mizimu* then once again have a minor place.

Once a woman has made beer for the *mizimu*, she continues to have the power to approach them on her own behalf, whether she is married or single. A man, however, makes offerings only so long as he continues to have a wife in his house. If she dies or departs, his household through which he established his ritual efficacy is broken. Widowers and divorced men, even though they had their own houses where they lived with their children or other relatives, had only one reply when questioned about the *muzimu* to which the house was dedicated: 'There is no woman here, and therefore there is no *muzimu*.' Women are important in Tonga social structure because through them descent is traced and membership within the matrilineal group is established. Men are important because of their position within a household, and the linkages which they as husbands and fathers establish between their own matrilineal groups and others in the community.

Mizimu are thought to be anxious to acquire for themselves households which are dedicated especially to their service. When a man has once installed a *muzimu* as house guardian, he may find that his household is still troubled by misfortune. The diviner may then announce that some other *muzimu* wishes to guard the house. The new *muzimu* may be installed along with the old, or the dedication transferred from one to the other. Or the diviner may announce that since the house is primarily dedicated to a *muzimu* of the father's line, the *mizimu* of the mother's line feel themselves neglected. They feel that they are not receiving sufficient offerings, that their names are called rarely, or only after the names of the *mizimu* of the father's line. They are therefore demanding that the men marry a second wife in whose house one of them may be installed. If a man does marry again, he usually places some *muzimu* of his matrilineal line in this house. It is spoken of as the house of his matrilineal line, whereas the first house becomes the house of his father's line, and he no longer propitiates his matrilineal *mizimu* there. Subsequent houses are also placed usually to the name of some matrilineal *muzimu*. However, no matter how many times a man has been married, if he has but one house at any one moment, this will usually be considered to be the house of the father's line if his father is dead. Moreover, the rights of his paternal *mizimu* over his homestead as a whole are stressed. When

TABLE II

Dedication of Huts to *Mizimu**

Muzimu of	1st House	2nd House	Subsequent Houses
Father	53	1	—
Some Member of Father's line . .	1	—	—
Mother's Brother	1†	12	—
Some Member of Mother's line .	4	6	5
Father and Some Member of Mother's line‡	8	—	—
Father's Father	7	1	1
Father and Father's Father‡ . .	3	—	—
Father, Father's Father, and Mother's Father‡	1	—	—
Mother's Father	1	—	—
Dedication Unspecified . . .	14	3	1
TOTAL	93	23	7
No Dedication§	86	17	1
No Information	33	7	4
TOTAL	212	47	12

* This information relates to the same 17 villages used in the earlier discussions of Succession and Taking the Spirit. It includes only households with a male head.

† This house was the only house of the informant at the time of the questioning, but the man had lost two wives in the previous two years, one through death and one through separation, and he had not yet changed the dedication of what had been the third house.

‡ Houses dedicated to more than one *muzimu* in this combination.

§ Some of these houses belong to men who consider themselves to be Christians and who therefore refuse to dedicate their houses to *mizimu* or to make offerings to them. Most of these live in the Mwansa and Ufwenuka villages which contain many strong Seventh Day Adventists. A few may belong to men whose wives have not yet been permitted to make beer. Where I could, I omitted such cases, but it was not always possible to make the distinction from the information recorded on the census forms.

beer is made for the *mizimu*, that provided by the first house may be drunk in the open space in front of the homestead. That provided by the house of the matrilineal line, should be drunk inside this house, for it is within its walls that these *mizimu* are important.

A few people, especially in the areas to the east and north-west of Tonga country, build an additional shrine for the *mizimu*, but this is done only if the *mizimu* themselves are thought to demand it. This shrine is the *cilyango* or 'spirit gate', made by planting three clusters of poles a few feet apart but in a straight line, and connecting them at the top by a cross-bar. The poles take root, and the shrine continues in existence as long as the homestead remains on the same site. Through the gates the spirits are thought to enter the homestead of the owner. The right-hand gate is used by the *mizimu* of the paternal line, the left-hand gate by those of the maternal line. When the owner moves, he builds a new shrine on the new site, though he may wait to do so until the ancestors remind him of his duty by sending sickness to a member of the household. If he dies, his successor may let the shrine lapse unless some misfortune is attributed by the diviner to the anger of the *muzimu* of the dead man at the neglect of his former practice. Occasionally a man may be told that though neither he nor any known member of his group has ever built a shrine, the *mizimu* have decided that it is time they received this honour. The new shrine is then built. Offerings are poured at the shrine when it is first built, and thereafter only when the spirits demand it. The usual offering place remains the doorway of the house, and the house itself is the essential shrine.[1] When it is abandoned, and the family build anew, some stick or other relic from the old house should be incorporated in the new, as a sign of the continuity of the family which it houses. Before and after the move to the new house, the *mizimu* should receive offerings to inform them of the move.

When a man makes an offering, though it is at the behest of a particular *muzimu*, he usually tries to propitiate all the *mizimu* who may be concerned with him. He calls first the house *muzimu*, then his guardian *mizimu*, his inherited *muzimu* if he has any, any *mizimu* which have endowed him with a special skill, the *mizimu* of his parents if they are dead, and then he usually adds three or four other names which he has heard older people call when they were making offerings. He asks these to bring with them all the *mizimu* of their line whose names he has forgotten. They are

---

[1] This is true also for other people in this area. See Richards, 1939, p. 357, where she refers to the Bemba hut as a shrine since the ancestral spirits of both husband and wife are thought to linger there.

thought to come behind the *mizimu* whose names are recited. Moreover, the Tonga argue, since the same names are given generation after generation, many *mizimu* will come when you call one name, even though you yourself know nothing about them. Men may call the names of *mizimu* although they do not know when the people lived, or where they lived, or who they were. This is not important. They are invoked because they are *mizimu*, and not because they are related to the one who invokes them in some particular fashion. In the invocation, the relationship between the one who speaks and the *mizimu* called is rarely mentioned.

Mizimu then are primarily concerned with the household and all that concerns it, and in the household the position of the husband is buttressed by the belief in the *mizimu*. Moreover, the authority of his father's line is enhanced above that of his mother's line, with which he is most closely associated. Here, as elsewhere, one finds that ritual authority is greatest where actual authority is weakest. For no one denies that a man is more closely associated with his own matrilineal group than he is with the group of his father, and that the rights of the mother's relatives over her children are greater than those of the father. Nevertheless, the Tonga say that the anger of *mizimu* of the maternal line is less dangerous to the living than the anger of the *mizimu* of the father's line. The former may make you ill, but they cannot kill without the consent of the *mizimu* of the paternal line. And within the household, the *mizimu* of the husband are supreme. They may send illness to husband, wife and children. If the *mizimu* of the wife should wish to punish neglect by sending illness to wife or child, the husband's *mizimu* may prevent them from fulfilling their intention, warning them that this house belongs to them and they will guard it against the intruding *mizimu*. It well behoves a wife to cater to the wants of her husband's *mizimu*, who will thus protect her against the malevolent intentions of her own *mizimu*. In their role as guardians of the household, moreover, the husband's *mizimu* will protect outsiders temporarily domiciled under the roof. The wife's children by a former marriage are thus ensured of some protection from the *mizimu* of their stepfather, so long as they remain members of his household. So also are other children who come to work for him and for a period are attached to the household. But their fathers are never completely displaced as the ritual guardians of their welfare, for wherever a child may live, the *mizimu* of its father's line as well as the *mizimu* of its own line have power to affect it. The diviner may announce that its illness is due to a *muzimu* of the father's line, and though beer for the offering may be brewed at the house where the child is domiciled, the father or his representative must be called to make the offering. The rights of the father to his child are thereby guarded, while at the same time the authority of the household head is recognized through the belief that his *mizimu* offer some protection to all who dwell within the house.

The *mizimu* also extend their protection beyond the household to all those living in the homestead, if these are ritually impotent. In former days, slaves came immediately under the guardianship of their owner's *mizimu*, and indeed one of the first acts that proclaimed their new status was the bestowing of a name from a *muzimu* of the owner's line. Young couples who have yet to make beer in their own house come under the protection of the *mizimu* of the head of the homestead, as do men who have lost their wives through death or divorce. Sons who settle with their fathers, or with a kinsman of their father, remain to some extent ritually dependent upon their father or his representative throughout their lives, for the *mizimu* of most importance to them are those of their father's line who must be approached through a member of the line rather than directly. Thus of the 22 men of other matrilineal groups living in D11's village, 11 are 'sons' on whose behalf he and his kinsmen should make offerings.

Sons and daughters are not bound to their father's immediate kinsmen by this ritual dependence. Any member of the father's matrilineal group who has established his own household may officiate. Indeed, if no suitable person is available, the Tonga allow a substitute to officiate. Their first choice would be a member of the father's clan, even though of another tribe, for they maintain that all members of the same clan are ultimately related and therefore they can appeal to the *mizimu*. When Reuben of Nampeyo and his wife first made beer for their *mizimu*, there was no one in the neighbourhood belonging to the matrilineal group of Reuben's father, a member of the Buffalo clan. The only Buffalo in the village was my Ila clerk, by then more or less resident in the village. Reuben asked him to make the offerings to the paternal *mizimu* and instructed him in the names to be called as he poured the offering. If no member of the father's clan is available, they turn to another type of substitute, someone who is a child of the father's clan, and preferably someone who is child of the father's matrilineal group. Samuel and Nehemiah of Nampeyo were making beer for the *mizimu* on the same day. Both men were sons of the Buffalo clan. Again the only Buffalo in the immediate neighbourhood was my Ila clerk. Samuel called upon the clerk to make the offering. Nehemiah asked an Eland woman who was the child of a Buffalo man to make the offering for him. One of these three men had matrilineal kinsmen of his father living within eight miles of the village. The other two had no paternal kinsmen anywhere within the vicinity as both were immigrants. However, many Buffalo people were living in the neighbouring district, perhaps three or four miles away, and these could have been summoned for the offerings. The men preferred to make the offerings through a local person, and this is usually the case. Thus the offerings which symbolize a man's dependence upon his paternal kin are made through members of his local group, whether or not these are members of his father's own matrilineal group. I think this is a significant clue to the nature of the cult of the *mizimu*.

We find a further clue in the fact that though the Tonga permit a child of the paternal clan to perform the offerings if no appropriate representative of the father's matrilineal group is available, nevertheless they deny that a person may make the offerings to the *mizimu* of his father's line on his own behalf, arguing that he is not a member of that line and therefore has no right to approach its *mizimu*. Nor would two brothers or two paternal half-brothers make the offerings for each other. The distinction, apparently illogical, must be due to the social nature of the rite—it is concerned with relating a person to others in the community rather than to the spirits of the dead. This also explains why in most cases the Tonga call upon those in the immediate vicinity rather than upon their true paternal kinsmen who may be living at a distance. If a man could make the offerings on his own behalf, he would be ritually independent of others. If he could depend only upon true members of his father's line, he might have to call upon people living outside the locality within which his life is spent. The principle of substitution means that a tie of ritual dependence can always be created between himself and others living near him, for though the Tonga communities are small there are only a few clans and the spread of clan members throughout the country makes it almost inevitable that some members of the father's clan will be found within the local community. If by any chance there should be no clansman, there will be a child of the clan.

The principle of substitution plus the dogma that a person is debarred from propitiating his paternal ancestors directly, thus allow the Tonga to indulge in the high geographical mobility which is so marked a feature of their society. At the same time it ensures that wherever a person goes he can and must establish some firm bond with another member of the community to permit him to call upon the other for offerings to the paternal ancestors which dominate his household and upon which he is most dependent for his ritual well-being. It is to these ancestors that he makes offerings most frequently, and therefore his dependence is stressed. We can understand, in this context, why the maternal *mizimu* have a minor role in the ritual, for these a man may propitiate himself, and in offering to them he is independent of the community. Where his direct dependence for assistance, in relation to others of his matrilineal group, is clearest, there is less need to stress a ritual dependence.

The formal differentiation of the two types of dependency occurs at a particular point in a man's life. It is the payment of the bridewealth for his first wife which establishes his household and permits him to initiate the offerings to the *mizimu*. Here the paternal line comes to the fore ritually. Until this time, the man has been dependent ritually as well as secularly upon both his paternal and his maternal relatives. But the chief material responsibility of the father's group ends with the provision of the bride-wealth for the first wife. Henceforth a man is a member of the community in his own right, and his chief legal identification will be with other members of his matrilineal group. His support will go largely in helping other members of his own group and in assistance to his and their children who are growing up. Since he is no longer directly dependent upon his paternal relatives for support, the ritual emphasis upon the paternal *mizimu* can be used to bind him closely not to his paternal kinsmen as such, with whom he may lose contact, but to other members of the local community within which he finds himself.

BECOMING A 'MUZIMU'

We have already said that not every person becomes a *muzimu* after his death. Paradoxically, a man is more certain of becoming a *muzimu* in relation to his own children than he is in relation to his matrilineal group. The dogma is that only fully adult men and women become *mizimu*, and this status is reserved not for those who have begotten children but for those who have made beer in their own house. Some say that it is sufficient to have cooked in the house, and that the beer is not important. But until such time, a man has not been able to make offerings to the *mizimu* so that they recognize his existence as a discrete personality, he has not been able to entertain fellow men so that his name and his household have become known. If he dies after this, whether or not he has begotten a child, he becomes a *muzimu*, able to join with other *mizimu* in approaching members of his matrilineal group with demands for beer and other offerings, in giving his name to children born of the group, in demanding the right to guard a house. The same is true of women, although a woman who dies before this stage is reached may still have the chance to become a *muzimu* of the matrilineal line when her children grow up. If a man leaves children, they will probably think of him as a *muzimu*, and install the *muzimu* as the guardian of their households. Indeed, the Tonga say that even if a man has never married, he may become a *muzimu* if he has begotten children for whom he has made the legitimization payment and to whom he has given a name from his line, for these children too, when they have grown, will remember their father. But his children belong to another matrilineal group. Unless they remain in close contact with some of their father's kinsmen, they will call upon other people to make offerings to their father's *muzimu*. His paternity then is irrelevant to members of his own group, and his *muzimu* need receive no recognition from them.

We can now see the significance of the stage at which a man becomes a *muzimu* of his matrilineal line. The dogma is that men become ancestral spirits through the wives with whom they establish a household which permits them to offer hospitality to men and to the *mizimu*, whereby they become distinguished from the household which begot them and the household with which they have been identified until this stage. Even though they die childless the perpetuation of their *mizimu* is said to be assured, for they have become personalities in their own right. But in actual fact it is in the households of their children that their *mizimu* find their chief shrines. Unless a man is an influential leader, his kinsmen will remember him after death chiefly because they summon him on behalf of his children. Children follow their mother on divorce, or if their father dies and their mother refuses to be inherited. Thus they are likely to drift away to other communities and lose contact with their father's kinsmen. The payment of the final instalment of the bridewealth comes several years after marriage when it appears that the union will be a permanent one. If the husband then dies, he can be succeeded by another of his kinsmen who continues the household. The children will probably remain in it. They grow up knowing their father's kinsmen. They are more likely to settle in the same neighbourhood with such paternal kinsmen. In all affairs that concern them, their father's kinsmen will be expected to co-operate with members of their own matrilineal group. So long as they live, they will make offerings to the *muzimu* of their father through the agency of representatives of his group. When his children are all dead, the bond created between the two matrilineal groups by the original marriage disappears, and the man who as husband and father created the bond is no longer socially significant. His group is then likely to forget him, and his *muzimu* coalesces with others of the same name. It is the establishment of a stable household which is the keystone to the structure built about the interests of the two groups in the offspring of a marriage. The household is thus rightly the focus of the cult of the *mizimu* as it is their shrine.

Elsewhere, I have pointed out that the chief factor making for local harmony within a Tonga community is the interweaving of ties between matrilineal groups within it by the fact that each group has children in many other groups.[1] These ties are in a state of constant flux as children are born of new unions and create new ties to bring groups together, while the offspring of former unions die and with them end the ties which centred in them. This form of the general society affects the structure of the cult of the *mizimu*. It is consistent with the short time span over which *mizimu* are remembered, for the important linkages between groups within a community alter with each generation. It is consistent with the dogma that the *mizimu* are general to the matrilineal group as a whole and not to some smaller unit within it, for it is the linkage together of matrilineal groups and not the union of segments within the group which is the basis upon which Tonga society is organized.

These linkages and the importance of men as heads of the households which are the basic local units influence the form of the cult. Nevertheless, women also see in it an acknowledgment of the primacy of their relationship to their children, and find a justification for the matrilineal system in the obligation of the maternal kin to take the *muzimu* of the dead. They know that it is through themselves, the mothers, that their children receive the spirits identified with them both in life and death, and it is through them and their kinsmen that these spirits are perpetuated. One night a group of us were discussing the ownership of crops and how husband and wife divide the product of their fields. A man then began to complain that his children belonged to their maternal line, and that while he could take bridewealth for his

---

[1] See Colson, 1951, pp. 150–1

daughters he would receive nothing in respect of their daughters. His wife remarked: 'Yes, but the matrilineal group takes it because if I should die, my father's side would not come to purify my husband. They would not come to take my *muzimu*. It is the matrilineal group that does the work. Therefore the children belong to the mother even if you take the maize.' Her husband snorted: 'To the mother! You mean the relatives take them.' She replied complacently: 'It's the same thing. They belong to us.'

The *mizimu* of the husband may be dominant in the household, but mother and children are united by the common fate of their perpetual *mizimu*—those drawn from the maternal line—in a bond very different from that which exists between a father and the children to whom he loans a *muzimu* for their lifetime only. The household which emphasizes the prerogatives of the father and the group to which he belongs is but a temporary affair, important though it is. So are the linkages between groups founded on paternity. The matrilineal group is permanent.

ANOMALIES IN THE CULT

So far, Tonga dogma about the *mizimu* has emerged as a reasonably coherent system of belief consistent with the social system. Those anomalies that have appeared are such that it is possible to explain them in terms of the system as a whole. We must now, however, turn to certain anomalies which seem to contradict both the dogma and the analysis presented of it.

Basic to the analysis are two statements: that the *mizimu* affect only members of their own line and the children of the line; and that each person at his naming receives a guardian *muzimu* from his own matrilineal line and from the matrilineal line of his father. Now there is no glossing over the fact that neither statement is absolutely true. Diviners sometimes attribute an illness to a *muzimu* unrelated to the person who is ill. Children frequently receive names which belong to the lines of their grandfathers or of even more remote ancestors. They sometimes are named after someone with whom they can trace no relationship whatsoever. The Tonga know that this is so. Indeed, they often say that they commonly name a son after their father. This name is not a nickname. It is a name associated with a guardian *muzimu* and is given instead of the name associated with the matrilineal group of the parent.

This means that many men go through life with a guardian *muzimu* from the paternal side which belongs to their father's father's matrilineal group. Less commonly children have a guardian *muzimu* not from their own matrilineal group but from their mother's father's group. And I have even known a woman to name her child after her own mother's father, the child's great-grandfather. The Tonga argue that this does not matter, for after all these *mizimu* too take an interest in the child, and can be appealed to on its behalf. They add that of course these *mizimu* must be propitiated by members of their own lines, and that a representative of the line in question would be summoned when the offering is to be made. This is simple enough if a child has received a name from its father's father, so long as it is a member of its father's household, for a member of that line will be present in any event to make the offerings to the paternal *mizimu* of the father. In later life, it implies a continuing link with the people of the grandfather. But by this time the guardian *mizimu* from both parents are overshadowed by the house guardians. Nevertheless, as the table on house dedication shows, men often have the *mizimu* of their grandfathers as house *mizimu*. Presumably this reflects the actual circumstances in which different individuals find themselves. Children frequently do grow up in close contact with their grandparents. They may continue to live in communities where the kinsmen of either grandfather are the important men. Their association with these people may be of the utmost importance to them, in establishing themselves within the community.

We may explain in the same way the fact that a child may sometimes be named after someone to whom it is not related. A man named after B2 is a case in point. His father was a foreigner of another tribe who moved to the Nampeyo area where B2 was the dominating personality. He brought with him a wife from another part of Tonga country who had no connection with any of the people at Nampeyo. After they had lived in the community for a number of years, under an alliance with B2 who recognized the foreigner as a possible rival and useful friend, B2 allowed the man to marry one of his sister's daughter's daughters. Then B2 died. When the first wife of the foreigner was in labour, the diviner announced that the *muzimu* of B2 wished to give its name to the child of his friend. The child received this name rather than a name from its matrilineal line. He has borne the name ever since, and proudly attributes his success to the *muzimu* of B2 which has presided over his destiny. When I questioned members of the matrilineal group of B2 about the matter, D11 answered somewhat querulously: 'Yes, you see that is just as I told you. Our names go into other groups and get lost to us. Now they have our name.' He obviously felt that in some way he and his kinsmen had a grievance, but they accepted the fact that the *muzimu* of B2 was the guardian of a man of another line. They were never called to make offerings to the *muzimu* of B2 on the man's behalf, for he was a progressive man and quite contrary enough to be extremely proud of his guardian *muzimu* while at the same time denying the existence of *mizimu*.

I found a number of instances where a diviner ascribed an illness to the wrath of a strange *muzimu*. One involved the wife of D11. Years before D11 had quarrelled with an old widow living in his village, and because she complained about the inroads of the cattle on her fields, he told her to move out. She went. Later D11 gave her field to his wife. Now the wife was ill. When they consulted a diviner, he announced that the illness was due to the anger of the old woman's *muzimu* which grudged her the field. Another divination ascribed the death of a man's wife to the anger of the *muzimu* of his first wife. The first wife died in childbirth, and her kinsmen appointed a young girl as her successor. The husband gave the child gifts of clothing, and at the time of her puberty ceremony he sent a goat to be slaughtered. But from the beginning, he doubted that he would actually marry the girl, and other people in the community seemed equally dubious. Finally, he married another woman, and his betrothed eloped with another man. When the second wife died in childbirth, the diviner announced that she had been killed by the *muzimu* of the first which was angry at the slight put upon her kinswoman.

The Tonga do not attempt to redefine their dogma about the *mizimu* to explain such cases. The divination is applied to the particular misfortune, and has no effect upon the structure of belief which relates to the groups within which people are organized. But then, even these groups are in a sense convenient myths of the Tonga. What they know are the multitude of relationships which exist between those living together in Tonga country. They define these relationships in their dogmatic statements about social structure. They are well aware that the dogma is not a completely accurate description of what happens, but it is sufficiently close for their purposes. The dogma of the *mizimu* is brought into conformity with it. They know that men do not always act in accordance with the dogma that governs their interrelationships with each other. They are not overwhelmed when confronted by evidence that the *mizimu* also sometimes act without reference to the dogma that relates them to mankind.

SUMMARY

In this chapter, it has been shown that various aspects of the Tonga social system are reflected in the set of beliefs they hold about the *mizimu*.

1. The affiliation of each individual with the two matrilineal groups of his father and his mother is reflected in the belief that a person receives at his naming a guardian *muzimu* from each line, which is important in determining character and actions. It is further reflected in the belief that all *mizimu* of either line may affect him.

2. The system of matrilineal inheritance, and the primary affiliation with the matrilineal group of the mother, is reflected in the belief that when a person dies his own *muzimu* is inherited by the matrilineal line, and has no power over members of the father's group.

3. The dogma that the matrilineal group is undifferentiated is

reflected in the belief that any *muzimu* belonging to the line may affect any member of it.

4. The lack of instituted formal leadership within the group is reflected in the belief that every adult may approach the *mizimu* of his matrilineal line on his own behalf, and in the fact that no one person acts as priest for the rest of the group or for any division within it.

5. The local dispersion of the matrilineal group is reflected in the absence of local shrines for the propitiation of the *mizimu*, and in the belief that they are present wherever living members of the line live.

6. The importance of the household is reflected in the belief that only men and women who have formed their own households become *mizimu* in their own right when they die.

7. The dominant role of the husband as representative of the household is reflected in the domination of his *mizimu* over the *mizimu* of the wife in household ritual.

8. The necessity for integrating people into a local community composed of members of many matrilineal groups is reflected in the stress upon the importance of the paternal *mizimu* for whose propitiation an intermediary is necessary.

CHAPTER II

CLANS AND THE JOKING-RELATIONSHIP AMONG THE PLATEAU TONGA OF NORTHERN RHODESIA[1]

FORMALIZED joking between clans has been reported from many tribes in British Central Africa.[2] Tew has attempted to place the joking between clans within the wider context of the funeral friendship which exists in one form or another from the Zambezi River in the south to Lake Tanganyika in the north and from the east coast to the Luangwa river.[3] Radcliffe-Brown has also dealt with the subject in his analysis of the general nature of joking-relationships.[4]

The Tonga are thus not unique in practising such joking. This chapter does not report any new phenomenon, nor shall I attempt within it to develop any new theory of the nature of joking-relationships. I am limiting myself to a description of the relationship as it exists among the Plateau Tonga. Despite Tew's suggestion that 'funeral friendship' should be adopted as a descriptive term to cover the phenomenon as it occurs in this area, I shall use the old form 'clan joking-relationship' since among the Tonga the funeral is only one, and perhaps not the most important, situation in which the relationship operates. Indeed, one could cavil at

---

[1] Material for this chapter was gathered during the same period and from the same areas as that for Chapter I. See page 1, note 1.

[2] Richards, 1937 (Bemba); Stefaniszyn, 1950 (Ambo); Melland, 1923, pp. 251–2 (Kaonde); Doke, 1931, pp. 197–8 (Lamba). Dr. Cunnison informs me that it is also found among the peoples living in the Luapula Valley. Among the Southern Lunda, joking occurs not between clans, but between two sections of the tribe, according to information quoted in McCulloch, 1951, pp. 21–2. Clan-joking has not been reported for the Ila, close neighbours of the Tonga with whom they share many customs. Instead joking is characteristic of the age group. See Smith and Dale, 1920, Vol. I, pp. 308–10.

[3] Tew, 1951. She gives references to the literature describing funeral friendships among the different tribes of the area.

[4] Radcliffe-Brown, 1940 and 1949. Both articles are reprinted in Radcliffe-Brown, 1952.

either term, since neither joking nor funeral duties effectively define the relationship. In many situations clans perform reciprocal services for each other. One might therefore call the institution, 'clan reciprocity', and those entering into it 'clan reciprocals'.

The Plateau Tonga are a Bantu-speaking people living in what is now the Mazabuka District of the Southern Province of Northern Rhodesia. Today they number between 80,000 and 120,000 people. To the east of them live the Valley Tonga of the Gwembe District in the Zambezi River Valley. They share with the Plateau people the same clan system and among them the institution of clan-joking also appears in the same form.[1]

Among both Plateau and Valley Tonga, descent and succession are in the matrilineal line. Today, they are organized into chiefdoms under Native Authorities instituted by the British Administration. Traditionally, they had neither chiefs nor other forms of instituted authorities to bind them into a tribe or some organized political body. Instead, though they recognized their common cultural and linguistic affinities, they were content to give their loyalty to much smaller groupings. These were of two types: small neighbourhoods composed of a few villages organized about a common rain-shrine and cult; and a large number of small groups based on kinship. The members of such a group were usually dispersed throughout a number of neighbourhoods. These groups I have called matrilineal groups to distinguish them from the much larger clans, which are known by the same term, *mukowa*.[2] The matrilineal groups were bodies which shared inheritances, bridewealth, and other privileges and responsibilities. Their members met together for common purposes, both ritual and secular. They acted as vengeance groups, and formed mutual assistance associations. Theoretically, all members of a matrilineal group were descended from a common ancestress, a few generations back, though usually her name had been forgotten, and those within the group were not able to trace their genealogical links with each other. Though I have written in the past tense,

---

[1] [Only a portion of the Gwembe people have clan-joking. In Mwemba it does not occur.]

[2] For further information on Tonga social organization, see Colson, 1951.

the matrilineal groups remain important elements of Tonga social organization, and many of their functions remain intact.

THE CLANS

The clan is a much less integrated body than the matrilineal group, and its functions are not as clearly defined. True the Tonga, even today, will argue that the clan system is of the greatest importance in their lives, but this is because they are usually thinking of the matrilineal group which is only situationally distinguished from the clan of which it forms a part. Still, though the clan is widely dispersed and owns no property, has no shrines, no common rites, no occasions on which all its members gather for some common purpose, the clan is the single unit in Tonga social life which has more than an ephemeral existence. Villages usually have short histories. Even neighbourhoods may shift their boundaries and composition within a generation. People move from one to another, and need not spend their lives within one village or neighbourhood.[1] Matrilineal groups may also be disrupted, and reform themselves into new groupings, as people become geographically separated and no longer maintain the old relations with their kinsmen. The clans alone are thought to be eternal. Most Tonga take them as a part of the natural order of things left to them by their ancestors from long long ago. Over most of Tonga country there is no myth which purports to explain the origin of clans or people. Both have always existed, or were created simultaneously. In the western areas, such as the present chiefdom of Macha, some people have a legend that the first people, already organized into clans, descended from the sky to light on a certain hill where their imprints may still be seen. Even in this myth, clans and people originate together. The only additional information they have about the development of the present clan system is that once two of the present clans were one, and then for some reason separated into the clans known as Baleya and Bantanga. This division again is said to have occurred

---

[1] Colson, 1951.

long before the memory of living men. Since then the clans have continued unchanged. There is no myth which gives one priority over the others or purports to relate its history.

This division into clans is considered to be an invariable human institution. The Tonga find it practically impossible to conceive of any society in which people are not divided into clans. Since most of the other peoples they have encountered also have a clan system, this belief is not surprising. Indeed, many of the same clans appear in other tribes, and foreigners who come to settle in Tonga country have little difficulty in fitting themselves into the Tonga clan system. They either belong to a clan which is also represented among the Tonga, or they find some way of equating their own clan with one of the existing Tonga clans. Thus, though Tonga country has always received influxes of people from other tribes, and today contains many foreigners who came first to work in the European areas near the railway and then settled in the Tonga reserves, the Tonga clan system remains unaffected. Strangers do not introduce new clans into the country. They find their place within the existing divisions, only fourteen in number.

The clan system then gives a common basis of understanding with people of other tribes, and makes Tonga society into an open system. For through their membership in the same clans, foreigners can find their place within Tonga society, while the Tonga can also associate themselves with other tribes if they leave their own territory.

Clan membership gives rise to only a few limited obligations and rights, which perhaps is why it is so easily extended to strangers. In the days before British Administration brought peace to the land with its ban upon vengeance and enslavement, the clans may have been more important in offering security to the man who ventured outside his immediate home area, for members of the same clan were expected to offer each other hospitality and assistance. It was considered unethical to enslave, or to hold in slavery, a fellow clansman, though a slave assumed his owner's clan without affecting their relationship. Today this aspect of clan membership is no longer of any importance. But the clan continues to function in other fields. It still governs marriage, to the extent that clan exogamy is rigidly maintained. I have recorded only three instances of marriage within the clan where there was no question of slave descent to complicate the issue. For a slave or a person of slave-descent is a quasi-member of the clan with whom marriage is permitted. The Tonga stress clan exogamy as the most important aspect of the institution. Almost fifty years ago, when missionaries first went among them and queried them about the nature of the clan, the Tonga said that the clan was an institution given to them by God so that people might marry properly.[1] And so they still view the matter. The clan system also provides a mechanism for finding acceptable substitutes for certain rites in which matrilineal kinsmen should participate if no one of the proper category is available. Finally, the clan system forms the basis for a system of joking-relationship and reciprocal services.

Before describing this, however, it is necessary to discuss clan names, and their association with certain animals. Twelve clans are found very widely throughout Tonga country, from the Zambezi River to the western borders. Two more seem to be found only in the western areas. In the north-west, the system of names seems to be rather different, and probably it is affected by the system of the neighbouring Ila. [The system also varies in the southern portion of the Gwembe Valley.]

Most of the clan names cannot be translated today, though they are assumed to refer to animals. Many of the clans have a number of names, any one of which may be used. Informants do not know why these multiple names exist, and they certainly do not seem to designate divisions within a clan, or local groupings. The same person may sometimes say, for instance, that he is a Mukuli, again that he is a Mutenda, and again that he is Muunga. When queried, he will comment: 'It is the same clan. It just has different names.'[2] Each clan is associated with a number of animals or natural phenomena. These are not totemic associations, since no one avoids or honours his clan animals in any way. The association between a particular animal and a particular clan is not invariable

---

[1] Personal communication from Father Moreau, S.J., who helped to found Chikuni Mission in 1905.

[2] [These are three different clans in the southern Gwembe.]

throughout Tonga country. In some areas, one clan will be associated with an animal which is attributed to quite a different clan in some other area. Occasionally even within a single area there is some disagreement between people as to the proper clan association for different animals. But in the main this difference of opinion seems to apply chiefly to what one might call secondary associates. Each clan is usually referred to as having one particular associate, and then informants remember to add that it also has others. These secondary associations are remembered chiefly in the praise names and slogans belonging to the clan and in clan-joking situations. Why the Tonga should have such a varied array of animal and other associates for their clans, I do not know. Possibly it results from the amalgamation of the various foreigners into the common clan system. Whatever the cause, the associations persist and appear in the joking situations.

The clans and their most common associates are given in Table III. Where an animal has been attributed by different informants to different clans, I have shown this by placing it within brackets.

TABLE III

Clans and their Associates

Clan	Associates
1. Bahyamba. . .	hyena, rhinoceros, pig, ant, fish
2. Batenda . . .	elephant, sheep, lechwe, (hippopotamus)
3. Baleya . . .	goat, tortoise, black vulture
4. Bansaka . . .	leopard, bee
5. Bakonka . . .	(eland), jackal, rain, zebra
6. Bafumu . . .	pigeon, frog, (hippopotamus), cattle
7. Bansanje . . .	hare, honey guide
8. Bayuni . . .	bird
9. Bacindu . . .	lion, grain
10. Beetwa . . .	crocodile, monitor lizard
11. Bantanga . . .	white vulture
12. Balongo . . .	baboon, (buffalo), scavenger bird
13. Bancanga . . .	bush-baby
14. Bankombwe . . .	(buffalo), (eland)

Clan names are used constantly in daily life. People are commonly addressed by their clan names, or they may be honoured by being addressed by the clan names of their fathers. Everyone, including young children, knows his clan affiliation.

CLAN JOKING

Each clan has a formal joking-relationship with a number of other clans. This is known as *bujwanyina*. A clan-joking relative is called *mujwama* (my fellow joker), *mujwanyoko* (your fellow joker), *mujwanyina* (his or her fellow joker). The term seems to be derived from the term for sister's child, *mujwa*, to which is added the possessive suffix.[1] Despite this derivation, the relationship is one which exists between clans, and it has no implication of kinship. Most people, indeed, say that where actual kinship exists, the joking-relationship goes into abeyance. Others claim that clan-joking relationships are of two types: one the formal unchanging relationship between paired clans, the other a particular relationship between a person and the clans of his mother's father and father's father. The latter type, they then go on to say, is not a true *bujwanyina* relationship but is only like it. Thus a woman who is Munsaka said that she had a clan-joking relationship with the Baleya, and then qualified this statement with: 'But they are not real *bajwanyina*. We have it because I am a grandchild of the Baleya. My father was born to them (i.e., her father's father was Muleya), and so at a Baleya funeral I can demand that meat be given to me. But my children won't have *bujwanyina* with the Baleya. They will follow only the real *bajwanyina* who are the Bansanje, Bahyamba, and Balongo.'

The confusion may occur because there is also a formal joking relationship between kinsmen of certain categories. This differs in kind from that of the clan-joking. Such joking exists between cross-cousins, between affines of the same generation and between grandparents and grandchildren. In the last category, the joking is extended to include all members of the grandfathers' clans. This type of joking is known by the term *ku-sobasyana* ('to cause to play'). It involves a good deal of teasing. Between grandparents

---

[1] The *bu-* prefix in Tonga seems to carry any abstract sense. See Hopgood, 1940, p. 30. Torrend, 1931, p. 461, gives the meaning of *mujwama*, etc., as 'my relative of a different tribe'. By tribe, he means clan. But I have found the term restricted to those with whom the speaker has a clan-joking relationship. It is not used for those who are considered to be kin.

and grandchildren it is confined largely to the exchange of pleasantries and sexual innuendos. Those indulging in it call out: 'You are my wife,' 'My wife get water for me,' 'You are my grandparents and so you must give me a wife (or husband).' Cross-cousins and affines of the same generation have the same type of verbal exchange, but they may also indulge in rough horse-play, practical jokes, and fondling.[1]

Clan-joking is quite different, and the bystander easily recognizes it and differentiates it from the joking appropriate between kinsmen. Clan-joking involves the play upon the presumed antagonism between the clan animals. It permits obscenities and rough words. It permits those in the relationship to call to each other: 'Your mother is dead,' 'Your mother's brother is dead.' Small children when they hear these statements may rush home weeping, thinking that a relative has actually died. Older people laugh and retort: 'Your mother is also dead.' Clan-joking also involves accusations of sorcery: 'You are a sorcerer! You are killing the people!' Such joking is called *ku-tukila* ('to use abusive language'). This is permitted only between those in a clan-joking relationship. If anyone else used these words to a person, it would be an insult. He would be called to account and made to pay damages before the matter was permitted to drop.

Some people may therefore assimilate the joking appropriate to the grandfather's clans to that of the clan-joking proper, but it is the relationship between paired clans which is the backbone of the system, and the one which most Tonga stress. Each clan is paired with a number of others for this purpose, and these in turn are paired with a number of others. This results in a web of ties between clans, rather than a division of the clans into a number of segments, each of which has a joking-relationship only with others within its segment. The pairing of clans is not invariable throughout Tonga country. Within the same small area, informants may differ as to whether certain clans are paired together. Nevertheless, there is sufficient consistency for people to be able to move from one section of the country to another without involving

---

[1] Age-mates may also joke together.

themselves in suits for joking with clans which do not recognize their right to enter into this relationship. The Tonga think that the pairing ought to be universal throughout the country, and they also maintain that it applies to all members of the appropriate clans and not to matrilineal groups or to local sections of a clan. They say that as soon as you learn that a man is a member of a paired clan you may begin to joke with him in the prescribed manner whether or not you have previously known each other.

I have found the clans paired for joking as follows:[1]

TABLE IV

Clans paired for Joking

CLAN	Bahyamba	Batenda	Baleya	Bansaka	Bakonke	Bafumu	Bansanje	Bayuni	Bacindu	Beetwa	Bantanga	Balongo	Bancanga	Bankombwe
Bahyamba		X	X	X	X	X	X		X		X	X		
Batenda	X			X					X					
Baleya	X								X					
Bansaka	X	X							X				X	X
Bakonka	X					X	X	X	X	X				X
Bafumu	X				X		X		X					
Bansanje	X			X	X	X		X	X	X				X
Bayuni						X	X		X	X				
Bacindu	X	X	X		X	X	X	X		X	X	X		
Beetwa						X	X	X	X					X
Bantanga	X								X					
Balongo	X			X					X					
Bancanga														
Bankombwe				X	X	X			X					

[1] These pairs were collected from informants in Monze chiefdom west of the railway, and in Mwansa, Chona and Ufwenuke chiefdoms to the east. In the north-west, in Mwanacingwala chiefdom, informants denied that *bujwanyina* was connected with clans, and I was never able to work out the system which governed it. These people are probably affected by their proximity to the Ila who do not seem to have clan-joking. In the Zambezi Valley, Valley Tonga [in the Middle River region] have the clan-joking pairs. During the month I spent in the Valley, I was working on other problems, but I did collect the following clan pairs: Batenda are paired with Bafumu, Bahyamba, Balongo; Bantanga are paired with Bayuni, Baleya, Bahyamba, Bacindu; Bayuni are paired with Bansanje, Bahyamba, Bakonka, Bananga, Bacindu, Batenda, Beetwa; Beetwa are paired with Bacindu, Bafumu, Bayuni; Bacindu are paired

If the Tonga are asked why certain clans joke together, they either refer to some antagonism between the associated animals of the two clans, or they relate a folk-tale which is said to describe the origin of the relationship. For unlike the clans themselves, the reciprocal relationship between them is thought to have come into existence after the origin of people. A Muhyamba, for instance, will say, 'We have *bujwanyina* with the Bansaka because they are bees who make honey, and we are ants who steal their honey. That is what we always tease each other with. And we have *bujwanyina* with the Baleya because they are goats, and we hyenas come and steal them from the house. And we have *bujwanyina* with the Bacindu because they are lions who kill meat, and we hyenas come carefully and eat alongside the lion when it is satisfied. And we have *bujwanyina* with the Bansanje because they are hares, and both hare and hyena are tricksters.' When joking partners meet they tease each other with such references, but among the Tonga the jesting does not turn on the counter-claims of the two clans to superiority over one another because of the relationship between their animal associates. The two are assumed to be of equal status. In this the Tonga differ from other tribes of the area who have the clan-joking.

The jest may be elaborated into a folk-tale as follows: 'We Bahyamba have *bujwanyina* with the Bansanje because we are hyena and they are hare. One day Hyena fell in love with a girl and asked her to marry him. She agreed. Then along came Hare who also wanted to marry her. She refused to marry him because she had already accepted Hyena. Hare said: "How can you marry him? He is my mount. I ride upon him." The girl then thought that perhaps Hare might make a better husband. Hyena came to see her. She refused to marry him, repeating that Hare had said he used Hyena as his mount. Hyena went off in a rage. He found Hare lying in bed claiming to be very ill. Hyena announced that they had a case and Hare must come with him to the elders to have it settled. Hare denied that he had ever claimed to ride upon

with Bayuni, Bahyamba, Balongo, Bantanga, Beetwa. Most of these pairings, but not all, were also found on the Plateau. Bancanga are found only in the west, and I had no opportunity to work out their joking-partners.

Hyena, and said it was impossible for him to come now as he was ill. Hyena insisted. Hare finally agreed, and said he would come if Hyena would carry him on his back. Hyena set off with Hare on his back. Hare suggested that Hyena should run so that they might get there faster. Thus Hare galloped up to the gathering, mounted on Hyena to whom he applied a switch from time to time. As they arrived, he shouted: "Well, see! Do I ride him?" And he jumped off. Since then Hyena (Bahyamba) and Hare (Bansanje) have had *bujwanyina*, and that is what they joke about.'

A similar tale relates the origin of the *bujwanyina* relationship between the Bahyamba, the Bafumu, and the Bansanje. 'One day there was Rhinoceros (Bahyamba), Hippopotamus (Bafumu), and Hare (Bansanje). Hippopotamus always stayed in the water and never came out in the daytime. Rhinoceros never went in the water. Hare went to Rhinoceros and said, "Why don't you go into the water and bathe? You would feel fine. I'll tell you what I'll do. Tomorrow morning I will bring a rope, and you will take one end and I will take the other. I will get in the water and we will both pull. If I pull you into the water that will mean that you will come into the water all the time." Rhinoceros agreed. Then Hare went to Hippopotamus and told him that he ought to come out of the water in the daytime, and that next morning he, Hare, would bring a rope and see if he could pull him out. So the pulling contest was arranged. Hare, out of sight of the contestants, so arranged the rope that Hippopotamus and Rhinoceros were pulling against each other. Then he ran away. Hippopotamus and Rhinoceros pulled most of the day. Then each began to wonder what could be wrong and if Hare could really pull this hard. They went to investigate and found each other. They said: "Ah, Hare has tricked us!" Since that day, these three clans—Bahyamba, Bafumu, and Bansanje—have had the joking-relationship.'

Another describes the origin of the joking-relationship between Bakonka, Bansanje, and Bacindu. 'One day Lion (Bacindu) fell into a pit trap. Jackal (Bakonka) came along and agreed to push a stick into the trap so that Lion could climb out. Lion was very hungry after his imprisonment. He announced that he was going to eat Jackal, who protested that this was no just repayment for his assistance. Lion refused to listen. Before he could eat Jackal, Hare (Bansanje) came along and asked what was happening. When he had heard the story, he asked Lion to show him just what had happened. Lion jumped into the pit. Hare grabbed out the stick and told Jackal not to help Lion out of the trap again. So they went off leaving Lion in the trap. Since then Jackal (Bakonka), Hare (Bansanje), and Lion (Bacindu) have had *buj-wanyina.*'

It would be pointless to give any more of these tales, which are all of the same type. They are said to explain the origin of the joking-relationship, but they are certainly not essential to it. Many people deny any knowledge of the tales and say that they carry on the relationship with their paired clans because this is a matter of tradition: 'Perhaps the old people knew how it started. We just know that it is the custom which they left for us to follow. So we follow it.' Even the very old may not remember the tales attached to their own particular joking-relationships. One old man of about eighty told me that he as a Muhyamba has a joking-relationship with the Bansanje. When I asked him why, he cheerfully replied. 'You must ask the old people. They never told me and I don't know.'

Certainly the tales give no clue to the importance that the pairing of clans has in Tonga life, for it enters into many situations, besides that of the formal exchange of insults and jests. Paired clans have reciprocal duties which they perform for each other. Whenever a man or woman has so misbehaved that he has brought upon himself the general condemnation of his community, it is through the clan-joking partners that his shame is brought home to him. This cannot be done through his own kinsmen—through the people of his own matrilineal group and the people of his father's matrilineal group—upon whom he relies for support and assistance. .Nor may it be done through his affinal relatives. For them to shame him would injure their permanent relationship which is built upon mutual respect and support. Perhaps their exclusion is also based upon the assumption that if the offender were amenable to the advice of his kinsmen, he would have so patterned his life upon their advice that he could not have committed his offence in the first place. In any event, his kinsmen are merely bystanders, and witnesses to his formal punishment, which is in the hands of his clan-joking partners. If a man repeatedly takes and wastes the property of his kinsmen, his joking-partners chide him with his folly and mock him for his stupidity. They make general play with his shortcomings and give them full publicity. If a man and woman commit incest, either by having sexual relations with a clansman or with some other prohibited relative, the matter is not allowed to rest. Their own kinsmen cannot proceed against them and force them to pay damages. But the man is forced to produce a goat which is killed. Then the woman must cook porridge, while the man cooks the meat of the goat. While they are thus at work, clan-joking partners stand about jeering at them for their misdeeds. They also take the blood of the goat and smear it on the bodies of the offenders, saying: 'Here is your incest!' 'Then everyone who is there will be afraid and think, "If I should ever do anything like this, they will give me the same punishment. I must never agree if someone who is my brother tells me that he wants me. I must remind him of what would happen to us if we did this wrong." So this is for punishment. It is the clan-joking partners who must make them ashamed of what they have done.'

The joking-partners also come to bring shame to any one who has attempted to commit suicide. But in this, as well as in cases of incest, and in certain other situations, the ritual serves not only as a punishment. It is also a means of averting the evil which would otherwise follow the kinsmen of those involved, or even the offenders themselves. So the clan-joking partners act even in situations where there is no thought of shaming since no offence has been committed. If a granary collapses under the weight of the stored grain, the joking-partners come and curse the owner while they remove all the grain in their baskets. This is said to prevent the death of the owner foretold by the collapse of the granary, for on a death mourners assemble and the granaries are emptied to feed them. Such occurrences—incest, suicide or attempted suicide, the collapse of a granary, and various others—are said to be *malweza*. This term is also used to refer to some subsequent misfortune which is attributed to the original occurrence. For these, the clan joking-partners assist to ward off the threatened misfortune.

At all funerals, joking-partners have a role to play, but they have a particular duty of burying the bodies of those who die as suicides or from leprosy, for these are considered to be *malweza*.[1] After most deaths, kinsmen and others living in the village of the deceased join together to bury the body, but they may not handle the bodies of lepers and suicides. Instead the joking-partners come to drag these out into the bush where they are thrust into an ant-hill and abandoned. For such people there is no formal mourning, nor do the people assemble. Relatives of the dead will probably kill a goat or a beast to feed the joking-partners who have officiated, and thus the matter ends. At other funerals, joking-partners perform certain rites at the grave, such as pouring a calabash of water over the grave, and again after the burial they have the duty of crying out to begin the renewed wailing. They also act the part of clowns, to release the tension of the mourners. 'If a Muleya dies, then we Bacindu go to laugh and joke. We say: "Well, he has died. Don't care about this! Perhaps you yourselves have killed him! You are sorcerers." Then a Muleya will say to us: "You too are going to die sometime. You also are sorcerers!" ' When cattle are killed to feed the mourners, joking-partners go out and play about with the bodies of the beasts. If a rich man dies and many cattle are killed, the first one is for the joking-partners, who may rush in and take the meat. They also speak out to tell the people that it is time to end this mourning and to disperse to their homes. If anyone else behaved in this fashion it would be a serious matter, which long ago might have led to his being enslaved by the offended relatives of the dead.

Joking-partners may also be considered to stand in a quasi-kinship relationship, but one which fits into none of the known categories of kinsmen. For this reason they can be substituted

---

[1] Valley Tonga informants denied that joking-partners had the task of burying suicides or lepers [or that they were called in to treat those involved in incest]. This custom is therefore probably confined to the Plateau.

whenever a kinsman of a particular category is not available to carry out his appropriate task. At funerals and on other occasions when a large number of people are gathered, it is the duty of the affines who have married women of the matrilineal group involved to cook the food and perform much of the other work necessary to the occasion. At one funeral when I questioned why different men were working, I was told of one: 'He is our joking-partner, but there are not enough of our affines here to do the work, so we told him that he must help us out and work like an affine. That is all right. He must help us because he is our joking-partner.' Again, when a man first obtains a new plough, he must take it to the field of his father, or that of some member of his father's matrilineal group, and work with it there before using it in his own field. A young Mweetwa said that when he got his plough he took it to the field of a Mucindu. I asked why he had so departed from custom, and he replied: 'But he is my joking-partner. I know I should take it to my father's field, but none of my father's matrilineal group and no member of his clan is living here. So I took it to the field of our joking-partner. That makes it all right for me to use it now in my own field.'

While the Tonga would argue that any joking-partner from any clan paired with your own might perform these services, in actual practice, of course, the people in one neighbourhood have worked out an informal arrangement by which only a few of the many possible joking-partners participate. All joking-partners in the area need not undertake the obligations. It is enough if only one appears, and no joking-partner may be sued for damages because he has failed to put in an appearance or perform his obligations.

Other aspects of the joking-partnership bring a much wider range of participation, since the joking-partnership also governs the relationships between people of different clans on other occasions. Various informants have told me that long ago it was forbidden to take offence at anything a joking-partner did. 'Long ago if my joking-partner was wearing a coat, I could go and spit on it, and he would have to give me the coat because I am his joking-partner. He would give it to me even if it was a new coat.

I could do this any time and not just at funerals.' Again, I have been told that theft was not recognized between joking-partners. Some said that if you impregnated a girl from a paired clan that you were not charged to pay damages. Her relatives simply cursed you up and down, and you paid nothing. Others said that this was not true, that you had to pay full damages. Today, certainly, no one pleads a joking-partnership as lessening his responsibility in such a matter. Informants also said that previously if you killed a joking-partner, you paid less than if you killed a member of some other clan. In times of famine, you could go to a village where you had joking-partners and beg for food and for seeds for planting. Indeed, you might go to the granary of a joking-partner and take the grain without permission. 'If I saw him, I couldn't give him a case because I would know that we joked together.' Old men say that they still observe this custom, but that the younger people do not. It was of considerable importance in the old uncertain days when famines were of frequent occurrence and there was no Administrative Authority to prevent starvation by the importation of grain. For if you begged food or seed in a village where you had no kinsmen or joking-partners, you were liable to enslavement. Joking-partners, like clansmen, were not expected to enslave each other.

In ordinary life, one would not urge a case against a joking-partner. The sign and seal of the relationship was the refusal to take offence, symbolized by the right to use crude and abusive language to each other. In kinship relationships, either consanguineal or affinal, one also should be slow to take offence, but this was because there were practical advantages from the continuation of the relationship which acted as a check upon anger and intemperate dispute. Even if anger boiled up, it would be curbed so that the relationship with its practical advantages could continue. In the joking-partnership, offence was outlawed from the beginning. If one of the partners did take offence and started to fight, then damages had to be paid. But this implied the end of the relationship. 'It is forbidden to fight with them. If you fight, it means that the joking-partnership is ended. You will be afraid to joke with them again because you will think "These people only

G

want to fight." ' Nevertheless, informants maintained that if a man found that his joking-partner was having an adulterous affair with his wife he would demand full damages without regard to the effect that this might have upon their relationship.[1]

Marriage between people belonging to paired clans was not only accepted. It was an approved form of marriage. 'That is our special place to marry.' Full bridewealth was paid, but marriage into a paired clan was considered to be a safeguard for the spouse who went to live amongst his or her affines, for though actual kinship ties, whether consanguineal or affinal, placed the joking-partnership in abeyance, such people had an added reason to protect his or her interests.

The existence of the joking-partnership, or clan reciprocity, therefore gave the Tonga added security in a world made up of small opposed groups, a world in which he found himself easily at odds with others and exposed to their vengeance. Against this he had only the security which could be offered to him by the willingness of his kinsmen to take up his quarrels as their own. But the joking-partnership meant that offence could neither be given nor recognized in dealings with a large number of people with whom he came into contact. From the table showing clan pairs, the wide range of joking-partnerships is apparent. If I had collected information more systematically I suspect that all the clans would have emerged as paired with at least half the available number of other clans. Thus the Tonga could move through a wide circle of relationships with security. He had to be certain of the clans with which he joked, or he embroiled himself in difficulties, but if he followed the simple rule that he joked where his mother joked, and not where his father joked, he was safe.[2]

This I think is the true significance of the paired clan arrangement among the Tonga, and perhaps elsewhere in Northern

---

[1] The Valley Tonga said that they ignored cases of adultery if a joking-partner was involved.

[2] Dr. Cunnison informs me that on the Luapula River, people may assume the joking associations of both parents, though they belong only to their mothers' clan. Elsewhere in Northern Rhodesia, people seem to be limited to the joking-partners of their own clan.

Rhodesia. It also has the effect of mobilizing and expressing public opinion through the mouths of joking-partners who by definition are not kinsmen and who are protected in the exercise of this function by the outlawing of retaliation against anything they may say. The joking-partnership is brought into the context of the funeral, because in the funeral all those who have responsibilities to a person during his lifetime are given particular roles in the ritual which surrounds his death. The funeral friendship is therefore only one aspect of the wider problem of how people may be organized into groups which may then be effectively related to each other, to ensure the well-being of a community.

CHAPTER III

RAIN-SHRINES OF THE PLATEAU TONGA OF NORTHERN RHODESIA

THE SOCIAL STRUCTURE

THIS is a preliminary report on the social and political significance of the rain-shrines as an integrating force in Tonga
society.[1] In a sense it is a misnomer to refer to them as rain-shrines,
for they are also appealed to on any occasion of general community disaster, such as epidemics or cattle plagues, but to the
Tonga themselves the dominant aspect of the shrines is their
efficacy in ensuring the proper rainfall.

The Tonga inhabit the railway belt on the Northern Rhodesian
plateau. They are affiliated linguistically and culturally with the
Ila of the Kafue plain, who have been described by Smith and
Dale.[2] Although the Tonga probably number over 80,000 persons, they are little known except for an occasional short note in
mission journals or government reports.

On the whole the Tonga might be defined as culturally a have-
not group. They have never had an organized state. They were
unwarlike and had neither regimental organizations nor armies.
They were and are equally lacking in an age-grade set-up, secret
societies, and social stratification of all kinds. The Tonga would
not even attract those fascinated by the intricate rules of lineage
organization, for while they have clans and smaller matrilineal
kin-groups, they have them in a characteristically unorganized
fashion which leaves the investigator with a baffled, frustrated
desire to rearrange their social structure into some more ordered
system. It is only in the rain-rituals and their associated shrines that
the Tonga show a half-hearted grouping towards the establishment of a larger community than that which existed in the village

---

[1] This chapter was read before the Royal Anthropological Institute in
January 1948.   [2] *op. cit.*

or in the ties of kinship. I think it important to study this nexus, not only because of the numerical importance of the Tonga themselves but because theirs is probably an extreme variant of a general Central Bantu culture type which seems characteristic of much of Northern Rhodesia, except where the more highly developed systems of the Congo or South Africa have impinged upon it. I should say that it is a type of society based on shifting cultivation with unlimited land and so little variation in land values in terms of the culture that no given spot possesses particular attractions.

From the earliest times of which we have any knowledge the Tonga have been settled in scattered villages throughout this countryside. A man might settle where he would, with his matrilineal kin, with his father's matrilineal group, with his wife's relatives, with a non-related fellow clansman, with a stranger, or by himself. Hence neither clan nor kin-group could be localized. The clans have no internal structure, no leaders, and no common rituals. Their only attributes, besides the bearing of a common clan name, seem to be the prohibition of marriage within the clan and the obligation of hospitality to all fellow clansmen. The kin-group was the unit which exacted vengeance, paid the fines for its members' misdeeds, functioned in inheritance, and gave assistance towards paying bridewealth or in meeting other emergencies. This kin-group is a small unit of matrilineally related persons, plus their former slaves, plus the matrilineal descendants of their female slaves. It differs from the clan in that all its members feel themselves to be related, although in some cases the genealogical connections have been forgotten, while the clan is composed of unrelated groups. Because the members of the kin-group lived scattered wherever they pleased to settle the kin-group was not a corporate entity in daily life. Equally it tended always to lose its members and to shrink back to a numerically tiny unit of perhaps two to three generations' span above its older members. Many shrank even further, as the dispersed members and their descendants moved farther and farther apart until finally all memory of them vanished. The diminished cells of kin began a new proliferation which in turn would give rise to dispersal and the vanishing of kin solidarity with its attendant responsibilities. Very probably a kin-group rarely numbered more than a hundred adult individuals at any one time, some of whom would be the attached slaves or their descendants, who within a generation or so were indistinguishable from the lineal descendants of the group. Not all of these people would live closely enough together for them to act effectively as a unit. The descendants of the slaves shared in the common right to move where they would and to live with whom they would, so that not even the slaves owned within a kin-group formed a stable core lasting more than a generation.

The village in which a man lived thus included some members who recognized no responsibility for his actions and for whom in turn he felt no responsibility. His loyalties to the village head were tenuous ones, based perhaps on gratitude for favours received, perhaps on kinship, perhaps on the ties which bound a slave to his owner. Only over his slaves did a village leader have the coercive authority which would force them to continue to live with him. When the head of a village, or indeed any other family man who still had effective kin, died, a successor was chosen for him, usually from among his matrilineal kin. It was quite possible, however, that the successor would come from among the slaves or even from the sons. The declared principle was always, 'We choose the one who will keep the people best.' The heir did not necessarily succeed to any position of ascendancy over village or kin. His adherents might split into small groups, move off on their own, or go off to seek other kin more congenial to them.

The kin-group theoretically was held together by the recognition of its common ancestral spirits, who had power to affect them all and only them. In practice this recognition had only a limited power to stabilize their relationships. Any adult woman, and any man who had a wife capable of brewing beer, could approach the ancestors; it was not canalized through one representative of the whole group. Moreover, the power of the ancestors was effective no matter where a man might settle. At the present time the ancestors follow the labour migrants to the Union of South Africa,

and the spirits of those who die there have no difficulty in returning to demand the attention of the stay-at-homes.

Since the village is composed of unrelated elements, the ancestral
spirits of any one kin-group cannot affect all of its members. I
have been unable to discover traces of ritual which might
symbolize the village as a corporate unit.

THE RAIN-SHRINES

Into this anarchy, some semblance of order is infused by the
rain-rituals, which effectively organize small groups of villages
for corporate activity, and which are able to impose sanctions on
offences affecting its organization. The districts over which a
particular rain-shrine or group of shrines held sway seem usually
to have contained only a few square miles and four or five villages.
One or two shrines, such as that of Monze, had a wide reputation,
and probably drew people from a much larger area. But there was
no hierarchy of shrines organizing the various separate cult districts into a country-wide system.

On the two or three days of the year when the rain-rituals were
being enacted, a general district peace was imposed in the name of
the shrine, which overrode the customary rights of the kin-groups
to exact compensation for offences against their members' persons
or property. In some districts this peace was instituted through a
ritual licence at this period, and the district refused to recognize
any offence save murder itself as culpable. In other districts the
customary code of behaviour remained in effect through these
days, but offences against it were subject to a fine paid to the
shrine or to the community as a whole through its elders, instead
of to the injured person or his kin. At the Monze shrine the
ground is covered with hoe-blades paid by those who chose the
ritual period to fight or commit adultery or take their neigh-
bour's goods. To the north-west, adherents to shrines in the
Mwanacingwala area were fined a fowl, a beast, or tobacco, which
was then distributed among the elders of the area. At the present
time the ritual peace has disappeared under the general peace
maintained by the Administration. Breaches of the peace or civil

cases arising during the ritual period now find their way into the Native Authority Courts, where they are treated on the same plane with cases arising at any other period of the year.

It has also become impossible for the elders to fine a man who fails to attend the ritual, though once the ritual was coercive upon all who lived within the cult area. Thus, in former days a man knew that at least once a year he must co-operate with his neighbours in a common ritual to ensure a benefit equally desired by all and which was for the common good. If feuds split the neighbouring communities so badly that it was impossible for them to co-operate in the ritual, the dissident sections could move into another district where they could co-operate, or the whole area might expect the visitation of drought, famine, epidemic, or other pestilence. The shrines were therefore effective in keeping the internal differences in the communities which they served within reasonable bounds. Occasionally during the rest of the year the community of the rain-shrine might be called into existence and its integrity reaffirmed. Disrespect towards the shrines even on non-ritual occasions might ensure general disaster for the community, unless the offenders were punished and a ritual cleansing performed. If it is discovered that someone has cut wood in the immediate vicinity of a shrine he is ordered to pay a black chicken. This is killed and eaten by the assembled elders of the shrine community. These fines are still exacted, although I have never heard of such a case coming into the Native Authority Courts.

In the Chona country, on the edge of the Zambezi escarpment, the highest hill in the area is regarded as a shrine. It is strictly forbidden for anyone to gather roots or wood in its vicinity, or to burn the grass upon it before the head of the rain-ritual announces that there is to be a communal hunt upon its slopes. In 1946 a foolhardy youth burned a portion of the hill by accident and then came to ask permission to burn the rest. He chose a day when the headmen of the area were assembled for another purpose. They screamed their rage at his impudence, put him in handcuffs, and threatened to make all the men in the district who were of his approximate age pay chickens for a general purifying feast. Finally, however, they agreed to fine only the offender. They maintained wholeheartedly their right to punish him. His act had endangered the whole community, and especially themselves as its leaders. If no retribution were made to the shrine, they could only expect when the rains finally came that their huts would be destroyed by lightning. During the same year others offended against this shrine. Finally the headman of the nearest village decided to move to a new site to escape the drain on his chickens and goats caused by the trespass of his people. The other people of the district were beginning to look at them askance and murmur that they were responsible for the prolonged drought which was endangering the crops. In the Mwanacingwala area the same drought was attributed by the chief to a sacrilege which he discovered—a pile of firewood at the base of a very large and very hollow fig-tree which is associated with the shrine of Luanga. He marched into the nearest village, which happened to have immigrated into the area a year or two before, asked its inhabitants about the matter, and told them that if they offended again they must pay a beast to the district. However, on this occasion they were let off with a warning, for they apologized profusely and said they had not realized that this particular tree was sacred though they knew and carefully respected three other trees which had been pointed out to them.

This same shrine of Luanga figures in the last big feud in this country. About 1910 some men found women cutting thatching-grass close to the sacred spot. The women came from a village only about three miles from Luanga, but belonging to the cult district of Ciboya. When the Luanga men told them they were trespassing at a sacred spot the women cursed them heartily in terms which left no doubt as to their opinion of Luanga and its people. The leader of Luanga went to demand an apology from his peer at Ciboya, who promptly spat in his face. The next step was an armed raid by the Luanga people in which several men were killed and the followers of Ciboya were driven from their homes. European intervention ended the hostilities, and the Ciboya people drifted back to their former sites. It is clear from the last two cases that those who live outside the cult area owe the shrine no reverence as a holy place for all Tonga, though any irreverence will be actively resented by the adherents to the particular place. It is regarded as an insult to the whole cult community. Once people move within the cult area they are expected to observe the taboos which surround the particular shrine of the place.

DESCRIPTION OF THE SHRINES

Since the largest social group ever mobilized by the Tonga is never of imposing size, we cannot expect that the shrines which symbolize the groups will be pretentious structures. And they are not. We can classify them into two general types, though both are referred to by the Tonga under the one term *malende*. One type has already been mentioned briefly. This consists in natural objects which have become sacred, though there is usually nothing to explain to the untutored eye why they have been selected out of the general landscape. Large hollow fig-trees are very apt to be sacred, and I know of one place where the sacredness has now been transferred to the hole in the ground left when such a tree was blown down. The Tonga of the area said, 'We can't lose our rain-shrine like this', and with no more ado continued to visit the hole. Such hollow trees are understandably sacred, for they are regarded as being dwelling-places of the spirits responsible for the rain. When the little huts at the man-made shrines lose their roofs, through wind or rot or the depredations of the browsing cattle, the spirits take refuge from the rain in the tree-hollows. It is more difficult to discover the motive for sanctifying other spots, such as the hill in Chona country, or another shrine in the same area, a spring which trickles out of the broken face of a rock above a watercourse which holds a small pool of water through the dryest spells of the dryest years. In Ufwenuka area also one of the rain-shrines is a spring. There the ritual is said to consist of throwing a tortoise into the spring's depths. I have not been able to discover that these particular shrines are connected specifically with any spirit, or in what the mechanism of their power consists. In the Chona country the same spirits are supplicated at both these shrines and at the artificial ones of the area, and the people claim they visit the spots at the present time because the first Chona visited them when he was alive and they are simply following the procedure he taught them to use in obtaining rain. But they do not seem to hold that the spirit of the first Chona dwells at either of these spots.

The other general type of shrine is man-made, and consists of small structures called *kaanda* (plur. *twaanda*), which literally means 'small hut'. They are not pretentious and are all built on the same general pattern—a circle of supports capped with the mushroom-like thatched roof which tops all structures in this area. In the Chona area I have seen two which have supports of upright slabs of stone. The later of these could not have been built after about 1880. The others I have seen are built with poles. Slender twigs are used in the Mwanacingwala area, where the shrines are tiny affairs, perhaps only thirty inches high when complete with thatched roof, and the shrines may vanish completely from one year to the next under the trampling of the cattle. Elsewhere substantial poles are used, which last from year to year, and some of the huts are large enough to admit an adult through the doorway, though no human being does enter once the shrine is built. Since the supports are set well apart, the contents of the shrine are always in clear view and there is little protection from the weather. However, the only permanent furniture are the pots, placed upside down near the doorway. These are the ordinary black pots of the area, indistinguishable from those used within the villages at the present time, though some of them may be of pre-European date. Two such pots should be found at each shrine, one for beer and one for the food for the communion feast which is a major portion of the ritual. Sometimes there are many more. They remain always at the site. Should they be broken, the ritual leader must seek new ones. My information indicates that he may acquire them in any way he likes, and they become ritualized only when placed within the shrine. They are found, incidentally, only at the hut-shrines. Nothing is placed at the natural ones. Another feature of most hut-shrines is the circling cluster of trees, planted when the shrine was first made. This is all. Through much of the year the shrines lie quiet and undisturbed, and their paths are overgrown.

THE ROLE OF THE SPIRITS

The hut-shrines are connected with definite spirits who are thought to have power over the rain through their intervention with Leza, the god who controls all things. Their origin, however, is diverse. Some shrines are said to be those of former *ulanyika*, or leaders. Formerly, when a man moved into an unoccupied section of the country he was regarded as having authority over those who followed him into the area. Just what his authority amounted to it is difficult to say, but probably it amounted to little more than an expectation that he would be listened to with respect. His status was essentially that of a first among equals, rather than that of a chief in the usual sense of the word. When he died, his kin and his neighbours might decide to honour him by building a shrine at his grave, but this did not necessarily become a cult-centre, and it might soon decay and be forgotten if the village moved away. If, however, the area suffered drought or other disaster within a few years of the leader's death, a diviner or prophet might announce that the spirit of the dead man was angry because the people had forgotten him though he had looked after the community during his lifetime. The people would then attempt to rectify their mistake and would either rebuild the shrine or begin a new one for him. Thereafter they might carry out the rites at the site each year before the beginning of the rains, simply to be on the safe side, or they might return to it only in another period of emergency.

Other shrines were initiated by people whom we may call prophets, or rain-makers, though there seems to be no specific term for them in Tonga. They are subject to possession by spirits. Through the prophets, the spirits make demands on the people, lecture them for their misdeeds, and demand the institution of new rituals or the better conduct of the old. Usually when the rain-maker becomes possessed for the first time he calls the people together and tells them to build a shrine for his spirit, which may be that of some important former member of the community, or sometimes of someone completely foreign to the area. Such spirits are called *basangu* and are regarded as distinct from the *mizimu* or ancestral spirits, though there are cases where the same spirits are addressed as *basangu* at the rain-shrines and as *mizimu* at the private household rituals. This is true if the *musangu* is that of a former member of the community. Such a man is honoured as a *muzimu* by his kin-group, who approach him, as they do any other ancestor, in private rites. He is honoured as a *musangu* by the community, which includes his kin-group, but as a *musangu* he is concerned with community affairs and not with the narrow sphere of individual or private matters. While the ancestral spirits affect only their own kin, the *basangu* can possess anyone they choose to enter without regard for the proprieties of kinship regulations, and they can afflict communities with drought, cattle epidemics, disease of epidemic proportions, or any other disaster of a general nature. I have never heard of *basangu* sending sickness to only one individual, or crop failures to the fields of only one person. For such misfortunes one accuses either the ancestors or the witchcraft of one's enemies. The only exception is that the *basangu* punish with illness individuals who violate their shrines and do not make restitution.

Aside from the regulation of the rain-ritual, the *basangu* seem chiefly concerned with combating the cultural changes which European contact and other influences are producing in Tonga country. In 1946 one announced that among the sins of the people to which the drought was due was the failure to follow the customs used by the *basangu* when they were living individuals, and it cited specifically the building of kimberley brick houses instead of the old-style mud-and-pole type. The Tonga, however, are not slavishly obedient to the whims of the *basangu*. This statement was met by jeers and the declaration that the times had changed. Another *musangu* announced that the previous rain-ceremonies had been ineffective because the ritual leader had bought the beast he sacrificed instead of killing one from his own herd. This was listened to more respectfully.

When the rain-maker is first possessed by his spirit, if it is a foreign one or one which does not already have a shrine within the immediate vicinity, he calls upon the people to build a hut-shrine for it and to participate in ritual at the spot. This will be carried out annually. After a few years it becomes institutionalized if it seems to be effective in producing rain. When the rain-maker dies the shrine continues to be visited under the leadership of some member of the rain-maker's kin-group. Another shrine may be built at the grave of the rain-maker, for he too is now considered to have become a *musangu* and to have power over the area. Such a figure was the Monze whom Livingstone described as 'the chief of all the Batonga'. Occasionally the original shrine of the *basangu* and the shrine of the dead rain-maker may coalesce, and both will be appealed to at the same place and at the same time.

A few other figures have been honoured in this manner. The first Chona is said to have had powerful magic, although he was never possessed by any spirit. He seems to have been able to dominate a fairly large section of the escarpment country. His shrine is still visited, though the cult community has now shrunk to three villages.

The hut-shrines are thus dedicated to two different types of spirits: the spirits of former leaders in the area, some of whom were rain-makers and some of whom had a secular and largely personal influence, and the foreign spirits who announced themselves through the rain-makers. All are called, in their public aspect, *basangu*. In some cases rain-makers in different districts have been possessed by the same *musangu*, but this imposes no connection between the resulting shrines.

Once the original figure is dead all such cults pass into the hands of his kin-group. The shrines of the indigenous leaders are in the hands of their own kin; the shrines of the foreign spirits are in the hands of the kin of the rain-maker whom they possessed. While the shrine affects the entire local community, the kin are regarded as the proper medium through which appeals may be made to the indwelling spirit. As officials of the cult they are the living representatives of the community itself, but their power and responsibility begin and end in the ritual sphere. They choose one from their group to decide when the rituals will be held and to direct the activities of the ritual period. Such a person may himself be possessed by *basangu*, but often he is an ordinary person without supernatural assistance. If he wishes to do so he may delegate his work to some more energetic person. His role is that of director and chief participant, but he can do nothing by himself. As far as I know, he never visits the shrines by himself, nor on any save the public occasions. Even then the *basangu* are only invoked for the public good.

THE RITUAL

The ritual itself is simple, and may be stripped even beyond the generally recognized proprieties of the occasion. I shall describe the rites as I saw them performed in the Chona area, as they followed the general pattern described to me by informants. However, each cult area slightly varies the basic pattern of the rites. Shortly before the first planting-rains of the year began in earnest, the man in charge of the ritual announced that it was time to prepare the beer for the *luinde*, as the ceremony is called. When the beer was ready the inhabitants of each village spent the eve of the ceremony dancing and singing rain-songs. They moved from house to house, calling out pleas to the *basangu* to send the rain. This is supposed to continue until the rain comes, and on this occasion the rain came conveniently about eleven in the evening so that we could get some sleep to prepare for the activities of the next day. The following morning the people set out equipped with axes, hoes, a chicken, and some meal. The women hoed the site to clear it of grass, while the men repaired the thatched roof which had fallen into disrepair during the previous year. The chicken was killed by striking its neck against the doorway of the hut-shrine, and it was roasted while the meal was being cooked. Then all joined in a communion meal, in which each received only a mouthful. Meantime the leader addressed the spirit at the shrine: 'Send us rain and good crops and health. We have done all the things you told us to do. We are still living in the way you showed us. We have not forgotten what you told us. We have not forgotten you. Send us rain. Help us.' When the meal ended the people returned to their villages. Since in this neighbourhood there are several shrines bound together in a common cult, each village went to the shrine nearest to it to perform this part of the ceremony.

When the people returned to their villages the dancing and singing continued intermittently through the day and evening. Early the following morning, when the light was first coming, young men carried a pot of beer to each shrine and left it there. Later in the morning the people went through the village again, singing the rain-songs and led by the drums. Then in a body they went to the village of the chief officiant and circled this village in the same manner. Each village in the area had sent beer to this central point, and here they spent the morning drinking the beer and eating the groundnuts which they had levied at each hut which had failed to make beer for the occasion. About noon the procession re-formed. It now contained people from all the villages in the district, and it moved from one shrine to the next in a specified order and manner, pausing at one point to circle a barely discernible mound, at another so that all participants could rub themselves with a white clay from the river bank. At each shrine they divided the beer, and as they drank they addressed the shrine with appeals for rain in formulae similar to that given above. An offering of beer was poured over the doorway of the hut, the people saluted the spirits by clapping, and then they danced around the shrine to show the spirits that they were happy. Such dances were either solos or by twos and threes, and were panto-mimes explained by the words of the accompanying songs. Some are intelligible to us as sympathetic magic, as when a woman sings and dances that she is delighted with her fine harvest. Others are less obvious. I am frankly puzzled as to why some are considered appropriate to the occasion. In one the dancer limped sadly about the shrine with a bundle on her head and sang that she had a case which she had taken to the District Officer and that she was heartily weary because all the district officials kept sending her from one to another. Other dances were obscene. After perhaps half an hour at each shrine the participants rushed down to some pool to bathe, and then returned to their villages to drink the remainder of the ceremonial beer.

This ended the ceremony. But if the rain fails to come, or does not last, then the shrines are visited again and again. At Chona the people went five times in 1946-7, although they did not always visit the same shrines. In desperation they consulted oracles. A woman was possessed by the spirit of the first Chona and ordered an innovation in the rite, the purchase of a black cloth to be placed on his shrine. On another visit a beast was killed. Finally, on the last appeal to the *basangu*, when no rain-clouds had appeared, one of the women turned just as they left the shrine of Chona I and announced: 'Look, your children will all starve and we will all die. You don't care for us. Now we are through with you.'

Participation in the rites is general. All members of the community are allowed to attend. At the Chona shrine the leaders urged all the people and not just the kin-group which controls the shrines to dance and pray for rain. They said: 'The rain falls on your fields as well as on ours. You must all dance.'

In this area a widening of participation is also obtained through a sharing of the control of the shrines with the kin-group to which the father of the person to whom the shrine is dedicated belonged. Thus for the full ceremony at all five shrines of the district six kin-groups must co-operate. This custom, however, does not appear to be typical of all Tonga country. But everywhere, whether the control of the rites is vested in one kin-group or several, the whole community should participate in carrying them out—men and women, people of all ages. Today elders complain that the rites are failing in efficacy because the missions have ordered schoolchildren and Christians not to attend.

One shrine is atypical of the area—that of Luanga in the northwest. Here only men and boys visit the shrine itself. Elsewhere there is no exclusion of women from any part in the ritual. Women as well as men have been possessed by *basangu* and become rain-makers, and some have shrines dedicated to them.

If you press the Tonga for an explanation as to why they perform the ritual thus, they say that they are carrying out the instructions of a particular *musangu*, or a particular rain-maker. They do not seek to draw any logical connection between particular acts and the end they desire to induce. It is enough for them that they are following traditional methods. If they do as their

H

predecessors did at this spot, then they can expect the desired result. Yet strangely enough, none of the shrines is regarded as deriving its sanctity from great antiquity, and myths concerning the first establishment of rain-ceremonies in the land are conspicuously absent. This is characteristically Tonga. They are a non-historical people in every aspect of life, and never more so than when they deal with the symbols of their ephemeral communities. None of the shrines I have traced can be said to have been in existence prior to 1850, although we do know that the Monze who apparently instituted one particular rain-cult was alive in 1855. The shrines which seem more important today are all associated with the cults of men and women remembered by those now living, or who lived only a generation earlier.

Since it is improbable that the rain-ritual and the associated shrines are recent cultural innovations, we must assume that shrines as well as their originators are mortal, and that in each generation some disappear while new ones are created. One can only guess at the causes of their extinction: their adherents may have been dispersed through epidemics or through the wars which devastated this area during the nineteenth century. Or the casual shift of villages over the land as fields became exhausted may have scattered the original village members to such an extent that they no longer represented a local community, and the shrines were too distant to be visited. Since rainfall is extremely localized, those who move some distance might well have good reason to doubt the efficacy of the rituals they had formerly practised. It may be noted that only in one area do the shrines tie their adherents to their immediate vicinity. The kin-group which controls the Chona cult assured me that if the leaders moved even four miles from the shrines the spirits would punish them with sickness. Elsewhere people laughed at the idea and said they could move where they would, though they should return each year to celebrate the ceremony. Thus in general the shrines imposed their peace on those who lived within the vicinity but had no effect in building up a permanent group tied to the area.

In other cases shrines probably disappeared as they were eclipsed by rivals instituted by new men, possessed by new spirits who clamoured for a chance to control the destinies of rain, pestilence, and famine. In some places we can see this process at work today. At Chona a first rite is performed at the shrine of Nangoma, mother of the present ritual leader. Hers is the most recent shrine now in existence. If after this all goes well with the rain, well and good. The Tonga are not people to concern themselves with rites for ritual's sake. It is only when the rains do not fall in a manner to satisfy them that they are driven to perform the rites at the four other shrines associated in this particular complex. Over a series of good years it is possible that the older shrines might be so neglected that they would vanish from the complex. But so long as they are remembered, it is always likely that in times of desperation the diviners will call upon the people to go back to the sites, rebuild the huts, and perform the rituals again. Or through a series of very bad years the attitude of 'You don't care for us, and we won't care for you' may swell into a general disgust and the shrine be abandoned as useless.

Very occasionally a shrine may survive its community. When the Mwansa people moved into their present area they found the decayed remains of an old shrine. They did not know to whom it belonged, or to what spirit it was dedicated, or indeed anything concerning the community which had performed its rites there, for that had vanished completely. But the Mwansa leader for some reason chose the ancient shrine as the centre of the rain-ritual which is now performed for his area, and today it is still visited, although the Mwansa people have since acquired two new shrines through more conventional methods.

Many districts at the present time thus have a number of shrines integrated into one cult. I am not satisfied entirely with my data on this point, but I think that this proliferation of shrines is characteristic today only in the cults controlled by the families of the chiefs and that other cults centre about only one shrine, or at least only one hut-shrine. This would suggest that the growth of such complexes is due to the conditions imposed by European administration. When the Europeans entered the country they tended to recognize the rain-makers or other such leaders as the Tonga authorities and to invest them with the status of chiefs, and thenceforth made this status hereditary in the matrilineal lines of the chiefs. Thus several successive members of the same family have been recognized and supported as leaders in a particular area, whereas in pre-European days it is quite possible, as it is today, that the next rain-maker who could speak with the voice of the *basangu*, and not merely as a shrine custodian, would appear in a non-related family, of a different clan, and in a slightly different area. His appeal would be to those who lived around him, and his influence or that of his shrine after his death might well serve to detach some of his neighbours from their alliance to an older cult centre and to draw them into a new community. Since the Tonga population was a shifting one, the new shrine which would represent the particular concatenation of population at this particular time could more truly represent the community than the old one. Control of the two cults would be vested in two different kin-groups and there would be little chance of their being integrated into a common complex unless the two communities which they represented were one and the same.

CONCLUSION

The system described above, overlaid though it is by the creation of hereditary government chiefs, is still the fundamental element in Tonga social structure. Authority in the last analysis rests on personal qualities, but some continuity is given to the society through the recognition that a man who has led the community continues after his death his interest in its welfare, and that his kin-group is the proper channel through which to approach him. But this recognition is only a sea-anchor in the society, which slows the drift and does not stop it. It creates a small community within which the rudiments of community law can be discerned and which forces its members to remember occasionally that they belong to a wider unit than the village or kin-group. Such communities endure for only a moment in time and then re-form themselves into new units. Unsatisfactory though it seems to us, it appears to be the only guise in which the Tonga could visualize authority. Indeed, at the present time, battered as the rituals are by the attacks of the missions, most modern chiefs tend to identify themselves with the rain-shrines as a prop to their authority. Monze, whom the Government accepts as Senior Chief of the Tonga, refuses to admit that any rain-shrines except those of the Monze line exist in all the Tonga country. Other chiefs refer only to those in the hands of their kin-groups and ignore completely the other shrines of the neighbourhood. They maintain that villages in all directions and in great numbers attend their rituals, although a little casual questioning among the surrounding peoples will narrow the influence of their particular cults down to only a fraction of their claims.

Since the Government pays little attention to the rain-rituals and seems unconscious of their role in Tonga life, this attitude must reflect a deep-seated tendency among the Tonga to equate rain-rituals with political integration.

CHAPTER IV

SOCIAL CONTROL AND VENGEANCE IN PLATEAU TONGA SOCIETY[1]

I AM here concerned with social control as it exists in Tonga society, where there are no obvious political institutions concerned in the maintenance of order. As in any society, control rests eventually on the sanction of force, here applied through a resort to vengeance on the part of an organized group if it feels that this is the only way to enforce its rights.

I am concerned with this problem because various people who have read the sketch of Tonga social organization which I have already published[2] have complained that they cannot see how controls can function in what seems at first glance to be an essentially unorganized society without clear-cut lines of allegiance to affiliate people to definite local groups. We understand the implications of the organized state with its delegation of authority to instituted leaders. Since the publication of Evans-Pritchard's studies of the Nuer, it has been possible to understand how stateless societies organized on lineage principles operate. But there are other forms of stateless societies, where the lineage system does not appear, and where no large group organized on kinship principles can be mobilized to enforce the rights of its members. Nor do local units relate themselves to each other through any genealogical hierarchy, or any system of perpetual relationships phrased in kinship terms. The Tonga form such a society. Since the terms of affiliation and alliance which operate within it are unfamiliar to us, it is difficult first for the field worker himself to see them in

---

[1] This chapter was read before the Royal Anthropological Institute on 27 November 1951.

[2] See Colson, 1951. In this and other earlier articles, I wrote of the feud as operating in Tonga Society. A talk on the feud among the Bedawin by Dr. E. Peters led me to reconsider my own material. I then realized that I had been using the term to cover isolated acts of vengeance, and that the Tonga did not, and could not, have the true feud.

their true perspective and then, when he has obtained an understanding of the principles involved, to find a method of making
them clear to others.

Europeans have found it difficult to understand Tonga organiz-
ation from the beginning of their contact with these people. Either they have attempted to find political authorities in the form
of chiefs, or they have dismissed it as an unorganized anarchy.
One who was in the area at the beginning of this century, when
British administrators were just beginning to exert their influence,
reported:

One of the chief characteristics of the Batonga race is its disintegration. They have never been known to act in combination as one race,
and the inhabitants of one village, and even of one family, will rarely
co-operate to attain some common end. Not even for purposes of
defence, nor to resist or avenge a wrong committed against one of their
number, will the Batonga unite; and in my early experience on the
Zambesi I have heard of the most atrocious murders being occasionally
committed with absolute impunity, owing to the disintegrated state of
society and absence of any central authority either in the district or at
the kraals.

To illustrate this I quote the instance of a man named Sia-masia, who
had quarrelled with another Batonga, by name Sinasenkwi, from a
neighbouring kraal. One morning Sia-masia observed the spoor of
two lions close to his hut, and, upon reflection, concluded that
Sinasenkwi had sent them by means of black magic. He thereupon
repaired to Sinasenkwi's village, and there, in broad daylight, in the
presence of all the villagers and of Sinasenkwi's relatives, stabbed not
only the suspected wizard but also his wife and one of his children.

When I inquired of Sinasenkwi's neighbours, why they had not
interfered, they replied that the quarrel was one between Sia-masia and
Sinasenkwi, and was no business of theirs.

In another case, the headman of a village having been stabbed in the
back, while entering a hut at a beer-drinking festival, his people were
appeased by a present of some goats from the murderers, and the matter
was allowed to drop.[1]

Despite this observer's emphasis on disintegration and anarchy,
the Tonga had their own methods of settling disputes and

---

[1] Notes by Mr. Val Gielgud, incorporated in H. Marshall Hole, 1905,
pp. 62–7. Mr. Gielgud apparently refers to the Valley Tonga, but similar
conditions prevailed among the people of the Plateau.

preventing general disorder, and even he comments that murders were occasional rather than frequent and that compensations was sometimes paid.

To understand how social control operates among the Tonga, it is first necessary to review the basic elements of their organization; we can then trace the interplay of these elements in an actual incident, and see how different systems of relationship act as checks on any general mobilization of one group against another, while at the same time influence is brought to bear upon the contestants to bring about a peaceful settlement of the dispute.

The Tonga, who occupy the Plateau in the southern province of Northern Rhodesia, live in small villages which are usually associated in little neighbourhood groups, called *masi* (districts) or *tusi* (little districts). Villages are sometimes compact settlements with a definite pattern; more commonly they are collections of scattered homesteads under the more or less nebulous leadership of a headman. Today, on the average, they number about a hundred inhabitants, and probably in the past they were even smaller. A neighbourhood or district may contain as many as seven or eight villages, but this seems to be the upper limit to which a neighbourhood can grow. Each neighbourhood may be separated from others of its ilk by bush or waste, or villages and fields may be continuous without any obvious boundary to separate one from another. The neighbourhood does not form a kinship unit, nor are the villages related to one another through any institutionalized system of kinship ties, fictional or real. The Tonga have always moved about freely, in search of new land, better village sites, or more congenial neighbours. The man who first comes with his followers to settle in a previously unoccupied area is usually termed the 'owner of the land' (*ulanyika*), and his heir may continue to receive respect for his primacy. But his control of the area is equivocal at best. Other villages which follow him into the area do not recognize that he has rights in the land which override their own, nor do they necessarily look to him to settle their disputes, to perform ritual on their behalf, or to represent them before the world. No headman, moreover, holds his position by virtue of his leadership of an organized body of kinsmen. The male members of his village will be related to him in a number of different ways: some will be his sons; others will be his matrilineal kinsmen; some may be related to him through his father. Others may be affines, the husbands of his daughters or his sisters, or of women related to him in other ways. Others will be the relatives of these men who have followed them, and not the headman, into the village, and they may have no direct tie of kinship with the headman. Still others may simply claim the tie of common clan affiliation with the headman or with some other member of the village. Finally there may be strangers who have come to settle in the village though they can trace no tie of kinship or clanship with any previous member to ease the strain of adjustment to the local life.[1] Each village than lacks the integration brought about by the centralization of unilineal kinship ties, and each neighbourhood is a complex of people, related to each other in a heterogeneous fashion. A man's place in his local community is affected by his kinship relationships to others in the community, but is not based upon these. His duties and rights in the community rise from the fact of his residence alone. Once he has moved into an area, has built his huts, and cultivated a field, he is a full member of the local group. He can look to other members of the group for assistance in ordinary daily activities. He is identified with the local community by outsiders. If he moves away, he loses this identification and joins with those of the new neighbourhood where he settles.

Local organization is dependent upon the general recognition that to till one's fields and tend one's herds it is necessary to live at peace with one's neighbours, and this recognition of common interests finds expression in rites in which it is incumbent upon all members of the community to participate, under penalty of mystical sanctions which may affect, not only the offender, but the community as a whole, or any member within it. And the mystical sanction had its practical expression in mob action against someone who was thought to be endangering the others in the community. Therefore members of the community were

---

[1] See Chapter VI.

expected to join together in the ritual for obtaining rain, for the eating of the new grain, for the festival of the harvest. They also joined together for a rite of purification if a slaying polluted the soil of the district with blood, or if a stranger died within the boundaries of the district. If any member of the community dies all are expected to take part in the mourning.

But the local group does not assume responsibility for the actions of its members in other spheres. This is left to groups organized on kinship principles. The exogamous matrilineal clans, twelve in number, are dispersed groups without leaders or a corporate life to impress upon their members the obligations of clanship. Clanship does not imply common responsibility, though it mitigates hostility between fellow clansmen. Effective organization is dependent upon much smaller groups composed of those who consider themselves to be descended by matrilineal links from a common ancestress, who recognize their common obligations and rights and who join in common action. This is the group which is held responsible for the actions of its members, and which in turn acts to uphold their rights and to avenge their injuries. This is the group which should undertake the work of vengeance if just claims are not satisfied. The group as a whole, and not any particular individual within it, is expected to provide bridewealth for its members, and it shares in the bridewealth received for its women members. The group as a whole has the right to inherit the estate of its members and, if the deceased is a married man, is responsible for the provision of a substitute to marry the widows and father the orphaned children. The group as a whole is responsible for the payment of compensation for the offence of one of its members and formerly, if it failed, the injured parties might retaliate against any one of them and not against the offender alone.

But the matrilineal kinsmen who form the group tend to be dispersed into different neighbourhoods, for though the Tonga are matrilineal, a man usually takes his wife to live in the locality where he had settled. And he is free to choose where he will go. His children may decide to settle with him, they may go to join maternal relatives, they may go off to live with others to whom they can trace some claim through kinship, or they may settle among strangers. And so, within a few generations, members of the group are dispersed across the countryside. But though they may live apart, they continue to act together and to form a group with common interests, so long as they remain in close enough contact to visit, to confer, and to share in one another's affairs. Membership is thus not directly governed by genealogical ties, and the exact degree of kinship is largely irrelevant in determining particular obligations to one another. A man belongs to a particular matrilineal group because he acts in common with its members, and he justifies his participation by the assumption of common kinship though he and others may not know the genealogical links between them. If he moves too far away to join with his kinsmen, or if he repudiates his obligations, he ceases to belong. Kin-groups are thus continually reduced in size by the shedding of those who through distance or the existence of quarrels find themselves no longer able to participate in group affairs. The continued existence of the effective kinship group is dependent upon general good relations throughout the area within which kinsmen are scattered, or their intercourse is blocked and the group is shattered.

The matrilineal group is held together by common interests in property and by expectations of mutual assistance if the need arises. It is also buttressed by the mystique of kinship, which posits supernatural sanctions to bind them to each other. There is the sanction of the ancestral cult, for the matrilineal ancestors may vent their displeasure on any member or on all. There is also the sanction of *malweza*, which in some contexts simply means a 'bad omen', and in others a supernatural retribution for an act or an occurrence which is thought to endanger the group. *Malweza* may strike any member of the offender's group, and not necessarily the offender himself. Incest, suicide or attempted suicide, physical violence by a man to his sister or by any person to someone of an older generation—these and many others are acts of *malweza*. After such an act, illness or misfortune suffered by any member of the group is likely to be attributed to retribution for *malweza*. The retribution can be averted only by a ritual peace-making which restores the integrity of the group. It may be necessary only for the offender and the one against whom he has offended to make their peace in a ritual manner. Serious cases require the participation of every member of the group, while wider public opinion must be faced through the jeers of the clan-joking relatives who are called upon to officiate in the rite.[1]

Joint responsibility of the group is thus extended into the supernatural sphere, and incidents which would require compensation and a public settlement if people of different groups were involved, are here a matter for ritual actions which restore the unity of the group. If a man slays his kinsman, there can be neither compensation nor vengeance. To exact either would require the division of the group, and the end of its common kinship. The taking of a kinsman's property gives rise to grumbling, and in some cases to hints that the taker must be a witch since he thus openly shows his disregard of a living man's personality. But it is not theft. Adultery with a kinsman's wife is incest and therefore *malweza* if the two men are brothers. In other cases, the aggrieved husband may avenge his wrongs by driving off a beast or two from the offender's kraal, and the offender would bridle his resentment and accept his punishment. If a man's expectations of assistance in bridewealth were not met, he could convert his quarrel with his kinsmen into a quarrel between them and some other group by eloping with a girl whose relatives would demand compensation from those identified with him. But there is no open forum in which the wrongs done by one kinsman to another can be proclaimed to the world, which in any event has no interest or obligation to see that justice is done, for where only kinsmen are involved, no outsider may enter.

Thus kinsmen, though dispersed, act as a unit as the local group or neighbourhood does not, and the cross-cutting of local and kinship ties give flexibility to the organization of society. However, the Tonga have further elaborated this cross-cutting of ties to bring about the relationship and interaction in set situations of each matrilineal group with others of like nature. This is done through the stressing of the role of the father. A man belongs to

---

[1] See Chapter II.

the matrilineal group of his mother, but he is a child of his father's matrilineal group and is identified with it also. And through the common interest which the two groups have in him, they are brought into association. Each group is expected to provide a portion of the bridewealth for the men, and they divide the bridewealth of the women. Both groups help to pay compensation if their child offends. If their child is killed, each group has a motive for extracting compensation, for each receives a share. Each group shares in the inheritance, and each has its role in the funeral ceremonies. The identification of a person with his father's group also receives ritual acknowledgment. A man may bring *malweza* upon his father's group as well as his own, for if he strikes his father, or any member of his father's group of an older generation, it is *malweza*. In return, he is dependent upon his father's group for his ritual well-being. Indeed he is more dependent upon them than upon his own matrilineal group, for he may approach his matrilineal ancestors directly. He is debarred from direct approach to the spirits of his father's line. Yet they may affect him, and indeed are considered to have a more powerful control over his life than have the spirits of his own line, and their anger is more dangerous to him and his than the anger of his matrilineal spirits. The Tonga say that if the ancestors of the paternal line are angered by neglect or by some offence against them, they will cause the death of the offender, and his maternal ancestors are powerless to protect him. If the maternal ancestors, however, are angered and wish to kill him, they must justify their action before his paternal ancestors, who will otherwise counter with: 'This is our child. You have no right to kill him.' But important as these ancestors of the paternal line are for good or evil, no man can approach them directly, for he is not a full member of their line. He must call upon some member of his father's group to make the offerings to them. Thus each matrilineal group depends upon the ritual offices of a number of other matrilineal groups for the well-being of its members.

This dependence is developed into a complex relationship, involving a large number of groups, for marriage rules force members of a group to seek alliances with the maximum number of other groups. Cross-cousin marriage is an approved form, but nevertheless the feeling is general that two closely related men should not marry women who are closely related. Nor do the Tonga approve of marriages which suggest that two groups are exchanging wives. It is impossible therefore for marriages, and the birth of children, to affiliate one group with only one or two others. Instead there is a dispersal of ties, and each person becomes a focal point upon which two groups achieve an integration of interests. A marriage is not an alliance between two people; it is a political relationship as well as a personal one, for each party to the marriage is identified with two groups, and all four are thus brought into association. These groups are: the husband's matrilineal group, and the group of his father, the wife's matrilineal group and the group of her father. The husband's two groups share in the payment of bridewealth; the wife's two groups share in the receipt of the bridewealth. All four share in the rituals that institute the marriage and mark its various stages; they are concerned in the sickness or the death of either spouse. And even after the death of the two whose union constituted the original tie between them, two of the groups continue to be affiliated in their common concern for the offspring of the marriage. At the same time, each of the four groups is bound by exactly similar ties to many other matrilineal groups. Bad relations between two groups thus force all the others with which they are in association to have an interest in the development of the quarrel.

Since members of matrilineal groups are dispersed through a number of neighbourhoods and marriages soon interrelate all those living in one neighbourhood, neighbourhood solidarity can be disrupted even though the original incident which provokes a quarrel between groups has occurred between people living in some other locality.

Still another set of ties exists which bind the people living in different localities to each other. These are brought about through the widespread lending of cattle, so that men herd cattle for friends and kinsmen living in various neighbourhoods, while their own cattle in turn are handed over to other men for herding.[1] I shall

---

[1] See Chapter V.

not elaborate this system of relationships here, however, since in the case described below herding ties were not stressed.

With this background, we can begin to understand the stresses which occur within the social system when a major crisis breaks the peace. Today, with the presence of the British Administration, the Northern Rhodesian police, the government-instituted chiefs with their courts and messengers, there is effective force to prevent the mobilization of units in vindictive action, but underneath this superstructure one can still see the interplay of the old forms of social control based on the interaction of kinship and local groups. These still work to reach a settlement over and above that which can be obtained through the courts. They are interested, not in the punishment of the offender, but in the re-establishment of good relations between the groups involved.

This will come out clearly in the particular case which I have chosen to present in illustration. It arose in 1948. It involved people of a number of different matrilineal groups, although those primarily concerned belonged to two groups, one of the Lion clan, the other of the Eland clan. Henceforth I shall refer to these groups as the Lions and the Elands, though it should be remembered that members of these clans belonging to other matrilineal groups were not involved even when they were living in the same community. The incident also involved people of a number of different local groups, though again two adjacent neighbourhoods were primarily concerned—Lupondo and Nampeyo. The incident itself was simple and direct; the issues were clear-cut, and the implications were accepted by all. *A*, a man of the Eland clan, living in the village of Gideon,[1] struck a man, *B*, belonging to the Lion clan, who also lived in Lupondo in the village of Moses. This was at a beer-drink. After lingering for a few days in a coma, *B* died as a result of the blow. The police were summoned. The body was examined by the government doctor. *A* was arrested and committed for trial. Eventually he was convicted of manslaughter and sentenced to a year's imprisonment which he duly served. But

---

[1] Names are fictitious, and following a convention of the Rhodes-Livingstone Institute are chosen from the Old Testament.

this is only a fraction of the case as the Tonga saw it. From the beginning it was not a matter of *A* and *B* alone. *A*'s trial and punishment were not a settlement of the issues involved, and neither group was primarily concerned in this aspect of the matter.

B was a young man, settled in his wife's village. A large number of his matrilineal kinsmen live in the neighbouring village of Joseph, whose headman is a Lion looked upon as the leader of their group. *B*'s father belonged to the Pigeon clan, and lived some 20 miles or more to the east in the district of Lupondo. None of *B*'s patrilineal kinsmen were living in the immediate vicinity of Lupondo, and the numerous Pigeons of other matrilineal groups did not concern themselves in the affair. *B*'s matrilineal kinsmen assumed complete responsibility, and summoned his father to come and join in mourning for their dead and in the decisions concerning what should be done.

A, a member of the Eland clan, lived in the village of Gideon, a Leopard headman who had married his mother's sister. His own father is Moses, a Hyena clansman, and headman of the victim's village. The majority of *A*'s close kinsmen live in the district or Nampeyo, which lies next-door to Lupondo. His mother and her sister married into Lupondo. After his mother's death *A* was reared by her sister at Gideon's village. His only sibling was living 30 miles away to the west, in the area where he had married, and though he was summoned to help in the settlement he took little part in the general discussion of the case. *A*'s mother's sister and her children all live in Lupondo. One is married to a Lion man of the same matrilineal group as his victim. Another who is married to a man of a different group lives in a village which contains many Lion people. Both had their children living with them. In their father's village, Eland and Lion people live side by side, and the Leopard people, of whom their father is one, are inter-married with both. In addition, there are other Eland people of this matrilineal group living in Lupondo villages.

At Nampeyo, where the majority of Eland people of this matrilineal group are living, the people have close ties with the people of Lupondo. One man, *D*, who belongs to the Eland group because his mother was a slave and he therefore took his father's affiliation, is married to a woman of the Lion group, a sister's daughter of the murdered man. Other Lion people are living in Nampeyo. Many of the Eland men are married to women from Lupondo, and their children have a stake in both communities. So numerous are the ties between the two groups that the people of Nampeyo almost automatically assume the obligation to attend funerals in Lupondo, though ordinarily you are only obliged to attend funerals in the neighbourhood, and funerals outside the neighbourhood if you are in some way related to the dead through an actual kinship or some affinal tie.

The leader of *A*'s matrilineal group is *C*, whose domination of the group is assured by a number of factors. He is a *musangu*, i.e. someone who under possession speaks for the spirits which control the rain and affairs of local import; he is a diviner with a reputation beyond his own area; he is a headman of a fairly populous village; he is an official in the Native Authority; he has a fair herd of cattle and, with his salary from the Native Authority treasury, he has sufficient wealth so that he is the logical person for his kinsmen to turn to in their difficulties. He is therefore considered to be their representative though many of them live outside his village, or his neighbourhood, or his chieftaincy. As soon as he heard the news of the assault and the expected death of the victim, he went immediately to Moses's village to see the man and to announce that he and his people were very sorry for what had happened, that it was one man who had injured theirs, and that they as a group did not back his action. The relatives of the victim listened grimly while the injured man groaned occasionally in the background. But they showed no overt hostility towards *C*. Their attitude was that they would wait for the death before they showed their hand.

Then *C* returned to his village complaining bitterly about *A* who had always brought trouble to them and had now crowned his evil-doing with murder. *C* said that he and other elders among the Elands had long since noted *A* as a trouble-maker. They had sent him into the army with the hope that he would be killed in action. He came back unharmed. When *A* was seriously ill in 1946, local gossip had it that the elders of his group were attempting

I

to kill him with sorcery to rid themselves of the trouble he caused them. Now their worst fears were realized. C said: 'I'm sorry. I always said that his life was bad. He always liked to fight, and he fought with anybody including women and children. So it is up to us to pay.' Again, he said: 'When your child marries, you take the calabash and announce to the spirits that she has gone to be married to such and such a man. Sometimes there where she is married, she bears a mad child. But it is our relative. So what can we do? We cannot say that we will not pay this case.' The other men who had gathered all agreed: 'Of course we are going to pay, but we shan't know how much we shall have to pay until the settlement.' Therefore, despite their general disgust with the murderer, they made no attempt to deny their responsibility as a group. C's brothers were too old to be active in the matter, and C therefore turned to their sons, who lived with their fathers, and informed them that they must help their fathers to pay the case. The sons agreed: 'Yes, we know that this must be paid. There is nothing to do but pay.'

Meantime, C was sending a constant string of messengers to Lupondo to inquire after the injured man; and in return he was receiving messages from his kinsmen living in Lupondo who were demanding: 'You must come and see the man whom A has killed. Why don't you come? Do you think that you will refuse to help us in this matter?' Then a messenger came back with the report that the man was dead, and that the Lion people had refused to greet him or the other Elands. Direct relationships between the two groups were now broken off. Because the body had been taken for examination, there could be no immediate mourning for the death, and the Elands did not know just how to proceed to indicate their repudiation of any attempt to deny their responsibility. Then Gideon of Lupondo, vitally concerned because he has both an Eland and a Lion wife, and among his children are both Elands and Lions, called C to try to come to some arrangement which would ease the local tension. C suggested that they call in the father of the victim, who was closely associated with the matter, but nevertheless not the one primarily concerned. The people of Gideon's village objected that they did not dare go to find him since the Lion people were no longer greeting the Eland people, and it was dangerous to go among them. Finally, however, they summoned the father to discuss the matter. Meantime C was informed that the killing was of local importance as well as a matter of the kin-group; for the people of Lupondo had maize in the pots to make beer for the harvest festival and they felt that they could not make their beer until the Elands had provided a beast to kill to cleanse the neighbourhood of the blood spilt within it. In this case, however, the Elands were able to counter with the argument that anything they did to cleanse the district would be useless since they knew that in the last six years three people had been killed in Lupondo and no steps had been taken to cleanse the district of their blood.

While they waited for the return of the body to Lupondo so that the mourning could be held, there was a general uneasiness in the two communities. As the people sat about their fires they talked of the fear that would have afflicted them long ago before the Europeans came and forbade armed vengeance. C said: 'Long ago, in a case like this, right after A had killed B, the people of B would be ready to attack us. First they would go to Gideon's village, because some of us live there, and they would try to kill some of them there and they would take all the women and children in that village to their village and shave their hair and give them new names. This would mean that now they were slaves. And after that B's people would come here, following the relatives of A. They would be coming with many spears, and we would have to be ready because we would know that if they came it would be only to fight. If they wanted to discuss the matter and settle the case without a fight, they could not come here and we could not go there. But they would send an affine, and we would send an affine. When the two men met, they would explain what each side wanted. But we could not go there ourselves, because they would not wait to find out what we were coming for and would start to fight right away. Neither could we send our affine directly to them, nor could they send their affine directly to us. The two must meet somewhere and talk the matter out.' When I pointed out that Gideon was not involved in the matter since he is a Leopard man, the answer was, 'Yes, but there are Eland people in his village, and the Lion people would try to get them. Then Gideon would start to fight them because he would want his children back. And they would come to us and demand that we help them pay to recover their children.'

While this was going on, the men said, there would have been a general disruption of community life. If a death had occurred, they would not have dared to go to the mourning if they knew that the Lion people were to be there, because they would be afraid that when the mourners danced with their spears before the house of the dead they would turn their spears on the Eland people. Nor would other groups welcome them at any gathering, for fear that fresh fighting would break out. Even today, they said, while they might attend the same funerals they would sit far apart for fear that when the people began to drink beer they would fight. Also long ago, they said, the Eland women married to Lion men and living in a community with other Lion people would be afraid to remain in their homes, and on first news of the disaster would be running away with their children to try to seek protection. 'They are afraid because their people have killed a Lion man.' Nor could they return until a settlement was reached, because when people started to drink beer the Lions would say, 'You have your child here, but you Elands killed one of us.' And they would start fighting with the Elands who lived with them. Only after compensation had been paid would the women be able to retaliate with the answer, 'Why do you talk like this? We have paid you.' Nowadays, because of the fear of the Europeans, women are able to stay with their husbands, and the Eland women living at Lupondo stayed in their villages, although they felt they still ran the risk of sorcery or poisoning if the people were very angry.

Nevertheless, though Eland women continued to remain with their husbands in Lupondo while they waited for the mourning to start, they sent constant messages: 'The Lion people are despising us. They refuse to greet us. They remind us all the time that we and our children are Eland, and we have killed their man. What are you going to do?'

And while the women were sending pleas to their relatives to settle the case in a hurry, their husbands were counselling their own kinsmen to accept a settlement: 'The Elands have killed our man, but if they agree to settle, we must settle. Look, our children are Eland. Our wives are Eland. Will it bring that man back to life for us to lose our wives and children? If you despise them for what one man has done, how can they live among us?'

So far as they could, members of the two groups tried to avoid each other, but this meant that some of them could not perform their obligations. D's wife was a Lion, and she went at once to her relatives to mourn with them. Her husband, an Eland, was required by the obligations of marriage to accompany her and take part in the mourning. It is his duty, along with all the other men who have married women of the line, to cook the food for the mourners and to perform the other necessary work about the place of mourning. He went, and got his brother, also an Eland, to accompany him. Then came word that mourning had started, and more and more people from Nampeyo who had kinship obligations to the Lion people went to the mourning. But the Lions sent no formal announcement that they were mourning. They were leaving the next step to the Elands.

C gathered members of his group and with them went to the mourning, where they were joined by Gideon and by the father of the murderer. First they went through the formal mourning dance, and then came to sit slightly apart from the silent group of Lion people. Between them sat a small group of men with ties in both camps. Then the Eland people and their children who had already come to mourn came out and joined C and his group, with considerable signs of relief. One old man, an Eland who had been living in Lupondo ever since his kinsmen had ordered him out of Nampeyo many years before, said that he had not been greeted by the Lion people since the whole trouble started. After a slight pause, the Eland group exchanged greetings with the group between them and the Lions. They called forward the head of the Lion people, and the men greeted each other courteously. The head of the Lion people brought the father of the victim, and again greetings were exchanged. C and others of his party spoke again and again of their sorrow, that this was indeed a serious matter which they thoroughly condemned, that it was only one man who had done wrong and not all of them. The father commented: 'Yes, that's all right. You are sorry. But I am the one who has lost a son.' After a general talk on the evils of this particular case and the increase of violence at beer-drinks, the leader of the Lions returned to his own group. C instructed his go-between Gideon who, as an affine of both the Lion and Eland people and the father of children belonging to both groups, was an ideal negotiator. Gideon relayed the matter to an affine of the Lion group, who in turn carried the words back to the waiting Lion men. Then the Lion affine withdrew, and the leader of the Lions joined the end of the neutral group. Gideon spoke to him and then to C and then he too withdrew, and C went to speak directly to the leader of the Lions. Relationships had now been restored between the two groups. C told them: 'We have heard that you are mourning. We have come to mourn with you, and to find out what you want from us.' The Lion people replied that they were not prepared to say what compensation they would accept until the court case had been settled. Then they would call upon the Elands to pay what was just.

Relationships having been re-established, the Lion and Eland men greeted each other, and food was brought to the visitors who ate. It was again possible for Eland and Lion people to meet and partake in the same rituals and in the same gatherings without danger of immediate hostilities. Each group had had good reason to desire this result, and each had been under considerable pressure from outsiders to settle the case. But it was only a truce, and a final settlement must wait upon the payment of compensation. Once the pressure of uneasiness and of general public anxiety was relaxed, however, the Elands were slow in paying. Normal relationships had been restored. They were no longer receiving frantic messages from their people living among the Lions that life was impossible until a settlement was reached. They began to find reasons why they should not give up their cattle. They argued that they too had lost a man, for was he not in prison? They suggested that the government law and its penalties had superseded the customary law of vengeance or compensation. They argued that they were poor in cattle and could not find the necessary animals to pay. They knew that the Government would not permit the Lions to raid them. They also knew that general public opinion was interested only in the settlement of the differences, and not directly in the matter of compensation.

But public opinion still held them to be at fault, and found its mouthpiece through the invocation of mystical sanctions. *D* had a child by his Lion wife. It fell ill and the diviner announced that the illness was due to the spirit of the dead man which was angered because compensation had not been paid. His spirit could not attack the Eland people directly, for they do not belong to his line, but it could attack them through their child born of a Lion woman. When the child died, the Eland were told that this was due to their recalcitrance about payment. In similar cases, when sickness or death afflicts a person who has a tie with both groups, public opinion through the voice of the diviner will continue to remind the Elands that their responsibility is not at an end. Indeed, it can point the moral still more strongly, for any member of the Lion group who dies, or any child of this group, whether or not there is a tie with the Elands, may also be announced as having died from the same cause, and those who are bereft of a child will hold that the Elands are responsible.

The forces that operate to enforce public control in Tonga society no longer have free play because the presence of the European administration prevents recourse to the final sanction of force through the institution of vengeance. Nevertheless, it is still possible to see in this case how public control is brought to bear upon the groups which in theory are free to settle their differences as they will. In a society of this type, it is impossible to have the development of the feud and the institutionalization of repeated acts of vengeance, for each act of vengeance, like each original incident, mobilizes different groups whose interests are concerned in the particular case and that alone. It would also lead to a general community disruption, affecting those who must live in the midst of the turmoil and yet are not directly concerned with it. Permanent bad relations then are only possible when the groups involved do not have kinsmen living together in the same local groups, and where they are not tied by the network of kinship and affinal relationships to the same matrilineal groups. Then it becomes possible for vengeance to operate without the drag of local obligations and the cross-cutting of kinship ties. But at this distance there is little likelihood of their members clashing. Where clashes are likely, local bonds and kinship ties intervene to force a settlement.

Tonga society, despite its lack of political organization and political unity, is a well-integrated entity, knit together by the spread of kinship ties from locality to locality, and the intertwining of kinship ties within any one locality. It obtains its integration and its power to control its members and the different groups in which they are aligned, by the integration of each individual into a number of different systems of relationships which overlap. When a man seeks to act in terms of his obligation to one set of relationships, he is faced by the counterclaims upon him of other groups with which he must also interact. This entanglement of claims leads to attempts to seek an equitable settlement in the interests of the public peace which alone enables the groups to perform their obligations one to another and a Tonga to live as a full member of his society.

It seems possible that the cross-cutting of ties also operates in the same fashion in societies organized on the lineage principle, and that a further analysis of the data would show that these societies obtain their stability not because their local groups are unilineally organized, but because of the presence within each local group of people with a diverse set of ties linking them to those in other areas.

This has certainly been of primary importance among the Tallensi, for whom Fortes reports:

In spatial relations every maximal lineage belongs to one set of adjacent lineages in the Bɔɣar cult and to a different set of adjacent lineages in the Earth cult. It has, therefore, two intersecting fields of politico-ritual relations so adjusted that its loyalties to the other component lineages of one field are counter-balanced by its loyalties to the component lineages of the other field. Both sets of politico-ritual loyalties are correlated with the same sort of social interests, symbolized in a single system of religious concepts and values. Their organization in two complementary configurations around polar symbols checks the dangers of disruptive conflicts that might spring from them. Thus the ties of clanship are regrouped around another axis of social integration. Every maximal lineage is a bridge between a *Bɔyar* congregation and a *Tɛŋ* congregation. In most cases, in fact, the component lineages of a particular *Tɛŋ* congregation all belong to, and in that context represent, different *Bɔyar* congregations, and vice versa. This is the fundamental mechanism of the remarkable politico-ritual equilibrium found among the Tallensi.[1]

The Tonga and the Tallensi are very differently organized, but the same principle of cross-cutting ties appears in both societies. I suspect that it is a general principle incorporated into most societies as a mechanism for ensuring the maintenance of order.

---

[1] Fortes, 1945, pp. 107-8.

CHAPTER V

THE ROLE OF CATTLE AMONG THE PLATEAU TONGA OF MAZABUKA DISTRICT[1]

THE Plateau Tonga are one of the few cattle-keeping peoples in Northern Rhodesia. They have had cattle for generations, but during the last half of the nineteenth century they lost much of their stock to Lozi and Ndebele armies which raided their territory. With the imposition of peace after British administration was established, the Tonga again built up their herds, to some extent through acquisition of European breeds though a remnant of the old native cattle survived to add its strains to the present heterogeneous Tonga herds. In 1948, records of the Veterinary Department showed a total of 210,204 cattle in the sixteen chieftaincies of the Mazabuka District, or 2·3 cattle for every Tonga man, woman and child.[2] Apparently the herds had almost doubled in the previous decade, since in 1938 Veterinary Departments estimates gave 148,485 native-owned cattle for this district.[3]

The area of the district in 1948 was computed at 7,600 square miles, with an overall density of African population of 12 to the square mile. However, a large area adjacent to the railway, which cuts through the district, has been taken over for European farms

---

[1] While collecting material for this chapter I worked mainly in four chieftaincies, Mwanza, Chona, Monze, and Mwanacingwala, and the material is most reliable for these four areas. I also visited, very briefly, Sianjalika, Ufwenuka, Siamaundu, and Chongo chieftaincies, and have talked with Tonga from every chieftaincy in the district.

[2] Information supplied by the District Commissioner, Mazabuka. The Tonga population of the district was estimated as 89,535 in 1948. The number of cattle per head of population is probably high for Central Africa. Among the Fort Jameson Ngoni the figure is about 0·3 cattle per person. I am indebted to Mr. J. A. Barnes for this information.

[3] *Veterinary Department, Annual Report for the year 1938.* Lusaka, Government Printer, 1939. This is an approximate figure and is the same as that quoted for 1936 and 1937. The district boundaries may have been altered during the decade so that the figures for 1938 and 1948 may not refer to exactly the same area.

and ranches, and the land available for the Africans and their cattle is much less than 7,600 square miles. The habitable portion available to them is still further reduced by arid unoccupied plains in Mapanza chieftaincy, the Kafue swamps, and the rugged country of the Zambezi Escarpment which lies along the eastern border.[1] The average population density is probably closer to 58·2, though locally in Mwanacingwala chieftaincy it rises to 137·7 per square mile.[2]

As might be expected, the district shows signs of over-stocking with subsequent deterioration of stock and developing erosion of the land. In certain areas, over-stocking was apparent at least as early as 1936. In 1945 a team of agricultural experts who made a survey of Tonga land usage pointed out while degeneration of grazing lands was not as marked as was to be expected from the concentrations of stock involved, nevertheless, over-stocking was locally severe and in all parts of the district probably incipient. They estimated that in Mwanacingwala, Sianjalika, and Mwanza chieftaincies, and probably also in Ufwenuka and Chona, the cattle population was already twice the stock-carrying capacity of the land. Chongo chieftaincy in the west seemed to have adequate grazing for its herds, but a further increase in the herds would reduce it to the same level as the other chieftaincies.[3] Since 1945, the herds have continued to increase. Moreover, since the survey, the Tonga have lost the use of grazing on Crown Land and on unoccupied farms in the European belt which had eased the strain on their own pastures.[4]

The deterioration of the herds has not gone unnoted. Some attempt has been made to improve the cattle by the introduction of good breeding stock. Government has distributed improved bulls. A few African farmers have bought good bulls from local European farmers, or occasionally have received them in gift from

---

[1] Information supplied by the District Commissioner, Mazabuka.

[2] W. Allan *et al.*, 1948, p. 30. Henceforth referred to as *The Tonga Report*.

[3] Cf. *The Tonga Report*, pp. 121-30, 114-17.

[4] From 1946 to 1950, farms were taken up at a rapid rate by new settlers. In some cases they found Tonga villages on their land. These were removed to the Native reserves.

European friends.[1] Good stock, however, is likely to die before the year is out due to the hardships of competing with native cattle for the over-crowded range.

The Administration is also aware of the problem of over-stocking and has begun to consider the advisability of enforcing a systematic culling of the herds to reduce the number of cattle to the stock-carrying capacity of the land. The Tonga themselves know that grazing is no longer adequate for their herds and that their cattle have deteriorated. They comment that 10 cows today give less milk than they got from 2 cows twenty or thirty years ago. They know that cows go dry quickly and that few families have milk from April to December. They say that their cows to-day rarely produce more than four calves before they are done bearing. They can see that the grazing has declined. They are quite capable of relating these facts and coming to much the same conclusion as the European observer. As one man put it: 'Today there is little milk because there is no grass.' Yet this does not make them willing to reduce their herds or to look favourably on de-stocking.

In part this is due to their sense of grievance over the loss of land to the Europeans. They argue that their pastures are over-grazed because they have less land than formerly and disregard the problems raised by the increase in the herds. But their resistance to de-stocking is also affected by their system of cattle ownership and the use to which they put their cattle. Cattle do not mean the same thing to Europeans and to the Tonga, and any failure to understand this can only lead to difficulties.

OWNERSHIP OF CATTLE

Only a few head of cattle are publicly owned. A man who has offended some ritual taboo of his local community may be fined a head or two of cattle, and these are then held by his chief, head-

---

[1] Tonga practice is to keep only a few of the male calves for breeding purposes. A bull calf is chosen on the basis of its own appearance and the calving record of its mother. All other calves are castrated for use as oxen. Not every cattle owner keeps a bull, and there may be only one to a village.

man, or ritual leader until they are needed for sacrifice on behalf of the community to end a drought or some other common misfortune. These cattle are dissipated again almost as soon as they are acquired and do not lead to the formation of large herds in public ownership. Another type of public ownership has developed in recent years as the Agricultural Department has purchased oxen for work in the gardens of certain approved schools. These are attached to the school and are supervised by the local teacher.

All other cattle can be said to be owned by individuals rather than by local or kinship groups. If you ask the Tonga about the ownership of a particular beast, they will always reply with the name of an individual, never with that of a group. Nevertheless, ownership does not have the same connotations of rights to independent action with respect to the property that it has to the European. The Tonga formulation would be: 'I own cattle. I belong to a kinship group. Therefore my kinsmen have the right to demand my assistance. My rights over my cattle are subject to the obligation which I have to assist my kinsmen.'

The Tonga distinguish between rights of ownership and rights to assistance. Rights of ownership apply to a particular beast or beasts; rights to assistance apply to a relationship between individuals. A man does not say, 'That cow belongs to my mother's brother and therefore it belongs to me.' He may say, 'That cow belongs to my mother's brother. My mother's brother should assist me and therefore I have the right to go to him and ask him to give me his cow if I need it.' As a result, an individual is subject to the demands of his kin for cattle no matter how he has acquired his herd. He may have acquired cattle through his own efforts, or by taking bridewealth for his daughters or for women of his kin-group, or by inheritance from members of his kin-group, or by collecting damages from those who have injured him in some way. The source of the cattle is irrelevant to the right of assistance. Indeed, it would be considered bad form for a Tonga to go to a kinsman and say, 'You have taken cattle for my mother, or my sister, and therefore you should help me.' It suggests a *quid pro quo* transaction inimical to the general bonds of kinship. Moreover, when a man dies his cattle become the common inheritance of his kin-group. Those which he acquired by his own efforts as well as those which he acquired through his kinship relations are part of this common estate. He has no right to will his property outside the group, nor can he designate his heir from amongst the members of the group.[1] His kinsmen divide the cattle amongst themselves, however, and each man considers that the cattle he receives are now his individual property and not the property of the kin-group.

To understand this system, it is necessary to pay some attention to the conditions under which it developed. It is only since the establishment of British administration that there has been a state organization which insures the safety of individual life and property. The Tonga had no chiefs, no public courts, no police system, no army. There were no public tribunals to which a man could appeal for justice. To maintain his rights, he was dependent upon the support of his kinsmen who would back him in an attempt to recover his property or to extort compensation for injury. They in return expected him to give them his support. The effective group of kin was a small number of individuals descended through females from a putative common ancestress. The genealogical links might be forgotten without effecting the validity of the claim to membership in the group.[2] Henceforth I shall refer to such a group of kinsmen as a matrilineal group. The Tonga refer to it as *mukowa*, a word which is also used for clan, species or type. Its members were considered both by themselves and by outsiders to have common interests which set them off as a unit. Furthermore, outsiders held them collectively responsible for each other's actions. If a man from group A offended a man from group B, group B might retaliate against any member of A to square the account. Thus a man had a vital interest in helping his kinsman. If the account were not settled, he himself might pay for the offence. Equally, if he refused to help his kinsmen when they were in trouble, they would refuse to help him when his turn came and might cast him out. He was then at the mercy of any

---

[1] For a discussion of the inheritance system of the Tonga, cf. Colson, 1950.

[2] For further discussion of the nature of the matrilineal group, cf. Colson, 1951.

outsider who wished to attack him. Or, to prevent possible involvement with other groups which he might offend, his own group might turn on him and either sell him into slavery or slay him. To deny the obligations of kinship was thus in a sense to outlaw oneself, since legal protection was dependent upon the support of the matrilineal group.

In such circumstances, the rights of ownership vested in the individual sink into the background. An individual had little incentive and less power to protect himself against acts by his matrilineal kin. If a kinsman took his cattle, he could get redress only if the majority of the group disapproved. Otherwise he was helpless. There was no outside authority to which he could turn to demand restitution.

With the institution of British administration about 1899, the necessity for the matrilineal group to stand united against the world began to disappear and the ties of kinship have weakened gradually as a result. Nevertheless, there still remains a strong sentiment attached to kinship and its obligations, which is in conflict with the growth of a desire for individual freedom both in action and in the use of property.

The introduction of courts and a police force not only freed a man from the need to rely upon his matrilineal group but also opened the way for him to sue his kinsmen and force them to restore his property or to pay him damages. Today, if his relatives take his cattle without permission, he has legal redress in the courts where the act is defined as theft. Nevertheless, a man is still reluctant to enforce the legal rights given to him by the new system. In 1947, a woman living in Mwanza chieftaincy brought suit against her matrilineal relatives for theft of a cow which they had been herding for her. After the initial hearing of the case, she withdrew the charge and decided to swallow her losses: 'They are my relatives and I can do nothing to regain my cattle.' It is said to be not uncommon for relatives even today to appropriate thus the cattle entrusted to them by the women of their group. Men also run this risk. In 1948, a young man, who was working as a government clerk in Lusaka, came home to bring suit against his mother's brother who had been herding his cattle. The mother's brother had used the cattle to settle an adultery suit of his own, and the young man demanded restitution. The Native Authority court which heard the case declared the matter a most difficult one. The counsellors admitted the legal rights of the nephew, but pointed out that he had a moral obligation to help his mother's brother. They finally succeeded in having the case transferred to another jurisdiction so that they need not pronounce a verdict.[1]

When a man grows old, he may find that his cattle have been seized by relatives now that he is no longer strong enough to protect his rights. They are undeterred by any thought that he might proceed against them in the courts. A wealthy farmer, rich in cattle, said one day that he hoped his favourite daughter would marry a good man who would look after him when he was old. I suggested that a son-in-law, no matter what his character, would be likely to offer asylum if only to have the use of the cattle. The man and the others listening laughed me down. 'Do you think that my matrilineal relatives would let me take the cattle with me? You can see for yourself—when a man grows old and has no strength, his matrilineal relatives come and steal his cattle and drive them to their own kraals. You can hear an old man shouting at them to bring back his cattle and grumbling about the theft, but he can do nothing and they take the cattle as they will until he has nothing left in his kraal. That was happening down here with the brother of Chifwebafweba. Before he died, they had already taken most of his cattle away from him.' Moreover, it is a common practice for a young man to steal a beast from his mother's brother to finance some enterprise of his own. Lads who run off to the labour centres of Southern Rhodesia or the Union of South Africa frequently finance their rail fares by the sale of a beast stolen from a matrilineal relative. Legally, today, the owner has the right to demand restitution, but usually he grumbles and threatens but does nothing. When the lad returns, his relative

---

[1] The plaintiff told me that he would not have acted against his mother's brother under ordinary circumstances, but he felt himself particularly aggrieved since it was his own sister with whom the mother's brother had committed adultery. This was incest and by his action his mother's brother had already denied their kinship.

frequently kills a goat or a chicken in his honour and avoids all mention of the stolen animal. The offender feels no shame and may refer to the matter cheerfully, as a custom of the Tonga.

In a sense, the theft is considered to be only an anticipation of rights to inherit, for the moment the owner dies his property reverts to his matrilineal group and every member may claim a share.[1]

Despite the obligations to assist his kin and the restrictions on his right to dispose of his property after death, the Tonga owner still has the right to administer his cattle as he sees fit during his lifetime. His matrilineal relatives have the right to complain if he refuses to help them; they do not have the right to interfere with his disposal of his property. If he wishes, he may sell his cattle and waste the proceeds. He may give cattle to his own children or even to those who are not related to him. He may kill his cattle for funerals, puberty ceremonies, or other ritual occasions. He may even slaughter them for food. He may send them away to be herded by other men. He should inform his matrilineal relatives of what he has done, but they cannot hinder him from his purpose save by persuasion or by threatening that since he has no care for his relatives they in turn will no longer consider him a member of their group or eligible for assistance. If feelings grow violent, a man will suspect his relatives of attempting to bewitch him and will attribute his misfortunes to their efforts, and this fear of witchcraft may stengthen the purely moral sanctions which lead a man to administer his herd in the interests of his matrilineal group.

A further proof that the Tonga system is based on individual ownership rather than on joint-ownership is the fact that women and children have the same right as men to own cattle, though they exercise it less frequently.

A boy is sometimes presented with a beast or two by his father or

---

[1] The matrilineal group of the dead man's father also has a claim on his inheritance. His own children usually are given one beast for their joint inheritance, though occasionally they receive more. Today the children could probably establish a legal claim to this beast which would be upheld by the courts.

K

some other relative. The original gift plus any increase then belong
to the child who exercises the same rights that an adult man does
over his property. He must be consulted before his cattle are sold,
traded, or killed, and could insist upon his right to dispose of them
as he sees fit. Usually he sends his herd to his matrilineal relatives,
however, lest his father should die and his father's heirs declare
that they belong to his father's herd. If he dies, his matrilineal
relatives will probably claim his property as their inheritance.
However, only an adult may claim the right to share in inheritance and in the distribution of bridewealth, and therefore a
child has not this means of gaining cattle.

Women receive cattle from a number of sources. Occasionally
they inherit cattle from their matrilineal relatives, although unless
the herd is large and the number of relatives small they are passed
over in the division of the inheritance. I have recorded only two
cases where women have accepted bridewealth in respect of their
daughters. Bridewealth cattle are therefore not a source of their
wealth. More frequently they purchase cattle with money
received as a gift or derived from the sale of beer or some crop.
In the western chieftaincies, women are more likely to have large
herds and some are counted as *baami* (wealthy people). In that
area, a wealthy man may give cattle to his daughter on her marriage. She is then the owner of these cattle and has the right to
use them as she will to assist herself and her children. This is an
important source. Sometimes a man gives a present of cattle to
his wife. In the western areas, a man may present a beast or two to
a wife who has brought him cattle through her adulteries, in appreciation of the role she has played in the increase of his herd.[1] If
he should later change his mind and try to recover the gift, the
women and her relatives would repudiate any claims to ownership that the husband might put forward. In the eastern areas, the
Tonga deny a husband would encourage his wife by giving her
cattle paid for her adulteries.

Among the eastern Tonga, women generally claim that they
do not own cattle. When I have asked a woman if she planned to

---

[1] The standard rate of damages paid by lover to husband is today 2 cattle
or £4.

use money she possessed to purchase cattle, the usual answer has been: 'I am a woman. What have I to do with cattle?' They also say that if men should hear them boasting of owning cattle they would be angry. Nevertheless, while ownership does not seem as common as in the west, some women do own small herds. At Chona village, no woman admitted to owning cattle. At Chepa village, among wealthier maize producers, six women admitted that they had cattle. One woman had inherited five from her full brother and had received another cow as a gift from her paternal half-brother. She increased her herd by the purchase of five cattle using money derived from the sale of her bean crop. Another woman built up a small herd from the increase of one cow originally presented to her by her father. The rest had received their cattle from various relatives. In a neighbouring village, the wife of the headman owned a number of ploughing oxen and several cows. Her husband originally gave her a share of the money made by the sale of maize which both had worked to produce. She purchased a cow and the herd came from the increase. In still another village a woman given money by her husband after the sale of their crop used her share to purchase a cow from her husband so that she might have cattle of her own. Among these people of the eastern chieftaincies, however, it is not common for cattle to be given to a woman on her marriage. If she does receive the use of cattle, the beasts usually are considered to represent a herding loan and not an outright gift. When the giver dies, his matrilineal relatives may claim the right to resume control of the cattle if they know of the transaction. Thus a woman in Ufwen-uka chieftaincy who received five cattle from her father and one from her father's brother hid the herd with her matrilineal relatives in anticipation of the demands which are likely to arise on her father's death.

In all areas, such cattle as a woman owns are her property, and her husband and children have no legal control over them. She must depend upon men to herd her cattle for her, and this presumably made her rights to cattle still less secure that those of a man in earlier times; but today the courts make her secure in her possession.

The consideration of the system of cattle ownership indicates that an individual has the right under Tonga custom to dispose of his cattle, and therefore to cull his herds. His obligations to his kindred, however, require that in disposing of his herds he keeps in mind his duty to assist his kindred with cattle to pay bridewealth or to pay damages if they are involved in difficulties. His independence of action is reduced thereby, especially if he wishes to be regarded as a respectable member of his community.

The Herding System

A further complication of the property system lies in the fact that although cattle are always owned by individuals, it is often difficult to establish the legal owner of a particular beast and usually quite impossible to discover how many cattle a particular man owns.

There are no adequate figures to indicate the spread of ownership among the population.[1] I would say as a guess that there are a few men who own several hundred head, many more who own from twenty to one hundred, still more who own less than twenty, and a few who own none at all; but that is as far as I would care to commit myself.

The Veterinary Department provides a break-down of the figure for total cattle population into number of head resident in each chieftaincy of Mazabuka District. In 1948, the cattle were distributed as shown in Table V.[2]

These figures, however, show only the number of cattle counted in each chieftaincy and do not show the number of cattle owned by the people resident in each chieftaincy. That is a very different matter.

I made a number of attempts to question informants about the number of cattle they owned and how they had obtained these, but abandoned the questioning as useless when even those who were usually co-operative and eager to help my work squirmed,

---

[1] The best indications, based on small samples, are contained in Table XXXVIII and Appendix II of *The Tonga Report*.

[2] Information supplied by the District Commissioner, Mazabuka.

denied, claimed to have forgotten and did everything in their power to be obstructive. They all denied any ritual taboo on counting cattle or announcing the number owned, but it was evident that on this subject I was up against one of the most deeprooted antipathies that the Tonga have. They are opposed to letting anyone, friend or foe or relative, know just how many cattle they have, or where the cattle are, or indeed how they were come

TABLE V

Cattle Population by Chieftaincy

Chiefs' Areas			Cattle		
			Male	Female	Total
Naluama	.	.	.	2,788	3,743	6,531
Mwenda.	.	.	.	4,390	5,044	9,434
Sianjalika	.	.	.	6,670	8,279	14,949
Mwanacingwala	.	.	8,153	10,493	18,646
Chongo .	.	.	.	8,735	10,721	19,456
Simuyobe	.	.	.	10,720	14,620	25,340
Monze	.	.	.	10,145	13,252	23,397
Mwansa .	.	.	.	5,200	6,827	12,027
Chona	.	.	.	2,119	2,779	4,898
Ufwenuka	.	.	.	5,273	6,733	12,006
Siamaundu	.	.	.	8,308	10,185	18,493
Moyo .	.	.	.	2,566	3,018	5,584
Mapanza.	.	.	.	7,944	10,705	18,649
Macha	.	.	.	1,257	1,594	2,851
Singani .	.	.	.	6,932	10,786	17,718
Siabunkulu	.	.	.	127	98	225
Totals .	.	.	.	91,327	118,877	210,204

by.[1] An inspection of the cattle kraals will do little to clear up the matter since a cattle owner rarely has all his stock in his own kraal, and some of the beasts in his kraal will undoubtedly belong to other men and women. This is due to the herding system.[2]

It is very common for Tonga to enter into herding arrangements. A man will send a beast or two to some friend or relative.

---

[1] In this they differ markedly from the neighbouring Ila of the Namwala District, who are said to boast publicly of the number of their cattle.

[2] Some similar type of herding system seems to be very common among cattle-keeping tribes throughout Africa. The Ila seem to have it. Cf. Smith and Dale, 1920, Vol. I, p. 386. It also occurs in South and East Africa. Cf., e.g., Peristiany, 1939, pp. 150-2. Schapera, 1937, p. 201.

If he owns a large number of cattle, he may have the greater number of his cattle herded by various clients. Even a small owner will probably have one or two head herded by someone else. In return, he receives cattle to herd for others. It is not a reciprocal arrangement whereby two men exchange cattle, but a system of wide ramifications. A sends cattle to B, who probably in turn has cattle being herded by C, D and E, and A meanwhile is receiving cattle from F and G. Herding links follow ties of kinship and friendship and reinforce these ties. They extend over considerable distances without regard to the boundaries of neighbourhoods or chieftaincies.

The actual owners of a portion of the cattle herded in any one chieftaincy may live outside its boundaries or even outside the district. Men who live in the Gwembe District, along the Zambezi where cattle do not thrive because of tsetse fly, may own cattle which are herded for them by men who live on the fly-free plateau of Mazabuka District. Thus cattle herded in Mwanza chieftaincy may be owned by a man living in Chipepo chieftaincy a good three or four days' walk away. In turn men living in Mwanza chieftaincy have some of their cattle herded elsewhere. One man had cattle in Munyumbwe chieftaincy, a two days' trip by bicycle from his home, and other cattle in Sianjalika, Chona, Ufwenuka, Chongo, and Monze chieftaincies, as well as a number herded by men living in Mwanza. A man questioned in Chona chieftaincy had cattle in Ufwenuka, Chona, and Mwanza chieftaincies, and was herding cattle for a relative living in Mwanza.

The herding arrangements may have started in the old dangerous days when it was better to split the cattle into small lots in different areas rather than run the risk that a raid against one kraal would destroy a man's whole herd. It also lessened the risks in case of cattle epidemics. It may be one of the reasons for the rapid spread of cattle throughout Tonga country again once the raids were over, since the raided areas could draw replacements from those areas which had escaped relatively lightly. In 1913 it was considered to be an ancient custom, and Tonga leaders informed government officials: 'It would not be possible to tell you how many cattle we have because no man keeps all his cattle in his own village. He herds the cattle of others and others herd his cattle: it is our custom of long standing. But we have many.'[1]

In the Tonga area where land was once plentiful and rights in land did not vest in any corporate group or authority, the existence of herding ties probably played their part in giving cohesion to Tonga society. A man rewarded his kinsmen by giving them cattle to herd; he attempted to bind others to him by the same method. In return he showed his friendship to them by caring for their cattle. Today the herding system still plays its part in maintaining bonds between people who often live in distant areas and see each other seldom. It is also a means of balancing the obligations of the individual to assist his kin against his desire to retain his property. The greater his visible wealth the greater the demands made upon him by his kinsmen. The herding system prevents his relatives from being aware of the extent of his wealth, which may help to reduce their demands for assistance. It also serves to hide a portion of his assets from his creditors and those who have a claim against him for damages. It is significant that when a man is ordered to pay cattle by the courts today, or when a relative begs for help in cattle, the usual reply is: 'I will try to find a beast.' A man does not admit that he has cattle in his kraal and has only to go and get them. He maintains that he will seek for cattle, but they will be difficult to find. When he is reminded that he has cattle in his kraal, he refers to other men as their owners and pleads his own poverty. Thus he delays and is sometimes able to evade the obligation. Moreover, others will be less likely to resort to self-help and drive off the cattle they regard as due them since they will not know which are his own cattle and which he is herding for others.

Herding arrangements have also a practical utility for those who participate. Men who have no cattle or not enough for their purposes are able to get possession of the necessary animals through the herding system. Large owners who have too many cattle for their own comfort find it a way to hold a maximum of stock with a minimum of hired helpers who require supervision. The large

[1] Quoted from a report by the Secretary for Native Affairs written in 1913.

owner relies upon the boys of his own immediate family with one or two additional youths whom he has been able to attract to his service for the care of the herd which he keeps at his own kraal and utilizes the herding system to care for the remainder of his stock. The scattering of his cattle into other areas also relieves the pressure upon the pastures and waterholes close to his kraal. The few cattle that he receives from other men do not balance the outflow from his own herd.

A herding arrangement may begin in a variety of ways. A man who needs ploughing oxen or cows for milk may approach a wealthier friend or relative and beg for cattle to help him. He may receive a beast or two, and if the arrangement proves satisfactory it may continue for years and even survive the death of the original parties to the agreement. Sometimes a man who has cattle seeks someone to herd them for him. A man who receives a share in the bridewealth of his daughters may pass on the cattle to other relatives. Sometimes he transfers his rights of ownership to the relative; sometimes he merely transfers custody. Once it was believed that a man became sterile if he drank milk from cattle given as bridewealth for his uterine sisters, and a father protected his sons from this catastrophe by sending the cattle elsewhere to be herded. Though the belief has largely vanished, the practice continues. In the eastern areas, when a man receives cattle of adultery from the lover of his wife, he usually seeks someone to herd them. The eastern Tonga do not look with approval on a wife's adulteries, and they despise the western Tonga for considering cattle of adultery as a way to wealth. They maintain that the husband should feel ashamed to drink the milk from such cattle, though it is not taboo to him, but still more important, they think, is the necessity to keep these cattle away from the wife lest she point to them as the source of her husband's wealth. They say that a woman is apt to sneer at a reminder of her sins if she sees cattle which she has brought through her adulteries leading to the increase of her husband's herd. It is best, therefore, to place the cattle where she cannot see them and be reminded of their origin, and where she will not know how they increase or if her husband sells one of the beasts.

When a man grows old and has no young sons or other dependants who will herd for him, he must send his cattle away to be herded by others or lose them entirely. Even young men will make herding arrangements from time to time when the need presses. If a man receives cattle in payment of debt, bride-wealth, or damages during the dry season, he will arrange either to have them herded by the original owner or by someone in the immediate vicinity, since it is useless to take cattle to a new home before the beginning of the rains has freshened the pastures; for the cattle will return to their familiar grazing grounds or go straying through the bush in search of pasture. The present-day veterinary rules also make it necessary to resort to a herding arrangement, for frequently a quarantine is imposed against the movement of cattle from one chieftaincy to another to prevent the spread of cattle disease. At such times a man who obtains cattle in another chieftaincy, or who wishes to move from his chieftaincy, must leave the cattle at their original home until the quarantine is lifted. A certain amount of surreptitious movement does take place across quarantine lines, but the Native Authorities are likely to take a severe view if the matter comes to light, and the owner will receive a heavy fine. In any of these situations, if the owner has no immediate need of his cattle and the arrangement proves satisfactory to both parties, a temporary herding arrangement may continue in force for many years.

The herding system is further complicated since the original herder may in turn transfer the beast further. Thus Sulwe of Shanamoonga Village in Chona chieftaincy received cattle to herd from a distant relative living in Ufwenuka chieftaincy. Sulwe has no kraal of his own and therefore placed the cattle in charge of his sister's son who keeps them in the kraal of the older man with whom he lives, Sulwe's paternal half-brother. They live in another section of the village, perhaps a mile from Sulwe's homestead. If anything happens to the cattle, the sister's son must answer to Sulwe who in turn is responsible to the owner. The owner of the kraal is not directly involved in the transaction. Matters may be complicated still further, for the beasts being herded may have some claim against them. If they were given originally as bridewealth, the relatives of the man who paid bridewealth have a prior claim against the cattle should the woman for whom they paid abscond. The identical beasts need not be repaid, but there is a claim against the cattle owned by the man who received the bridewealth. Frequently when suit is brought in a Native Authority court, the argument involves owner, claimant, primary herder, and secondary herder.

Recognized rights and obligations regulate the herding system. The owner does not pay the herder for his care of the cattle. The herder has his repayment in the use of milk from the cows and in the use of the oxen in ploughing. If a beast dies, he usually receives the major portion of the meat. He also has the manure for his fields if he wishes to use it. But the increase of the cattle as well as the original beasts remain the property of the original owner. The herder is responsible for the cattle while they are in his care and for any damage they may cause. If the cattle raid a field, the herder may be made to pay the whole of the damages awarded, though occasionally an owner will pay a share proportionate to the number of his cattle involved in the raid. The herder is not liable for accidental deaths to the cattle in his charge, even should these be caused by the carelessness of his herd-boys, but if he deliberately kills a beast or disposes of one in any way, he must repay the owner. If the two men are in a kinship relationship or are close friends, the owner may present the herder with an occasional beast from the increase of the cattle or permit him to kill a beast for some ritual occasion. He is not obliged to do this. If the herder should use a beast without the owner's permission, he is liable to be sued for damages even though the two men are relatives. He remains responsible for the cattle until he returns them to their owner or until he produces evidence that they have died in his hands. In the latter case, he should take the skins to the owner and explain the manner of the deaths to prove that he is not at fault.

Despite these safeguards, owners claim that they are always at a disadvantage in a herding arrangement: 'If you send your cattle to be herded, when a beast dies in the herd it is always one that belongs to you and never one owned by the herder. Never were so few calves born to a cow save one that is being herded. To give out to herd is to give indeed.' It may be true that herders succeed in acquiring a certain number of the calves born to the beasts in their care, and that they deceive the owners about the number of cattle that die, and this is particularly likely to happen when herder and owner live far apart and may not see each other for several years. Nevertheless, the legal position is clear. No matter how long the arrangement may continue, the owner has always the right to resume his cattle including their increase. If the cattle increase in the herder's hands, the owner may take some of the progeny and hand them on to another herder.

Eventually, a large owner will have cattle being herded away which have never been in his own kraal, and his heirs, indeed, may have little knowledge of the ramifications of his ownership. On his death, his matrilineal group will assemble to discuss his property and attempt to trace the cattle that have disappeared into the herding arrangements. Where a member of the group itself has cattle, he will probably be allowed to retain possession as his portion of the inheritance and they then become his own property. Where an outsider is concerned, the cattle are usually called in to be divided out again amongst the heirs. Occasionally the group may continue the herding arrangement with the chief heir in the position of the original owner. If the herder dies, the owner usually recalls his cattle. Occasionally he allows the herder's heirs to appoint another in his place, and again the arrangement continues as before. In either case, the link that binds herder and owner is emphasized at the funeral when the surviving partner brings one of his own cattle to kill in honour of the dead, which should then in turn be replaced by another beast from the dead mans herd. Cattle links, like kinship links, are respected by the Tonga.

The perpetuation of the herding system is possible only in a situation such as is found among the Tonga where people are interested in ownership of cattle rather than in immediate possession. Once a man has satisfied his immediate needs for ploughing oxen and for cows for milk, he is free to use his cattle to build up, or enhance, his links with other men and thereby his influence. He retains his rights of ownership so that he may draw upon these cattle if need arises. The fact that he may lose economically through embezzlement by the herder is in this system of minor importance. This contention is supported by the behaviour of the Tonga in another though somewhat comparable situation. When a man has been awarded cattle by a court or by arbitration between the matrilineal groups concerned he is often in no hurry to put himself in possession of the cattle. He knows that when he does make his demand that he will be able to enforce his claim, and so he is content to let the years pass with occasional trips to remind the other man that he still owes the debt. The Tonga are eager to establish a claim to cattle but are prepared to let the claim lie dormant for long periods of years. The claim remains good, and can be inherited, so long as there are witnesses either to the original transaction or to the subsequent acknowledgement of the claim. In such cases, the claimant loses the increase from the cattle awarded to him, but only in very recent years have men begun to claim that they should receive more cattle for a long unpaid claim. The courts have yet to come to any clear decision on the point, but it is an indication that the Tonga are beginning to think of their herds in terms of economic transactions rather than as the material means of building up a network of social ties.

It is obvious that the herding system will lie in the way of a thorough culling of the herds which a policy of de-stocking would require. A man may always take refuge from a demand that he dispose of particular animals by declaring that they are herding cattle and not his own property, and this very often may be true. If an official suggests that a given beast be slaughtered, the owner may live some days away and the herder has no right to sell or slaughter an animal on his own initiative without the owner's permission. The owner, while he had a right to dispose of the animal as he pleases, would probably hesitate to deprive the herder of his charge unless he himself felt the pressure of necessity, either to meet some obligation or to exchange for food in times of starvation. Equally, since the owner has no immediate benefit from some of his cattle—perhaps the larger portion of his herd in the case of a large owner—he has less incentive to seek to improve quality. A cow that gives more milk will not help him since the herder will drink the milk. Better oxen will benefit the herder rather than the owner. A reduction of the cattle, even though he now has better quality stock, may mean that he must retrench on the number of his herding arrangements, and thus lead to a diminishing of his influence.

On the other hand, the system ensures a more uniform distribution of cattle among the population. Probably many families have milk cows and enough oxen for ploughing because of the herding system. It may also disguise the concentration of cattle in the hands of the wealthier men and make the Tonga less conscious of any possibility that the wealthy may own more cattle than the land can carry.

USE OF CATTLE

It is obvious that until recent years the Tonga desire for cattle was not conditioned entirely by the practical benefits derived from their possession. Forty years ago, little or nothing was done to turn them into what the European would regard as an economic asset. The Tonga milked their cows to provide sour milk for food and butter for use as an unguent; they ate the meat of those beasts that died or were killed for ritual purposes. They used cattle hides for mats and cut the hides into thongs for ropes. But such utility did not determine the importance of their cattle to the Tonga, and the Tonga did not examine stock in terms of ability to meet these practical ends. They admire and extol cattle for beauty of form, strength, and size, and cows for their reproductive records. I have yet to hear them comment on milk records or beef production as criteria affecting their judgments of particular beasts, though they have begun to appraise them in terms of their market price.

By the older Tonga, at least, cattle are valued for quite different reasons. They are important in a social context and in the ritual that dramatizes social ties. In earlier times this was their chief role. In the western chieftaincies which seem to have escaped the full brunt of the raids and where cattle have always been most numerour, cattle were used for bridewealth as an important element in the series of transactions which created a new family group. They were killed to celebrate the emergence of a girl from her puberty seclusion and her entry into the status of a marriageable woman. They were killed during the mourning for the death of mature members of the community, and the number killed varied with the importance of the dead to the community. Occasionally cattle were killed at the rain-shrines when the community mobilized to ward off a common disaster, such as drought or pestilence. They were transferred between individuals and groups to nullify hostile acts such as adultery, theft, bodily injury, and murder, which threatened the good relations between the groups. In the latter case, in default of cattle, slaves or even full members of the offending group were substituted. Cattle were also used to bind people together in herding arrangements. In the eastern areas, where the raids left few cattle, goats and chickens were used for much the same purposes.

Tonga still visualize the importance of cattle as arising from their use in these situations. If you ask a Tonga why he wants cattle, he is likely to reply: 'They are a good thing to have. They help you if you are in trouble.' To some extent their importance in these social contexts has even increased in recent years. The outlawing of feuds and the institution of courts and police have made it unnecessary for individuals to rely upon their matrilineal groups for physical support. Today it is their mutual right to inherit each other's cattle and other property and to receive assistance in paying bridewealth and damages which checks the breakdown of the matrilineal groups. To a large extent, the Tonga have used their increased herds to further their customary interests. The number of cattle passed in bridewealth and in payment of damages and the number slaughtered for ritual occasions have increased steadily with the increase in the herds. This is especially noticeable in the eastern chieftaincies. In 1900, cattle were rarely included in bridewealth. Today four cattle are commonly included in the payments. In 1900, the emergence of a girl from her puberty seclusion called for the killing of a goat or chicken. Today the occasion is celebrated commonly with the killing of two head of cattle. Some people have begun to slaughter a beast or two for a wedding. In

1900, the funeral of an important man might be honoured by the slaughter of five to six cattle. Today twenty-five cattle may be killed during the mourning for a headman to feed the crowds who come to mourn, and the funeral of even a small child may see the slaughter of one or two head.[1] Probably today several thousand head are slaughtered annually for funerals, weddings, and puberty ceremonies. This allows for a small-scale culling of the herds. Good stock was killed until a few years ago when the Native Authorities began to enforce a rule that a permit is required before breeding stock or working oxen may be killed. While the rule is occasionally ignored, most people go to a good deal of trouble to obtain a suitable animal: an old or barren cow, an ox incapacitated by blindness or some other physical defect. They trade good stock for useless animals, or purchase them with money—a development, incidentally, which makes a man value animals which he otherwise might be prepared to slaughter.

The value attached to cattle because of their role in social life has not been untouched by the various developments which have Christianized some Tonga, educated more, and led most of them to exploit their soils and their proximity to the railway by developing as cash crop farmers. Indeed, the old men say that the over-stocking problem will solve itself on their deaths since the young people are interested only in money which they can turn immediately into goods such as clothing, gramophones, bicycles, beer, tobacco, and food. 'They are fools and will never get cattle the way we have done.' Young men rather agree: 'We young men have money, but the old men have cattle. Today cattle are too

---

[1] The eastern Tonga say they kill cattle at funerals to feed the mourners and that traditionally those who came to mourn had the right to seize and kill any small stock they saw about the homestead to satisfy their craving for meat. They might continue the mourning until everything had been consumed. Children were forbidden to eat funeral meat, but otherwise there was no restriction on its use. Today even this rule has faded. In the western districts, some of the cattle slaughtered were not used to feed the mourners and the meat was allowed to rot. I was told at Mwanacingwala that this was formerly their custom and that they had begun to eat funeral meat to cater to the European's peculiar ideas that one should not waste cattle without recompense. In both areas today, mourners eat their fill at a funeral and at a big funeral they may return home laden with fresh meat which they proceed to cook at home for general consumption.

dear for us to buy. If we can buy eight oxen for ploughing, then we are content and think we have done well.' But I noticed that when I asked even the more sophisticated young people to name the wealthy Tonga that they replied first with the names of the big cattle owners and only later did they think of wealthy farmers who sold large quantities of maize but had few save working cattle.

Their attitude, and to some extent that of their elders, is conditioned by developments which have increased the importance of cattle in Tonga economic life. It would be a mistake to look only at the social value of cattle and to forget the development of this new aspect of Tonga life. The European missionaries and farmers who settled in the district early in this century taught the Tonga the use of oxen in drawing the plough. In the decade between 1910 and 1920, many changed from axe and hoe cultivation to plough cultivation, and today almost every Tonga depends upon plough and oxen for planting his crop. About 1920, they began to use oxen in transport, first to drag the rough homemade sledges which they learned to fashion and which are still important items of equipment, and then to draw the scotch carts and wagons which wealthier men were able to purchase. They are dependent still upon ox transport to carry their maize to the buying stations and to some extent to transport goods from the trading stores back to their villages. Possibly for this reason oxen today are valued more highly than cows. Young men who are beginning to build up their own herds usually begin with oxen, and only after they have sufficient oxen—from four to eight—do they consider the possibility of buying cows.[1]

Manure from the herds has also become important. Until recent years, abandoned kraal sites were planted to tobacco. Today in many areas, the more progressive men cart manure to their fields in an attempt to maintain the fertility of their soil. This gives new emphasis to the desire of each man to have his own herd and his

---

[1] In the eastern chieftaincies, every ox is broken to the plough. Men with many cattle wait until an ox is two years old before beginning to use it. Those with few cattle may put a yearling ox to the plough. It is possible that in Simuyobe and Mwanacingwala only a few are broken for this purpose and the rest are kept to gladden their owner's eyes, as among the Ila.

own kraal, where his rights to manure will be unquestioned. In some areas, those who are not interested in transferring manure to their fields may still be interested in its possession since they can sell their kraal sites to more progressive men.

The existence of a market for cattle must also be considered. Most Tonga feel that cattle should not be sold unless there is some urgent need for cash. During the famine of 1950, many people sold cattle to finance the purchase of food or traded their cattle for maize to those in areas fortunate enough to have a surplus. Other men, however, turn their cattle into cash to finance business ventures. In January 1950, a man who sells chickens to the markets in the Copper Belt of Northern Rhodesia, sold his ox for £7 10s. because he needed money to buy chickens for shipment and his middleman was late in forwarding money for previous shipments. Others have sold cattle to pay for ploughs, cultivators, scotch carts, or bicycles. The general sentiment today favours these transactions, though someone who sold his cattle to buy beer, clothes and food from the trading stores would be despised as worthless. I remember at a funeral listening to a group of men commenting freely upon their host and the dissipation of the cattle which he had inherited from his mother's brother: 'He bought beer and chickens. He drank up all the money· he didn't spend on chickens and other things to eat. He wanted to eat chicken all the time. And he killed the goats one after the other and ate only a bit and then killed another. He bought everything he wanted from the store: clothes, shoes, sugar, tea, bread, and everything like that. If anyone came along and asked him for money, he reached in his pocket and pulled out 2s. 6d. and gave it to him. Oh, he was a big man for a time!' Their contempt could only be matched by that of a real New Englander for a man who lives on capital.

Nevertheless, men have begun to consider cattle as property to be transferred for cash with which to obtain the many new requirements they now have.

The demand for cattle at the moment appears to be unlimited, and over the past decade prices have increased steadily, or sometimes by leaps and bounds. The Tonga say that only a few years ago they got 10s. to 20s. for a good ox, and that today a similar animal may fetch £7 or £8. They can get more money today for the scrubbiest scrub animal than they could a few years ago for a fine beast in good condition. Cattle therefore are regarded as a good investment in which one may more than double one's money with any luck. Even a bull calf which has just been weaned brought £3 in 1950, while a yearling ox might sell for £4. A cow of corresponding age might sell for 5s. to 10s. less. Most people, however, avoid selling young stock, if they can, and sell their old or defective animals.

The Tonga are eager to buy from each other, either to build up their own herds, or for re-sale to European buyers on the railway line, or to slaughter themselves. The competition between Europeans and Tonga probably plays its part in keeping up the price of stock, and as the Tonga have received more and more money with the increased price of their maize in recent years they have had the cash to develop considerable internal trade in cattle. European dealers find it worth their while to send African buyers through the reserves to search out cattle for them. The Tonga also drive cattle in to the hamlets on the railway line. In 1948, 4,563 head of stock were purchased in the reserves under permit by European cattle buyers, local butcheries and farmers.[1]

There are no African butcheries in the reserves as yet. None the less the Tonga have begun to compete with European buyers for slaughter cattle. This applies particularly close to the railway line where the people are most sophisticated. Men buy up old stock which they slaughter. They trade the meat for maize and then dispose of the maize at a profit at the buying stations. Men also convert their own stock into cash in this way when an animal is old or for some other reason has become useless. Even a portion of the meat killed for a puberty ceremony or a funeral may find its way into the market if the owner decided that a whole animal is too much to sacrifice to his social obligations. It is therefore quite possible today for a man to invest in cattle, get the full value from the beast in the form of work or calves, and then recoup

---

[1] Information supplied by the District Commissioner, Mazabuka.

himself for more than his original investment by slaughtering the animal when it can work no more and selling the meat.[1]

Progressive Tonga are well aware of these possibilities, and consider cattle a good investment for their spare funds. I have heard young men insist in court that they want damages in cattle rather than money: 'If he gives me money, I may only gamble it away. If he gives me cattle, then I shall have something to help me.' Young men have pointed out to me that banks and postal savings accounts pay only an infinitesimal return each year on deposits.[2] They argue that if they place £5 in a postal savings account, they receive in return a few pence on their investment. If they use the same money to buy a cow, with luck they should have a calf which can be sold for £2 or more. If the cow dies, they may still be able to sell the meat for sufficient to cover their original investment. Men away at work, including teachers and government clerks, send money to relatives for investment in cattle, saying that it is the best investment known to them despite the chance that the cattle may die or the relative embezzle a part of the herd entrusted to him.

All sections of the community are likely therefore to offer strenuous objections to any suggestion of de-stocking. Cattle have retained their ritual and social importance over the years, and at the same time have received a greatly increased economic importance, which is most evident to the progressive elements in the community who have least appreciation for the role of cattle in ritual. Most Tonga, however, probably value their cattle for both reasons—with an emotional response to the social aspect which is incomprehensible to the European and at the same time with a cupidity born of their economic value which is only too understandable.

---

[1] Hides are also sold to European buyers, and give a small but welcome cash income. Formerly when cattle were killed for ritual purposes, the hides were usually cut up with the meat. Today the hides are removed and sold. Hide buyers make a point of attending funerals and puberty ceremonies to obtain the green hides which sell for more than dry ones. There is also a very small trade today in milk.

[2] A few Tonga do have postal savings accounts.

GRAZING LAWS

Customary rules concerning land ownership and land usage are also hostile to the growth of an appreciation of the need for de-stocking.

So far, we have paid no attention to ownership of pastures or to organization to control the use of grazing. These are matters which have not concerned the Tonga until recent years, and which today concern them only because of pressure from the Veterinary and Agricultural Departments. Traditionally all land was open to grazing, except when it bore crops, and grazing was free to anyone who needed it. It was not restricted to members of a village or a neighbourhood or a chieftaincy. Men naturally tried to graze their herds as close to their own homes as was feasible, but they were not prevented by any customary law from going further afield. No organization existed which could restrict the movement of cattle or limit the numbers grazing on a given area. This is still largely true today.

As a result, it is possible to let the cattle roam freely once the crops have been harvested and they can do no further damage to the crops. So during the dry season, cattle are left to roam as they will through the fields and the bush. No attempt is made to bring them back to the kraals at night, and many of them stray far from their home pastures, especially in a dry year or in a year when the regulations against burning the bush have been evaded and the pastures near the village have been burned bare. Even the cows are left to roam, for only during the rains is there sufficient milk to warrant milking, and the rest of the year there is no need to bring them to the kraals. Just before the rains begin, the owners begin their search for strayed beasts, which may take them far afield. Each man is responsible for tracing his own cattle, unaided by others.

The Tonga do not have the cattle law of the southern Bantu which holds the inhabitants of a homestead responsible for strayed animals whose tracks can be traced to the homestead but not beyond. Instead, it lies to the owner to prove that his cattle are in a given kraal, which is not always an easy matter. If he asks too diligently about the whereabouts of a strayed animal, the man questioned may decide that he is being accused of theft and sue the owner for slander. Those who may have seen a straying animal are not eager to suggest its possible whereabouts, since if their word is produced as evidence they too may find themselves involved in the suit. Recently the Native Authorities have ordered that strayed animals should be brought to the chief and held in his kraal until claimed by their owners, but this rule is often evaded and the owner must still seek far for his cattle.[1] But complicated as this may make the life of the cattleowner, from one point of view the most serious problem is the loss of time spent in searching for the animals and the possibility that the owner will not be able to take advantage of the ploughing rains because he has yet to locate his cattle. Moreover, strayed animals are often found in poor condition and quite unable to do the heavy work of ploughing.

In areas which are short of grazing and water during the dry season, the residents take advantage of the right to graze their cattle anywhere in Tonga country to drive their cattle to more fortunate areas. This seems to have been very general in the past. In the eastern chieftaincies, the people of the Escarpment country brought their cattle westward to the Magoye River for water and pasture without protest from villages located along the Magoye. Today, however, the Government has built dams in many parts of the country and the old custom of sending cattle to dry season camps has disappeared in the east. It still continues in the western chieftaincies. Cattle camps are built along the Kafue by the people of Simuyobe, Mwanacingwala, and Chongo chieftaincies. Occasionally the people of Sianjalika also send their cattle to the

---

[1] Identification of strayed stock is the more difficult since the Tonga have yet to adopt a system of adequate identifying marks. All the cattle of a chieftaincy are branded with a mark identifying them as a resident in that chieftaincy. This is done by the Veterinary Department. A few individuals have their own brands and have purchased branding irons from a European blacksmith who works in Monze. Most people depend upon ear marks, which are also used for goats and pigs, but while these are sufficient identification within the immediate locality, they may not be helpful if the animal strays a long way. In general, identification depends upon a minute description of the appearance of the animal and the owner's ability to pick it out from the other cattle in the kraal.

Kafue. The Mapanza people are said to send their cattle to the Mutama basin. At the Kafue camps, the cattle may be placed under the care of Twa herders, but more commonly the Tonga merely receive permission from the Twa residents of the Kafue margin to build their camps near by. The men then take it turn about to visit the camp, where they stay for about two weeks before being relieved by a fresh contingent from the village.[1]

Customary law which allows the free range of cattle also permits such dry season movements and the transit of the cattle throught the intervening country to reach new pastures. It permits the ranging of cattle during the dry season when no crops are in the fields. And it prevents the growth of any particular sentiment about improving the grazing of a particular area. Thus though a man may be aware that a limitation of the number of cattle would allow him to breed better stock, he has no incentive to limit the number of his own cattle. Their place would be taken by the cattle of his neighbours or even of people from more distant areas, or by cattle moved in on herding arrangements to take advantage of the lessened strain on the available pastures.

The Strain on the Social System

Not only is Tonga country over-stocked for the carrying capacity of the land. There is evidence that there are more cattle today than the Tonga can cope with successfully with their present methods of organizing the care of their cattle. This aspect of the problem has received little attention. Probably neither administrative officials nor the Tonga themselves are aware of the implications for the management of the herds of the present trend towards family rather than village groups as the local units. The Tonga live today very often in small groups, which may consist only of one man whith his wife, or wives, and their children. The small group finds it difficult to provide the labour required for both agricultural activities and the care of the herds.

---

[1] Cf. also *The Tonga Report*, p. 117.

THE ORGANIZATION OF KRAAL GROUPS

The matrilineal groups are not organized into local bodies which undertake the care of the cattle owned by their members. Although the Tonga recognizes his obligations to his matrilineal kin, and their obligations to him, he is under no necessity to settle with them. Instead he lives where he chooses, with his maternal relatives, his paternal relatives, his affinal kin, or occasionally with friends who are bound to him through common clanship or perhaps through no tie whatsoever. This apparently has always been true of the Tonga. Today he is apt to settle on his own, and many villages consist of various small clusters of one or two huts scattered at some distance from each other. In the eastern chieftaincies it seems that there has always been this tendency to scatter. In 1913, when a government official commented on the scattered villages along the upper Magoye River, he was told, '. . . it is our custom to live so. Otherwise we might quarrel if we all lived close together. Then our cattle must graze.' [1] However, the scattering was not as extreme as at the present time, and even in this area informants remember some large compact villages built around a central cattle kraal. In the western chieftaincies this seems to have been the common village plan.

In the description of kraal groups which follows, I shall deal largely with the eastern area which I know best. In the western chieftaincies of Mwanacingwala and Simuyobe, large compact villages are still common, and the kraal groups tend to be larger than in the east. This may be due, in part, to the necessity to send the cattle of these chieftaincies to dry season camps along the Kafue margins.

The men who live in a compact village, or in the clusters of a dispersed village, are likely to belong to different matrilineal groups, and therefore have no rights over each other's cattle. Even where two or more men of the same matrilineal group are living close together, they may show considerable independence in caring for their individual property, especially if they are men of

---

[1] Quoted from a report by the Secretary of Native Affairs for 1913.

middle age who have established their own independent families. Nevertheless, for various reasons several men may decide to unite to build a common cattle kraal and to arrange for the common herding of their cattle. I shall refer to these groups as kraal groups.

To illustrate the organization of kraal groups within a village I have chosen a village located in Chona chieftaincy on the edge of the Escarpment. It is relatively conservative and also relatively compact. In 1950 the village had a population of 146 men, women, and children, the populations being distributed as follows:

				Males	*Females*	*Total*
Children*	.	.	.	33	33	66
Adolescents	.	.	.	13	3	16
Adults .	.	.	.	26	38	64
TOTALS .	.	.	.	72	74	146

* This heading includes all children below the apparent age of fourteen.

The genealogical chart, page 155, includes eighteen of the twenty-six adult males. They are affiliated to six different matrilineal groups, but some tie of kinship, either consanguineal or affinal, connects them all and relates them to the headman, No. 1. The other eight adult males have no such tie. The women of the village are not shown on the chart save where they serve as a link relating the men. The diagram, page 154, shows the placement in the village of the huts and cattle kraals. Huts numbered S1, S2, etc., are inhabited by the unrelated men living in the village.

Nineteen men have cattle in the kraals attached to the village. Probably one or two of the other men own cattle, but these are herded at some other village, and their owners are not members of the kraal groups in this village. Men who have no cattle are not connected with a kraal group. Kraal groups are composed as follows:

1. *Kraal A.*—S1 has his own kraal. He lives in a cluster approximately half a mile from the main village with only one other adult male, the insane son of his wife's mother's sister.
2. *Kraal B.*—No. 7 is regarded as the owner of the kraal. He is

joined by 17 and 18, his two adult sons, who are teachers and spend only part of the year in the village. When they are away, they leave their few head of cattle with their father.

3. *Kraal C.*—No. 8 is regarded as the owner of the kraal and owns the majority of the cattle kept within it. His is the second largest kraal in the village. With him are 2, who is married to his classificatory sister, and 11, who is married to his full sister. His married son, 16, lives with him but owns no cattle and refuses to work to maintain the kraal.

4. *Kraal D.*—No. 1, the headman, is regarded as the owner of the kraal, which is the largest in the village. He owns the majority of the cattle attached to it. He is joined by 6, his brother's son, and by 12, his sister's daughter's son.

5. *Kraal E.*—No. 5 is regarded as the owner of the kraal. He is joined by 3 and 4, his mother's sisters' sons, by 10, his father's brother's son, and by 13, 14, and 15.

6. *Kraal F.*—S6 has his own kraal.

It is significant that kraal group membership depends upon personal preferences rather than kinship affiliations. The genealogical chart showing the kinship links between those living in a village does not enable one to predict the number or the organization of the kraal groups. No. 2, for instance, joins with 8 rather than with 3, 4, and 5, who are his closest kinsmen. No. 6 remains a member of the kraal group of 1, his father's brother, though it would be equally possible for him to join 7, his sister's husband, or to attempt to persuade 17 and 18, his sister's sons, to join him in a new kraal. No. 5, unlike 6, has left his father's brother to join a kraal group consisting of two close matrilineal kinsmen, one paternal kinsman, and three very remote kinsmen.[1]

Since personal preference plays such a large part in the membership, kraal groups tend to break up and reform over the years. The history of this same village illustrates this point. The village

---

[1] On the chart, 13, 14, and 15 are shown only as affinal kin. There are also consanguineal links. Their mother was the headman's mother's mother's brother's daughter. Their father belonged to the headman's matrilineal group though the genealogical links have been forgotten by all concerned.

DIAGRAMMATIC MAP OF VILLAGE

SYMBOLS:

○   huts

⬭   cattle kraals

N   marks huts inhabited by single women.

Huts joined by connecting lines belong to one man.

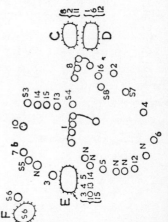
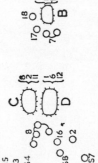

DIAGRAM 2

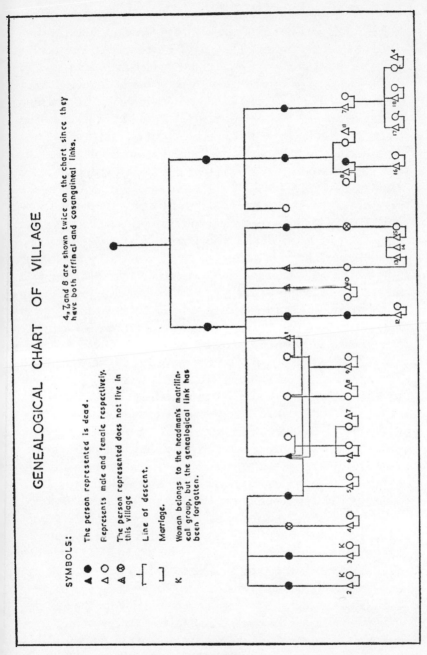

GENEALOGICAL CHART OF VILLAGE

SYMBOLS:

● The person represented is dead.

△ ○ Represents male and female respectively.

▲ ⊗ The person represented does not live in this village

⌐ Line of descent.

⌐ Marriage.

K Woman belongs to the headman's matrilineal group, but the genealogical link has been forgotten.

4, 7, and 8 are shown twice on the chart since they have both affinal and cosanguineal links.

DIAGRAM 3

moved to its present site in 1938 or 1939. Previously it had consisted of scattered clusters. These now drew together into a compact village with only one kraal group, which included 1, 2, 5, 7, 8, 12, and 15. The other men shown on the genealogical chart were then young boys. The kraal group, and village, also include two brothers of 8 and one brother of 7 who have since moved away to other villages; the father of 13, 14, and 15; the first husband of 11's wife; and a matrilineal kinsman of 1. The last three have since died. The first split in the kraal group occurred about 1941 when 7 and 8, and possibly their brothers, formed a kraal of their own; 7 later returned to the main group, but 8 continued to maintain his own kraal and persuaded 2 and 11 to join him. Then 5 formed a kraal with 3 and 4. About 1947–8, 13, 14, and 15 joined them. In 1950, 10 also left the kraal group of the headman to join this new kraal. Meantime two unrelated men moved in and retained their own kraals rather than join a group already established in the village. S6 moved into the village in 1947; S1 came in 1948. In 1949, 8 moved a short distance from the main village and formed his own kraal, separate from that controlled by 1. About the same time, 9 moved to another village and took his cattle, which had been in 1's kraal, with him. The present arrangement is unlikely to be any more stable than the earlier ones. In 1950, 13 and 14 were establishing themselves in other villages where they lived much of the time returning home only to plant and harvest their crops. It is unlikely that they will long continue their attachment to this village or to a kraal group within it. Meantime as the young boys grow up and gain cattle for themselves, they will change the composition of the groups. Moreover, as the young men who today are minor members of the groups succeed in finding herd-boys to care for their cattle, either with the growing up of their own sons or by drawing to themselves their sisters' sons, they will be able to break out of the present kraal groups to establish their own kraals.

The kraal group is an arrangement to provide for the building and maintenance of the cattle kraal and for the provision of herd-boys to care for the cattle during the growing season when they must be herded to prevent damage to the crops. Kraals are roughly circular enclosures built of poles and brush. All members of the kraal group are expected to contribute material and to help in the work of building the enclosure. Thereafter they are all expected to share in the work of keeping it in repair, of moving the brush and poles to a new site when the kraal must be shifted because of the accumulations of manure. Members must either work themselves or provide a substitute. Each member is expected to bear a full share of the labour, rather than a share proportional to the number of cattle he has in the kraal. Each man should also provide a herd-boy, or several, if this is possible. If a man has living with him either sons or other relatives who are at an age to herd cattle, these become part of the common pool of herd-boys attached to his kraal group. However, not all members of a kraal group are able to provide herd-boys, and this does not restrict their right to have their cattle housed and herded.

To turn again to the kraal groups described above:

Kraal A: S1 who has his own kraal has two sons who herd for him.

Kraal B: 7 has two sons and a daughter's son who herd for him. During school terms, he also has his brother's son who stays with him and attends school.

Kraal C: 8 has one son who herds for him, and two classificatory sisters' sons. 2 has one son and one daughter's son who herd. 11 does not contribute a herd-boy to the pool. However, he appears to do more work than either 8 or 2 in maintaining the kraal and usually supervises the milking.

Kraal D: 1 has two sons as permanent herd-boys and another son who herds when he is home during school vacations. He also supports a classificatory sister's daughter's son who lives with him and herds. 12 contributes no herd-boy and does not seem to take any larger part in the work of the kraal. 6 has a sister's son who lives with him and herds.

Kraal E: None of the men have sons who herd. All the herding is left to two boys, sister's sons of 3. Occasionally a sister's son of 4 will spend a few weeks in the village and then help with the herding.

Kraal F: S6 who has his own kraal has no sons, and he depends upon his two sister's sons who live with him and herd his cattle.

The herd-boys work in rotation, each boy taking his turn, though when enough boys are attached to the kraal group several boys will herd together. The work is apportioned by the number of boys, rather than by the number of men in the kraal group. If two men form a group and one has two herd-boys and the other only one, each boy will do roughly a third of the work. During the time that he is on duty each herd-boy is usually in charge of all the cattle of his kraal, no matter to whom they belong. If he shirks his work, his guardian is expected to discipline him. Interference by other members of the group may lead to quarrels and a break-up of the group.

The pooling of labour and of herd-boys by the members of the kraal group has obvious advantages for all concerned. The man who owns many cattle receives the assistance of other men in building and maintaining his kraal. The man who has only a few head need not go to the labour of constructing a separate enclosure for his herd. Men who are unable to attract enough young boys to herd their cattle can obtain assistance from others in the village. However, it should be emphasized that while labour is pooled, the use of cattle is not. Each man sees to it that his own cows are milked, and he is under no obligation to divide the milk with others of his kraal group. Each man uses his own oxen for ploughing and cultivating, and is under no obligation to assist the other members of the group. In actual fact, of course, they do assist each other, since anyone who feels dissatisfied with the arrangement can always pull out of the group and join another, or perhaps set up his independent kraal.

Kraal groups do not control rights to pasture, since this is open to all, and a man who withdraws from his kraal group therefore does not lose access to the grazing grounds. The assistance given by one man to another within the kraal group is always phrased as due to the generosity of the giver rather than to his obligation to assist a member of the group. In Kraal Group C, for instance, 2 had no milking cows in 1948. His wife constantly sent to 8 to beg for milk. 8 finally wearied of her petitions, which annoyed his wives, and informed 2 that he could milk two cows and have the milk. He did not give the cattle to 2, but merely assigned him the right to milk the cows, and this loan is revocable whenever 8 wishes. He also provides 11 with milk and allows him to use his oxen for ploughing and other work.

Today the kraal groups must also deal with the problem of the division of the manure which accumulates in the kraal. Traditionally kraal sites were used for planting tobacco, and this is still done in some areas. Each member of the group might receive a strip of the area, or the largest cattle owner in the group might take the whole of the site for his own. In many areas today, the manure is used to maintain the fertility of the fields, and the right to a share in the manure may give rise to numerous quarrels. In this village manure rights are not a problem, since only 1 and 8 use it on their fields. Elsewhere in the hilly country along the Escarpment, not all men find it necessary to use manure in their fields, but they may still consider it an infliction if someone else takes manure from their common kraal. Thus John of Shanamoonga village in Chona chiefdom originally kraaled his cattle with those of his affinal relatives. He was the only member of the kraal group who wished to use manure on his fields, but when he began to take manure from the kraal, they began to complain, 'John is growing rich from our cattle.' He therefore withdrew from the kraal and built his own. In other areas, the owners of a kraal have worked out various arrangements to govern the division of manure.

At Chepa village, in Mwanza chieftaincy, two different systems are in use. One kraal group is composed of Simon and Peter, two full brothers; their paternal half-brother, Jonathan, and their mother's sister's son, Reuben. The four men have divided into pairs and each pair takes manure every alternate year. During the year in which a man may not take manure from the kraal, he attempts to buy up kraal sites from less progressive neighbours, an expedient which is becoming more difficult as the use of manure spreads. They divide the manure equally, although the different men do not have comparable numbers of cattle. Jonathan who has only a few cattle receives the same share as Simon who has five or six times as many. In the same village, the headman and those who share his kraal mark the surface into rough divisions, roughly proportional to the number of cattle each man has in the kraal. Each man receives a share each year, but the headman, who is the largest owner, receives the lion's share. In the western chieftaincies of Mwanacingwala and Simuyobe, few men use manure and it is not a matter of argument. Elsewhere, it is becoming an important element in the desire of men to have their own kraals and thus leads to the break-up of the kraal groups.

In many villages, the kraal groups are even smaller than those described above, and more and more the work of maintaining a kraal is coming to fall upon one or two men and such half-grown boys as live with them.[1] This is occurring at the same time that the herds are increasing and the work involved likewise mounts as larger kraals are required. Probably the individual kraal of today is often larger than the village kraal of an earlier generation, though the former must be maintained by one or two men and the latter could depend upon the efforts of many. The Native Authority, moreover, has passed a ruling that the size of kraals must be increased to prevent the crowding of animals into inadequate enclosures. So far, this seems to have had little effect, but once enforced it will make the maintenance of the individual kraal still more difficult. At the same time, in many areas suitable timber is becoming short and men wishing to build or repair a kraal must go a good distance to find materials. In the more progressive villages, wealthier men have begun to discuss the possibility of buying wire to surround the kraal in place of brush, and this would ease some of the problem, but only for the wealthy. Men who cannot afford wire, and these are in the vast majority, may be driven back into larger kraal groups as the shortage of timber prevents them from maintaining their own kraals. The

---

[1] I have information on the number of kraals attached to 13 different villages scattered in Chona, Ufwenuka, and Mwanza chieftaincies. The village described above has the largest number of men per kraal (26/6 or 4·33) of any of the thirteen. The mean number of men per kraal is 3·09 over the thirteen villages.

major factor, however, that prevents kraal groups diminishing further in size is the difficulty of obtaining herd-boys.

THE STRUGGLE FOR HERD-BOYS

Cattle are usually herded only during the season between the planting and the harvesting of the crop, a period lasting roughly from some time in November to June. The cattle owner is then faced with the urgent problem of finding young boys who will herd his cattle for him. He himself must be in the fields if he is to produce a crop, and has little time to supervise the boys and the herds. It is a time when major conflicts within the family group are likely to arise, as the boys attempt to evade their herding duties and the men grow more and more resentful as they see their cattle straying through the bush and invading the fields.

The conflict, and the problem of finding herd-boys, has been always at least latent in this area, but it has become more and more apparent with the increase of herds, the diminishing of grazing, and the increased competition for herd-boys with the disappearance of large kraal groups.

In earlier years, when the Tonga feared the raids of predatory beasts on their herds, they assigned young men to the task of herding. Men continued to herd cattle until they married, at about the age of twenty-five, or even later, and the younger boys were inducted into their duties as members of a group of herders headed by adults. Today young men refuse to have anything to do with herding, and if necessary go off as labour migrants to establish their independence. I have heard boys of fourteen and fifteen complain that they are now too old to be sent out with the cattle and that the work should be passed on to a younger child. Their complaints are ignored, but it is rare in the eastern districts to see a boy who is over sixteen who is still herding and most herd-boys are youngsters from about the age of seven to fourteen.[1]

---

[1] In the western chieftaincies which send their cattle to the Kafue margins this is not true. Because of the danger from lions among the Kafue margins, older men take an active part in the herding at the cattle camps, and younger boys are present only as servants and apprentices who look after calves. Even so, they do

M

Often the boys are most reluctant herders whatever their age and are only kept at work by the threats, and sometimes the physical chastisement, of their elders. Small boys, from about five to seven years, are allowed to go out as they please, and no effort is made to force them to remain with the cattle. Older boys may be driven to the cattle kraal by an irate parent or guardian who flourishes a stick or cattle whip. The boys argue that herding is hard work with few compensations. For various reasons, herding is indeed harder work than it was a generation ago, though the Tonga adult tends to ignore the new difficulties and blames the boys for their laxness.

Fewer boys are available to share the duties today, partially because of the refusal of older boys to do their share, partially because of the encroachment of the schools. Families eager to send their sons to school attempt to arrange herding duties so that all the children have an opportunity to attend. This is possible since classes in the village schools are staggered, some meeting in the morning and others in the afternoon. But in some cases, all the boys of the family, or even of the kraal group, would be in school during the same hours. The child who must be kept from school to herd resents his position, even though he himself loathes the thought of school and prefers herding to class-work, and he has harder work coping with the cattle than if he had assistance from the other boys.

The dispersal of the village into isolated clusters, and the diminishing size of the kraal groups also play their part in the difficulty of herding. Where all the boys of a village or of a large cluster may be sufficient to perform the herding duties without any undue burden on any one child, the smaller kraal group is usually short of boys and probably has to send out the herd under the care of one small child. The one boy herding alone is likely to

---

not go to the camps until they are about twelve years old, at a time when their age-mates in the east have long been active herd-boys. Boys of eighteen and older are still herding cattle without complain. though their chance to escape is quite as good as that of their fellows in the east. However, the herding at the Kafue camps takes place during the dry season when the men are free from agricultural work. I failed to investigate herding arrangements during the growing season.

be less efficient, as well as more thoroughly bored, than were the herd-boys in the days when five or six boys might herd together, and where the older boys had an informal hazing system for initiating younger lads, which may have made life more strenuous but certainly more interesting. At the same time there was an opportunity for closer supervision of the herds, and the older boys had more opportunity to pass their wood lore and cattle lore to their younger mates. Today when one small boy, perhaps only nine or ten years old, has solitary charge of a herd which may contain as many as fifty beasts, the life is hard and less likely to contain mitigating moments of excitement. Sometimes boys from various kraal groups will take their herds together, but it is more common to herd alone.

Herding is also made more difficult by the increase in cultivation which has cut into the land available for pasturing the cattle. The boys must be on constant guard less their cattle stray from the grazing areas into the neighbouring fields which encroach on all sides.

The boys who are herding the cattle usually have little immediate interest in the animals which they herd. A boy has no assurance that he will ever inherit or have the use of any of the cattle he is expected to tend, even though some of them belong to his own guardian. If he is herding for his father, he knows that he will not inherit; for his father's heirs are the members of the matrilineal group and not the sons. If he is herding for a matrilineal relative, he knows that his rights to inherit are only the same as those of any other matrilineal relative, including those who have never cared for the cattle. His elders may tell him that he is earning cattle for his bridewealth, but he is aware that his father and his matrilineal relatives will feel a duty to provide in any case. The Tonga child, therefore, does not feel the same identification with the herd, or with the fortunes of his family, that a child does in a patrilineal system where his work leads eventually to his own advancement. When the Tonga child complains to his mother about the trials of herding, she is likely to sympathize and comment that she sees no reason why he should work for his father since he cannot inherit. If he is herding for a matrilineal relative, he knows that the wife and the older children resent his presence as a reminder of the ultimate inheritance of the matrilineal group.

The resentment of the boys sometimes crystallizes against the cattle in their care, and this may lie behind the accidental deaths to which cattle are liable during the herding season when the too vigorous wielding of the long cattle whip may kill a calf, or the beating of an older beast may cripple it so that it has to be killed. The boys also abandon their herds to wander through the bush and into the fields while they fill themselves with sweet-stalked kaffir corn stolen from the fields, or search for honey in the bush, or start small bush fires to hunt for birds. These games receive added zest from their appetites; for few take any food with them to the bush, and they depend upon milk and such products as they can discover on the roam to tide them over until the return to the village in the late afternoon. At night, if a beast or two is missing from the herd, the boys are likely to worry very little. Then the men may spend the next day or so searching for strayed beasts, or facing indignant cultivators who have found the cattle eating the maize in their fields. At night and during the day, the cattle are thus left relatively free to raid the fields. Meantime the men grow more and more indignant with the boys, accusing them of making no attempt to earn their keep, forgetful of their own youthful delinquencies and also of the increased difficulties of herding.

If the herding presses upon a boy too heavily, he takes refuge with other relatives, thinking perhaps to lighten his work. For instance, a boy of ten was lying on the ground one day sulking after a berating by his father. His age-mates speculated as to whether or not he was planning to run away to his 'own home' (kwabo), by which they meant to his mother's brothers who lived some ten miles away. On the other hand, boys living with their matrilineal kin may abscond to their fathers or to their father's relatives or to other matrilineal kin. And either lot may go off to distant relatives or to strangers, for such is the demand for herd-boys that they are assured of a welcome. If they find their refuge no better than their original condition, they will again run off, either back to their homes or to some other village. To some extent, however, they are likely to be able to force a better bargain from distant relatives or from strangers than they can from their own parents or immediate matrilineal relatives, even though they do not become hired labour. They are given their food and clothing by the man for whom they work, though the clothing may not be abundant, and they also expect that when they mature the man will consider himself responsible for at least a portion of their marriage payments or the fines and damages which they are likely to accumulate in adultery and paternity suits. Many of them, however, return home again within a few months or years. Others remain on with one man until they are adults, and some then settle permanently in his village. There is no formal agreement, however, which binds the boy to the man for whom he works, and some men use the situation to take advantage of the boys. They work them hard during their early adolescence and then make life more and more difficult as the boys mature, in an effort to drive them away before they are quite old enough to claim assistance for damage suits or marriage.

Many boys attempt a further escape. They run away to find work on European farms in the neighbourhood or with the Indians who live in the railway hamlets. For such work, a boy receives a small cash payment each month which allows him to clothe himself more handsomely than his own parents or the relatives to whom he may attach himself will usually think necessary. This work, however, will not give him a claim to assistance on his marriage payments, for he no longer is working in the same system of kinship obligations which governs work done for other Tonga. It is a short-term solution, but one which appeals to lads who are still too young to be concerned with marriage. It is therefore common for a boy to depart without warning, leaving his herd to wander in the bush and his guardian to find another herd-boy to take his place.

The village used in the previous section illustrates the difficulties faced by the Tonga in providing adequate numbers of herd-boys for their cattle. Only nineteen boys were available for herding duties all the time. A boy of about seven occasionally went out with the others but could not be trusted to remain with the herds and was not considered in the planning of duties. Another boy of about nine occasionally herded with the others, but he was feeble-minded and could not be induced to work for any length of time. Frequently he ran away to relatives for a few days or weeks and then ran home again. At a rough guess the boys were herding about 250 cattle, but the cattle were not divided evenly among the kraals. Only eight boys were sons of members of the kraal group, and only five men had sons in the village who were of an age suitable for herding. Five other boys were considered to belong to the village and to be resident there—all of them sons of men in the village—but two were at school most of the time and three had gone away to work. The men had managed to bring in other boys to work for them. These were either grandsons or matrilineal relatives. Some of the latter were so distantly related to the men for whom they herded that their genealogical links were quite unknown; others were uterine sister's sons. Other children on whom they had a claim refused to come to them. 12 had a son of fourteen, who as a small boy went to live with a younger brother of 12. When he was about thirteen, he ran away to work on a European farm where he still works. He has never herded cattle for his father. 8 has two sons who left him when their mothers were divorced, and though they occasionally visit him for a day or two, they never stay for any length of time with him.

A few boys remain with the same cattle throughout their herding lives and learn to know them intimately; others shift from herd to herd, affected both by their own mobility and by the changing kraal group membership of their guardians. In 1949, Kraal C had five herd-boys: Mark and Mathew, classificatory sisters' sons of 8; Jacob and Joseph, sons of 2; and Peter, daughter's son of 2. By early 1950, Mark and Mathew had run away to work on a European farm; and Jacob had vanished to work for a distant matrilineal relative who lived some twenty miles or more away. None of them had any intention of returning in any immediate future. To replace them, 8 managed to secure his own son, a lad of about seventeen, who had been living with matrilineal relatives in Lusaka, and two other boys of his matrilineal group. One was the son of his mother's mother's sister's daughter's daughter; the other was the son of a very distant classificatory sister who had come to live with him after her divorce. The last boy made at least one attempt to run away during the year.

The mobility of the boys is partially produced by the conflicts implicit in the Tonga kinship system, since a child is affiliated both to its father and to its own matrilineal group and has the right to live with either. The situation is made more acute by the present competition of fathers and matrilineal groups, as well as by unrelated men and by those completely outside the system, such as Indian store-keepers and European farmers, for the labour of the boys. It does not lead to an efficient herding system.

There are few signs that the Tonga are evolving any method of coping with the situation. In the Mujika area of Mwanza chieftaincy, and perhaps elsewhere, a few men have been forced by the shortage of boys to send their herds out in the care of small girls.[1] Traditionally girls and women should have no contact with cattle, and were not allowed to approach cattle kraals. The Tonga maintain that this is only a matter of custom and that neither women nor cattle can be harmed by the contact, but nevertheless they dislike the expedient of using girls for herding duties. A few men have attempted to protect their own fields from the cattle by fencing with brush or quick-growing plants, but this is not general and does not release the field-owner from the obligation to see that his own cattle are herded to keep them from the unfenced fields of others. There is no general interest in fencing. The Tonga say that this would be a major undertaking possible only for those who have considerable labour, and impossible for a man who works by himself with the assistance of a wife and small children.

Meantime the damage done to the growing crops reaches considerable proportions. The owner of the damaged field may sue the owners of the marauding cattle and receive compensation for the damage, but in many areas the cultivators swallow their losses

---

[1] Men occasionally herd for a day or two in an emergency, but this is uncommon.

on the principle that ultimately the damage done by their own cattle will offset what they gain from the suit. At Chona village, for instance, one family lost most of its maize for three years running because of cattle damage. In each year their store of grain was exhausted before the next crop, and they either had to buy food or exist on the charity of their relatives. The third year they were furious and said their say to the owners of the cattle, but they refused to demand compensation. Others are not as long-suffering, but only a small proportion of the damage done is reported to the courts or made the subject for compensation.

Those Tonga who live adjacent to the European farm strip have further difficulties, since their cattle often stray on to European land. The result depends upon the particular relationships established between the European farmer and the Africans. A few Europeans consider it both courteous and good sense to stay on good terms with their African neighbours and it is understood that strayed stock from either side of the boundary will be returned to the owner without action being taken. In practice this may mean that the European is the loser financially, but he gains in general good relations with his neighbours. Other farmers order straying cattle to be rounded up and have them sent to the cattle pound. The owners are required to pay a fee to redeem their cattle. If a beast is not redeemed within a certain period of time, it is sold and the owner receives no compensation. The laxness of the herding may therefore result in serious financial loss to those Tonga who live near European land.[1]

---

[1] Occasionally a European takes advantage of Tonga customary law which does not restrict pastures to residents of a particular area and allows his herds to graze into the reserves. Near the Magoye there was still good grazing in July 1950, when I passed that way with several Tonga. They pointed to a large herd grazing along the margins of the road, well within the reserve, and commented, 'Mr. X has sent his cattle to our grazing again. He wants to save his own for later in the season, and so he sends his cattle to eat up our grass.'

THE DESIRE FOR INDEPENDENCE

Despite the difficulties faced by the immediate family group in coping with the labour involved in agricultural production, the upkeep of the homestead, and the management of the cattle herd, the break-up into individual family groups continues. Various motives are involved. Some of them have already been mentioned, such as quarrels over the division of manure and over the delinquencies of herd-boys. Families also move away from the main village to build their own homesteads because of quarrels over chickens or annoyance at the depredations of the pigs and goats owned by their neighbours.

Of more importance, however, is the desire, on the part of the men to become the head of an independent unit and thus gain in status. As long as a man remains within an established village, or a section of a village, he is regarded as a subordinate of the established head of the village or section. His subordination may be of little practical moment. He may neither assist nor be assisted by his head. He may act quite independently. Nevertheless, he will be identified with the head by other members of the community, and will feel that he has not yet achieved an independent status, which will entitle him to recognition by other Tonga as an important member of the community.

He gradually establishes his own identity by differentiating himself from the household and interests of the older man with whom he lives and upon whom he has been dependent as an unmarried boy and as a young married man. He first acquires his own hut and his own fields and granary. When he has completed the payment of his bridewealth and his wife's relatives give permission for the couple to cook and to make beer, he establishes his independent household under the aegis of his ancestors, whom he can now approach for the first time with offerings. The next step is reached when he can build his own cattle kraal, a step which calls for a special offering of beer to the ancestors. When he can build his own homestead, separate from a cluster housing other men, he has progressed still further. From then on his status increases as he can attract other men to accept his leadership and settle with him. But other men are also ambitious and desire the independence of their own homesteads. Today there is little pressure to keep them within a larger cluster, and the homesteads with their attendant cattle kraals proliferate.

Thus as the cattle have increased, the units which supervise the herds have grown smaller until today they are probably attempting to cope with more cattle than they can effectively manage without some change in their methods of cattle management.

SUMMARY

This chapter has dealt with the role of cattle among the Tonga in an attempt to understand Tonga attitudes toward suggestions of de-stocking and to consider the strains placed upon Tonga organization by the possession of large numbers of cattle.

The Tonga recognize individual rights to cattle and most cattle are owned by individuals rather than by groups. Nevertheless, the Tonga social system requires a man to balance his rights to dispose of his property against his obligations to assist his kinsmen, and particularly the members of his matrilineal group. While he has the recognized right to dispose of individual animals, he is expected to consider the requirements of his kin before he disposes of any major portion of his herd. Men scatter their cattle through a system of herding arrangements which spread the possession of cattle widely throughout the community, while at the same time the owner retains his prior rights to resume possession or to dispose of his property. The man in possession of a beast may therefore have no right to sell it or dispose of it in any way, and the man who has the right of disposal may live at some distance. This system is possible since the Tonga value cattle for their role in symbolizing social ties rather than for their immediate utility. Today this view of cattle is still strong though it is beginning to break down with the development of new uses to which cattle can be put and also with the development of a cash market and the need for a cash income.

The possession of large herds clashes with the trend towards independent homesteads composed of small family groups. The small groups are short of labour for building and maintaining cattle kraals, and, still more important, find great difficulty in providing a sufficient number of herd-boys to herd the cattle during the period between planting and harvesting. There is a constant competition for the labour of herd-boys, who move from group to group or run off to work for Europeans and Indians in neighbouring areas, with resulting inefficiency in herding.

CHAPTER VI

RESIDENCE AND VILLAGE STABILITY AMONG THE PLATEAU TONGA[1]

THE importance of the village as the significant local unit among many Central African peoples has been noted by a number of observers.[2] Nevertheless, villages are not necessarily enduring units with stable populations tied to particular localities. Among some Central African peoples, villages may shift from spot to spot, while through them stream a succession of inhabitants brought together by a variety of motives for limited periods of time. In this chapter, I shall examine the shifting population of certain Plateau Tonga villages to see what light can be thrown on the factors leading to changes in village composition in this area. I hope that the chapter will encourage further research into village instability and that it will provide guidance for field workers in collecting and analysing their material.

The Plateau Tonga are a matrilineal people who live in the Mazabuka District of the Southern Province of Northern Rhodesia. Traditionally, the Tonga had a mixed economy, combining shifting cultivation with the possession of herds of cattle. Today, they are turning to a cash crop economy, based largely on the sale of maize.

The Tonga population is highly mobile. People shift freely from one village to another and from chieftaincy to chieftaincy. Data from sixteen villages in Mwanza, Ufwenuka, and Chona

---

[1] For the material in this chapter I worked from four villages, located in the chieftaincies of Mwanza, Chona, Monze, and Mwanacingwala. Two of the chieftaincies lie to the east of the railway line, two to the west. For quantitative data, I am relying chiefly on material collected during the second tour from sixteen villages in Mwanza, Ufwenuka, and Chona chieftaincies, all in the eastern areas.

For a general account of Tonga social structure, cf. Colson, 1951.

[2] Cf. Gluckman, Mitchell, and Barnes, 1949, pp. 89–106. Barnes and Mitchell have made intensive studies of village organization among the Fort Jameson Ngoni of Northern Rhodesia and the Yao of Nyasaland.

chieftaincies indicate that about 36 per cent of the adult men and 20 per cent of the adult women live in their natal villages. Table VI is constructed from censuses made in these sixteen villages.[1]

TABLE VI

Population Mobility

Age	Males			Females		
	Nat. V.	*Oth. V.*	*Total*	*Nat. V.*	*Oth. V.*	*Total*
21–30 Years .	41	37	78	35	87	122
	(52·5%)	(47·4%)	(100·0%)	(28·6%)	(71·3%)	(100·0%)
31–40 Years .	34	52	86	22	68	90
	(39·5%)	(60·5%)	(100·0%)	(24·4%)	(75·5%)	(100·0%)
41–50 Years .	16	36	52	5	57	62
	(30·7%)	(69·2%)	(100·0%)	(8·0%)	(91·9%)	(100·0%)
51–60 Years .	5	24	29	3	31	34
	(17·2%)	(82·7%)	(100·0%)	(8·8%)	(91·1%)	(100·0%)
61–70 Years .	5	21	26	2	19	21
	(19·2%)	(80·7%)	(100·0%)	(9·5%)	(90·4%)	(100·0%)
71– Years .	1	9	10	4	11	15
	(10·0%)	(90·0%)	(100·0%)	(26·6%)	(73·3%)	(100·0%)
TOTAL . .	102	179	281	71	273	344
	(36·2%)	(63·7%)	(100·0%)	(20·6%)	(79·3%)	(100·0%)

These figures show only a minimum mobility; for many of those who were living in their natal village at the time of my census had not lived there all their lives. Moreover, many people had previously resided in two, three, four, or more villages. I have not attempted to quantify the data on number of moves, however,

---

[1] I or my assistant, Mr. Benjamin Shipopa, interviewed every adult resident in these villages at the time we made the census with the exception of three men and one old woman. This meant repeated trips to the villages until we had found and interviewed all those who had been away at their fields or at beer drinks or funerals or on short visits to other villages when we first began the work.

Both relatively conservative and relatively progressive villages are included among the sixteen. Twelve of the sixteen villages were in existence at the time that Civil Administration was first organized, about 1903. One village was recognized officially in the 1920's, two in the 1930's, and one in the 1940's.

In the Table *Nat. V.*, stands for those living in their natal villages; *Oth. V.*, for those living in other than their birth village.

since these are incomplete. In some cases, those who continue to reside in their birth village have moved further than those who have transferred their allegiance to another headman; for a village itself may move some considerable distance from its original site. One of the villages included in the census had moved some twelve to fourteen miles from its former site; another had moved over twenty miles. Some people who have spent their lives within a mile or two of their birthplaces have yet transferred their allegiance to some other headman, and are thus shown as living in another village. Table VI, therefore, reflects shifts in village allegiance rather than movement from one area to another.

The high mobility shown in Table VI may be due in part to good historical reasons, rather than to any peculiar feature of Tonga social organization. In the nineteenth century, the Tonga were heavily raided by Lozi and Ndebele armies which scattered the people and disrupted many villages. Later, in the early years of the twentieth century when British occupation had restored peace, a railway was built through Tonga country. Land on either side of the railway was taken for European settlement, and the Tonga who lived in this strip were ordered to move into areas which had been set aside as Native reserves. Some Tonga went to work as labourers on the European farms, and later when they left their jobs some of them settled close to the farms on the borders of the reserves among people whom they had met during their years of work in the vicinity. A further motive lay behind this settlement; for a market for maize developed with the opening of the mines on the Northern Rhodesian Copper Belt. The villages on the borders of the reserves were closest to the railway line and to trading stores and buying stations where the people could dispose of the crops which they began to grow for the market. In the eastern reserves, therefore, a drift occurred into the areas closest to the railway line. This only accentuated a general east-to-west movement which had been going on for many years. Immediately to the east of Mazabuka District lies the Gwembe District, inhabited by the Valley Tonga. They occupy the country lying between the Zambezi River and the Escarpment. Periodic famines drive the Valley Tonga to take refuge among their relatives on the Plateau and there many of them remain. Population pressure was therefore greatest in the eastern districts and led to a steady westward migration across the Plateau. The bulk of the Tonga population today, even in the western chieftaincies, trace their descent from those who fled from the Gwembe famines.[1]

To indicate something of this westward drift, I have constructed Table VII, where I have classified into their birth chieftaincies all adult men and women living in seventeen villages located in three areas; Chona chieftaincy on the edge of the Escarpment (5 villages); Mwanza chieftaincy, on the edge of the eastern reserve (8 villages); Monze chieftaincy towards the western borders (4 villages). The accompanying diagram (p. 177) gives a rough indication of the relative locations of the different chieftancies and shows the position of the villages used in constructing the Table. The diagram is not drawn to scale. For the purposes of classifying the people into chieftaincies, I have assumed that the borders of the chieftaincies extend to the railway line and thus ignore the intervening strip of European farms.[2]

From Table VII, it is clear that the major drift has been from east to west, though the actual movement had been rather greater than is shown in the Table; for within each chieftaincy there has been a westward movement.

In the western chieftaincies, a counter movement has occurred bringing people from the west into areas more adjacent to the railway line. Moreover people from western Northern Rhodesia have been moving into Tonga country, apparently attracted by its proximity to the railway line. In the Katimba area, on the western borders of Monze chieftaincy, for instance, I found small settlements of Lovale,[3] as well as many Lozi. Lozi are also common in Mapanza and Chongo chieftaincies.

Throughout Tonga country, there have also been movements

---

[1] Cf. J. Gordon Read, 1935.
[2] The boundaries of the chieftaincies, as well as the chieftaincies themselves, represent administrative convenience rather than Tonga tradition.
[3] The Tonga follow Europeans in using this general term to refer to people of a number of different tribes: Lwena, Chokwe, Lunda, Mbunda, and Lochazi, who are found chiefly in the Mwinilunga and Balovale Districts and in neighbouring portions of Portuguese West Africa.

TABLE VII
Birth Chieftaincies of Adults in Seventeen Villages

Birth Place	Chona		Mwanza		Monze	
	Males	Females	Males	Females	Males	Females
TONGA CHIEFTAINCY						
Naluama . . .	—	1 (0·7%)	—	—	—	—
Mweenda . .	—	—	1 (0·8%)	—	—	—
Sianjalika . . .	2 (1·9%)	3 (2·1%)	2 (1·6%)	6 (4·1%)	—	3 (2·7%)
Mwanza . . .	3 (2·9%)	6 (4·2%)	46 (38·3%)	62 (49·7%)	—	2 (1·8%)
Chona . . .	68 (66·0%)	87 (61·7%)	19 (15·8%)	19 (15·8%)	—	—
Ufwenuka . .	7 (6·7%)	19 (13·4%)	14 (11·6%)	14 (9·6%)	8 (8·8%)	6 (5·5%)
Shamaundu	2 (9·9%)	5 (3·5%)	11 (9·1%)	9 (6·2%)	14 (15·7%)	22 (20·3%)
Moyo . . .	—	—	—	—	3 (3·3%)	5 (4·6%)
Siabunkulu . .	—	—	—	—	—	—
Singani . . .	—	1 (0·7%)	—	—	1 (1·1%)	1 (1·1%)
Mwanacingwala .	—	—	—	1 (0·6%)	—	—
Chongo . . .	—	2 (1·4%)	4 (3·3%)	6 (4·1%)	—	1 (0·9%)
Simuyobe . .	—	—	1 (0·8%)	1 (0·6%)	3 (3·3%)	3 (2·7%)
Monze . . .	2 (1·9%)	4 (2·8%)	5 (41·%)	9 (6·2%)	47 (52·8%)	45 (41·6%)
Mapanza . . .	—	—	—	2 (1·3%)	2 (2·2%)	12 (11·1%)
Macha . . .	—	—	—	—	1 (1·1%)	1 (0·9%)
FOREIGN AREAS						
Gwembe District	13 (12·6%)	13 (9·2%)	14 (11·6%)	11 (7·5%)	2 (2·2%)	3 (2·7%)
Southern Rhod. & South Africa	—	—	2 (1·6%)	4 (2·7%)	—	2 (1·8%)
Other (including Northern Rhod.) . . .	6 (5·8%)	—	1 (0·8%)	1 (0·6%)	8 (8·8%)	2 (0·9%)
TOTALS . . .	103 (100·0%)	141 (100·0%)	120 (100·0%)	145 (100·0%)	89 (100·0%)	108 (100·0%)

DIAGRAM 4

Relative location of the Chieftaincies in Mazabuka District

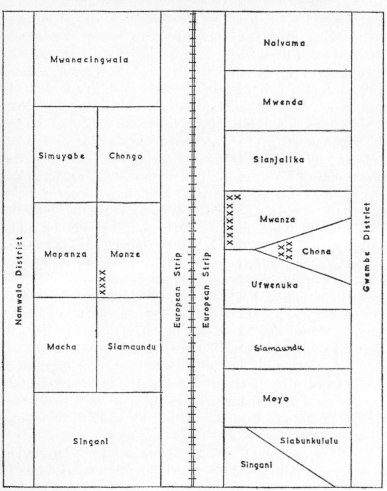

⊞ Railways.

✕✕ Villages used in the construction of Table VII.

N

into areas which were either unoccupied or only sparsely settled fifty years ago. Immigration and the natural increase of a population no longer beset by wars or killing famines have brought the Tonga to a stage where they must utilize all the cultivable land at their disposal. In the western chieftaincies, new settlements have been made as people have found the means to exploit relatively waterless areas. Everywhere, save on the Kafue margins, fields, villages, and herds of cattle have replaced the grazing herds of game in former hunting grounds. Little cultivable land is left unclaimed today, and shifting cultivation is no longer possible. In some areas, it is already difficult to provide sufficient fields for the young people who are growing up in the villages, and the stranger finds it difficult or impossible to obtain fields. In the eastern areas, I have frequently heard men say, 'The soil in the west is good. They can grow much maize there. We would like to move west, but the land is all taken and we can get no fields.' This, however, is a recent development which may in the future restrict population movements to a minimum.[1]

Wars, population increases, loss of land to Europeans, the new economic opportunities based on the sale of crops, have all played their part in shifting people from village to village and from area to area. But they are not the only forces at work. Villages away from the railway line, which have been least affected by the new economic opportunities and touched not at all by the loss of land, even so are not integrated bodies with permanent populations bound together by specific ties of kinship. Factors inherent in Tonga social organization must therefore be at work to produce the mobility which is so characteristic a feature of the Tonga village.

The Tonga system of land-holding has been permissive to the existence of a shifting population, and it in turn is based on the assumption that land is plentiful and can be had by clearing unoccupied bush. Until recently, land was a free good, to be freely taken and as freely abandoned again. Neither communities nor individuals owned land in any absolute sense. Each man took what

---

[1] For a further discussion of land shortages, cf. *The Tonga Report*.

he required for cultivation, used it for as long as he wished, and then abandoned it again. Whereupon, some other member of the community or a stranger recently come to live nearby might take possession. Land was not sold or rented, nor was it inherited. Ownership of land, therefore, did not tie men or women to a given locality. Those who wished to move could do so with the assurance that they could always find land in some other place. Only recently has the situation altered, and the Tonga are still reluctant to recognize the implications of present-day land short- ages, and the increased value of land which has been stumped and manured.[1]

Other material considerations to attach people to one area are lacking. Even today few people have any major investment in fixed capital equipment, such as burned-brick houses, wells, or fruit trees, which attach them to one spot. Most houses are of pole and mud or unburned brick construction and rarely last as long as ten years before they are past repair and must be abandoned.[2] Few families have more possessions than can be moved in a single wagon-load, including the food to last them until the next harvest for their chief wealth lies in their cattle which move themselves. It is therefore not a major undertaking to move even considerable distances.

Ritual attachments to given localities are also slight. A few ritual leaders are bound to the vicinity of the local shrines where they officiate. The vast majority of the people are more concerned with the cult of their own ancestral spirits, who are thought of as accompanying their descendants in their wanderings rather than as attached to a particular spot. Ancestral graves are of no import- ance to this cult, and the sites of the graves are ignored and then forgotten.[3] Moreover, each fully adult person may approach his

---

[1] Formerly there was no capital investment in land; i.e. land was not stumped or manured and after a short period of cultivation it reverted to bush fallow.

[2] Recently a few men have employed African builders to construct their houses and have bought nails, cement, and other materials to be used in the construction. If these men move, they try to sell their houses, and I have recorded a number of cash purchases.

[3] A few graves become shrines in local cults, but this does not localize the ancestral cult in which such men also figure. Cf. Chapter III.

ancestors on his own behalf and is thus independent of the ritual offices of his kinsmen.

European administration probably has had little direct effect upon the mobility of the population. It is axiomatic that all Tonga live in villages, since the Administration insists that all people must be attached to some recognized headman, whose village they then constitute.[1] A man who wishes to join a village must have the consent of its headman and should also notify his old headman of his intention to move. He should also register his move with the District Office, though few are in any immediate hurry to fulfil this requirement, and many men only do so after they have already spent several years in the new village. If a man wishes to form a new village, he must find nine other tax-paying males— that is, able-bodied men over the age of eighteen—who will join with him and accept him as their headman before he will receive recognition by the Administration, which may, however, refuse recognition if the secession will leave the old village short of tax-payers. These are the official limits placed upon the formation of new villages and the movement of men from one village to another. Apparently no official check is placed upon the movement of women and children. Movements within a village are theoretically confined to an area of a square mile, as all members of a village should live within 'hailing distance' of the headman's hut. Many people, however, successfully ignore this ruling and build their huts where they will.[2]

The Tonga themselves know no reason why a man should not live where he will. Traditionally, only slaves were bound, and they were bound to their owners rather than to a given piece of land. All others were free to move, and even young children could not be denied the right to move from relative to relative. No rule of residence bound a man or woman to one set of kinsmen rather than to another. The Tonga are matrilineal, but tend to be viri-

---

[1] In the last few years, provision has been made for men recognized as improved farmers to live in their own homesteads away from any authorized village. This has had little effect as yet and can be ignored in this discussion.

[2] Cf. *The Tonga Report*, pp. 34–58. The 'ten-taxpayer' rule was repealed in 1945, but this has had little effect in this area.

local, since the husband usually takes his wife to live with him wherever he has settled. His own choice of residence appears to be unrestricted. He usually prefers to settle with those to whom he can trace some bond of kinship, but he is eclectic in his use of kinship ties, rather than bound to follow matrilineal or patrilineal links to the exclusion of other ties. Sometimes he settles in the village of his stepfather, if he has followed his mother on her remarriage. Sometimes he follows a married sister or other female relative and settles with her husband and his kin. More commonly he follows some consanguineal tie of his own, though this may be a remote one and his closest kinsmen live elsewhere. The only kinsmen with whom a man never comes to settle are his own children. In twenty-one villages for which I have census information, I found no single instance of a man joining a village because his son or daughter lived there.

Table VIII shows the way in which different types of kinship play their part in determining residence of adult men. The data relate to the same men who were used for constructing Table VI. The column headings are as follows:

M, settled with Matrilineal kin.
P, settled with Patrilineal kin.
W, settled with Wife's kin.
A, settled with Affinal kin, i.e. husband of some female relative.
N, no kinship link with others in the village when he first settled there.

Table VIII over-emphasizes the importance of patrilineal ties, since all men living in a village with their fathers or their fathers' relatives were classified under this heading whether or not they also had matrilineal relatives in the village. In some cases, a man is classified as living with his wife's relatives, but his sons are classified as settled with patrilineal relatives since they are living with their father. This is obviously arbitrary, but some choice was necessary, and this seemed the most useful one.

Patrilineal links seem to have a slightly stronger pull than matrilineal links in determining residence, though this tendency is reversed in the older age-groups. One cannot argue from this that the Tonga are shifting from residence with matrilineally related kin to residence determined by patrilineal ties. Rather it seems that young men often settle with their father, especially if the mother is still alive and living with the father. When the father dies, or when the mother leaves him, then the sons may go off to join matrilineal kinsmen or to settle on their own. The strong tie to the paternal side is largely a personal one with the father himself rather than with the paternal kin in general, while the sentiment towards the maternal kin is much more diffuse and is

TABLE VIII

Kinship Links Determining Village Residence of Adult Males

Age	M	P	W	A	N	Total
21–30 Years .	29 (37·1%)	42 (53·8%)	2 (2·5%)	3 (3·8%)	2 (2·5%)	78 (100·0%)
31–40 Years	25 (29·0%)	38 (44·1%)	4 (4·6%)	11 (12·7%)	8 (9·3%)	86 (100·0%)
41–50 Years .	18 (34·5%)	16 (30·7%)	11 (21·1%)	5 (9·6%)	2 (3·8%)	52 (100·0%)
51–60 Years .	8 (27·5%)	6 (20·6%)	5 (17·2%)	4 (13·4%)	6 (20·6%)	29 (100·0%)
61–70 Years .	10 (38·4%)	8 (30·7%)	3 (11·5%)	0 (—)	5 (19·2%)	26 (100·0%)
71– Years .	7 (70·0%)	1 (10·0%)	1 (10·0%)	0 (—)	1 (10·0%)	10 (100·0%)
Total . . .	97 (34·5%)	111 (39·5%)	26 (9·2%)	23 (8·1%)	24 (8·5%)	281 (100·0%)

attached to all matrilineal kin rather than to some specific individual. In support of this argument, my evidence shows that a man living with paternal kin is usually living with his own father;[1] if he is living with matrilineal relatives, he may be living with anyone of a large number of people and it is impossible to predict from a glance at his genealogical connections which particular relative he will join.

Residence of a particular individual is determined not only by his general kinship ties, but also by his particular history which

---

[1] Or the man who has taken the place of his dead father by inheriting the name and widow or widows of the deceased.

may be very different from that of his own full siblings. Elsewhere I have described the competition for small boys which hinges on the need for cattle herds.[1] A man who has no sons of an age to herd cattle, or who needs extra assistance, will try to attract other young boys to come to work for him. He will exploit any tie of kinship, and will be glad to obtain the children of his own matrilineal relatives (who may then be linked to him by either a matrilineal or a patrilineal tie), the children of his wife's relatives or her small brothers, his wife's sons by a former marriage or by a lover, the children of his father's relatives, the children of distant clansmen. Occasionally, he may succeed in obtaining children who have no kinship link with him whatsoever. Many of the boys who come to herd his cattle may not stay with him for any length of time, but others may remain with him until maturity, whereupon he is expected to provide them with cattle for their marriage payments. Today he may also need to allot them a portion of his fields if there is no unoccupied land in the neighbourhood which they may clear for themselves. When the boys marry, they usually find wives in the village or at least within the neighbourhood of their guardian's homestead, and thus have a double attachment to the area. Sometimes the guardian moves on to find new fields or to escape quarrels in the village, and the young men who have settled with him may remain behind in the old village, though they may now have no immediate kinship tie with any other member of the village. It is probably in the area closest to the railway line that the growth of villages through the attachment of herd-boys is most marked; for here live the wealthier farmers who are most likely to attract youngsters to work for them.

The wealthier men are also the ones who make the most effort to keep their own sons with them and prevent them from drifting off to join other relatives or to work for the Europeans in the adjacent farming belt. This, however, gives rise to stresses which may lead to changes of residence. These men are faced now with a lack of new land to be exploited and from their own fields they

---

[1] Cf. Chapter V.

make provision for their sons and for their maturing herd-boys. Quarrels arise as they are thought to be favouring one or the other, and dissident members may move away.

Men move, however, for other reasons. Quarrels and dissensions arise from other motives besides the possession of land and the use of equipment. Quarrels about women are common and may lead neighbours to move some distance apart. Others move because a series of deaths or other misfortunes have been laid to the witchcraft of some member of the village, and they seek safety in distance. Today in villages where Christians ban the brewing of beer, and therefore offerings to the ancestors, pagan members may decide to move to villages where they can carry on their old practices.

People not only move from one village to another. They also move from site to site within the village, now combining with one set of neighbours to form a cluster or section within the village, now combining with another set to form another cluster, now building a separate homestead.

In the preceding pages, I have given a general account of factors leading to village mobility. In the following section, I shall trace the history of one village to show some of the forces at work to change the physical plan of a village as well as the network of relationships which binds its members together. I shall pay particular attention to the events of the period from September 1946 to July 1950, a time during which I had the village under observation. I have chosen this particular village because it is the largest for which I have detailed information over the four-year period, because it has a strong headman who attempts to hold his people to him and who discourages a break-up into small isolated clusters, and because the village was founded only in the 1930's and there was therefore an opportunity to learn something about its original composition.[1] The village is located in Mwanza chieftaincy on the borders of the Tonga reserve, close to the European farming belt.

---

[1] I have similar detailed information for six other villages: three in Chona chieftaincy and three in Mwanza chieftaincy. I also have information on changes in three other villages in Mwanza, but little reliable information on the motives lying behind the changes.

Many of its members are adherents to the Seventh Day Adventist church. It also has an unusually high proportion of progressive farmers, and the average income per family is well above the average for all the villages in my sample. Many of the people in the village show little sympathy for traditional values, particularly for the ritual of the ancestral cult or the local rituals of the rain-shrines. A few resolutely refuse to believe in the reality of witch-craft. Many dislike the Tonga system of matrilineal inheritance whereby their property will pass on their deaths to their matrilineal relatives rather than to their own sons, but tension over inherit-ance is today fairly common throughout Tonga country. In some respects, therefore, the village is atypical, but it shows about the same number of changes, and for similar reasons, as do the other villages for which I have information.

For convenience, I shall refer to the village as Ndaba, the Tonga equivalent of 'so-and-so'. The genealogy facing p. 206 traces the kinship links between members of the village and the headman; for it is difficult on a two-dimensional chart to show all the links which connect the members to each other. For instance, B4 and B8 have married full sisters; the wives of C17 and C3 are full sisters and the mother's brother's daughters of C24 and his sister, the wife of C6. C27 and C19 have married full sisters. The genealogy is therefore incomplete, but it does show those ties which the people themselves stress when asked why they are living in this particular village. It shows people who are not resident in the village only if they are important as links between residents. Only adults are shown.

Ndaba village was founded about 1935, when B10, the present headman, withdrew from a neighbouring village with his follow-ers and received recognition by the administration as a headman. At that time there was still unoccupied land in the neighbourhood which could be taken by incomers. B10 and his immediate follow-ing continued to till the fields they had acquired when they were living in the old village, and also took new fields into cultivation. Later comers and those who have grown to maturity in the past decade have had to obtain fields by begging from the men of the village or from men of neighbouring villages. Today the fields held by residents in the village are interspersed amongst the fields held by men in some five other villages.

B10 was born in a village some fifteen to twenty miles from Ndaba and originally came to the area to work on an adjacent European farm. He settled in a village close to the borders of the farm and gradually began to attract followers, many of whom worked on farms in the area for some years before obtaining fields and starting to work for themselves. B10's first mature recruit was his younger full brother, B8. After the smallpox epidemic of the late 1920's destroyed their birth village, some of the survivors came to join B10 and B8 in the new area. Their widowed sister, B9, arrived with her small children. Their father's daughter, B7, who had left her husband, came with her small children, and her brother, B6, who was then an unmarried youth. B10 and B8 also undertook the care of C9 and his six sisters, the orphaned children of their full sister. B10 also fostered two other youths, B3 and B4, who were at loose ends after the death of their mother and the return of their Shona father to his home in Southern Rhodesia. These boys were parallel maternal cousins of B6, but were not related to B10 who was only their mother's sister's husband's son. When B10 decided to form his own village, he persuaded B20, the husband of another paternal half-sister, to join him. B20 had been working on a European farm up to that time. Another recruit was B10's wife's brother, the father of B1 and the wife of B2, who died a few years after joining the village. B10 also brought in C15, a remote matrilineal relative. These people formed the nucleus of his own section of the village. They built their huts in a long row facing the river. There they were joined by B13, who had lived in this area since childhood and who now left his old village, some two miles south of Ndaba, to join the new village along with C21, a close matrilineal kinsman, and C27, the adult son of his dead brother. B10 and B13 claimed matrilineal kinship, but the link was forgotten and very possibly never existed.

From this nucleus the village has continued to grow as the sons of the original members have matured and founded their own families, and as the men have brought in other relatives and a few strangers. B4 traced his father to Southern Rhodesia where he had married a Shona woman of his own tribe. After one visit, B4 brought back his younger half-brother, B2, to herd his cattle. When B2 grew up, he married the orphaned daughter of B10's wife's brother. B2 later returned to Southern Rhodesia and brought back his brother's son, C1, who has since lived with B3 and worked for him. At the present time B2 and B4 have with them two other lads from Southern Rhodesia, descendants of their father, and B4 has also attracted a young matrilineal relative of his wife. These lads work for the two men and will probably settle in the village.

When B10's father died, B10 brought his mother to the village and with her came the maternal grandmother of C19. C19 accompanied his grandmother and remained to grow up in the village and to settle there. B10 also persuaded his kinsman, the father of C20, to lend him C20 as a herd-boy for his cattle and begged C18 from other relatives for the same purpose. Both lads settled in the village. B10 also brought C15 in to herd cattle. The latter had come from the Gwembe District as a small boy to live with a matrilineal relative in the eastern part of Mwanza chieftaincy. B10 found him there and persuaded him to shift his allegiance, though their kinship is admittedly untraceable. B10 was able to lure other matrilineal relatives from their home in the Gwembe District: C13 came and later brought his younger brother, C12; C10 came on his own initiative; C11 was brought by B10 when she was still a small girl to assist with the household and field work. C16, who was born in Shamaundu chieftaincy, found his way to the area as a teacher in the local school. B10 and he claimed matrilineal kinship, and B10 persuaded him to settle in the village where he was joined by his old mother, B11.

In the meantime, B13 had traced his paternal half-brother, B12, who had been working for 38 years as a farm labourer in Southern Rhodesia. His sister's son, C23, visited him there and persuaded him to return to Tonga country to settle near his brother. He returned with his two Shona wives and most of their children, though the older children remained in Southern Rhodesia. C22, young and unmarried, joined him.

Earlier, B16 had joined the village. Indeed, he may have been one of the original members. He worked with B10 on the European farm, and B10 gave him his sister's daughter in marriage. B16 later brought his mother's sister's son, B15, into the village, and B15 in turn brought his sister's son, C29, to work for them. All three were from the Gwembe District. B14, who could trace no direct kinship links with anyone in the village, decided to settle with B10 because they had known each other from boyhood. B17 also seems to have joined the village because he and B10 originally came from the same area, but later he married another of B10's sister's daughters, thus strengthening his link with the village. He in turn brought in his old mother, A3, and his sister who was married to C22, a classificatory sister's son of B13. C22 had been living in his wife's village and now moved with her to live with her brother and mother, in a cluster at the opposite end of the village from B13. B20, the husband of B10's paternal half-sister, also brought other kinsmen. He had taken his mother's sister's son, B19, and his mother's brother's son, B21, to work for him while they were still small boys. When they were grown and married, they settled near him in the village. He was also joined by a more remote matrilineal kinswoman, B22, who came to live with him after divorcing her husband. She brought with her her young son, C30. C14 came to the village as a follower of his paternal half-sister's husband, C15. When C15 decided to move westward to Chongo chieftaincy in search of new land, C14 remained behind though he no longer had any direct kinship links with anyone in the village. His wife, however, came from a neighbouring village and had relatives in Ndaba.

In 1946, the village was composed of the following spatially discrete socially recognized clusters of dwelling huts:

1. B17 with his wife, his old mother (A3), his sister and her husband (C22).
2. C21 with his wives.
3. C14 with his two wives; B14 with his wife.
4. B16 with his wife, and his mother's sister's daughter's son (C29) then unmarried.
5. B2 and B4 with their wives and dependent herd-boys.

6. B21 with his wife.
7. B20 with his three wives, his mother's mother's sister's daughter's daughter (B22) and her son (C30).
8. B19 with his wife.
9. B10 and B8 with their wives, their mother (A1), their widowed sister (B9), their three sisters' sons with their wives (C5, C6, C9), the married son of B10 (C8) with his wife, their unmarried but adult sons (C3, C4, C7); their father's daughter (B7), her mother's sister's son (B3) with his wife and his father's son's son (C1); their more remote matrilineal relatives (C17, C12, C13) with their wives, and C12 and C20 who were unmarried boys; and their matrilineal kinswoman (C11) who was an unmarried woman but had borne a number of children by C8.
10. C18 with his wife.
11. C19 with his wife.
12. B12 with his two wives, and his sister's son (C22), an unmarried boy.
13. B13 with his two wives, his son (C24) with his wife, and his brother's son (C26) with his wife.
14. C25 with his wife.
15. C27 with his two wives.
16. C16 with his wife, and his old mother (B11).
17. B15 with his wife.
18. B6 with his wife.

The listing gives the number of clusters in which the members of the village lived, and the placement of the huts is shown in the accompanying diagram of the village as it was in September 1946. In the eleven years of its existence, the village had already undergone considerable change. The long line in which it was originally built had been broken, and the people had begun to build in small clusters of two or three huts. C16, B15, and B6 had moved some distance from the main part of the village, the first two to live near their fields and the last to live closer to his work on the adjacent farm. There may have been other motives, however, behind their moves. B6 was generally thought to have moved,

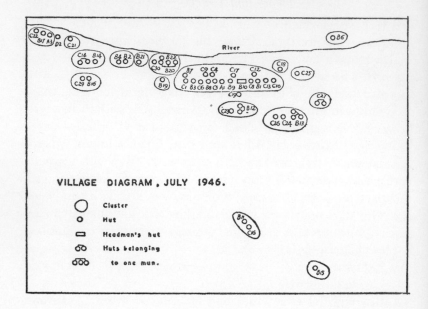

VILLAGE DIAGRAM, JULY 1946.

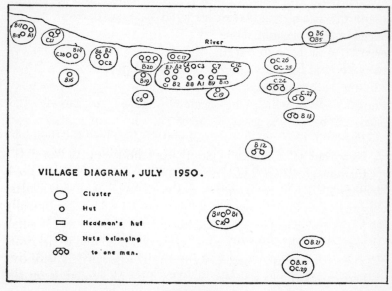

VILLAGE DIAGRAM, JULY 1950.

DIAGRAM 5

and to have moved well outside the immediate vicinity of the other huts, because of a quarrel with B20, his sister's husband, with whom he built originally. He caught B20 in adultery with his wife. The two men quarrelled, and B6 hurriedly moved out to avoid further discord. He may also have been willing to move to avoid embroilment in the quarrel which had already developed between B20 and B10, who was headman and the paternal half-brother of B6. B20 had lost two other members of his immediate homestead, though they had been content to move only a few yards away and seemed to consider this sufficient demonstration of their independence. B21 and B19 had quarrelled with B20 over cattle for their marriages, over fields, over use of equipment and stock, over rights to their own labour. They withdrew from B20's homestead to build a few yards away. B19 cheerfully admitted that he had moved to escape beatings which B20 still dealt out when he was drunk regardless of their dignity as married men and heads of families. C21 had moved well away from B13, with whom he lived originally, to build his homestead somewhat separate from the rest of the village. He claimed he moved to escape the village pigs which ravaged his mango trees, and he fenced his new site and planted mango and banana trees. C25 also moved from B13's section, to live closer to the small tearoom owned by his brother, C26, for whom he worked.

In the four years that followed, the village saw many more changes, most of which are indicated by the diagram showing the placement of the huts in 1950. The changes are enumerated below.

1. B17 went off to work in Southern Rhodesia and was gone for two years while his wife and his mother and C22 and his wife struggled to maintain the homestead. He returned in 1949.
2. In 1950, C22 had a final disastrous quarrel with his wife, which hinged on his recent failure to beget children. She went off to live with her sister, some twenty miles away, and C22 spent part of his time with relatives in Ufwenuka chieftaincy and the rest of his time as a visitor in the cluster of B13, his mother's mother's sister's son.

3. B18 who had been living in Chongo chieftaincy left her husband when she became ill and came to live with B17 and A3, her father's sister, in 1949. She claimed to be possessed by *basangu* (spirits) and began to prophesy and to treat those who were brought to her from surrounding villages. Many people in Ndaba objected to her presence because they feared that those brought for treatment would die in the village. B17 finally threatened to move if he heard any further protests, and B18 remained in the village.

4. D2, sister's son of C22, returned from working in Johannesburg in November 1946. He built himself a small hut halfway between the huts of C21 and C22. He soon went off to work in a nearby railway hamlet, but meantime he had married and had built another hut in B13's section, which he inhabited between jobs.

5. C21 inherited a wife on the death of a remote matrilineal kinsman in 1947. He brought her to live with him, and with her came the old mother of the deceased husband. The latter died in 1949, and her hut was abandoned.

6. C14 moved out from the cluster in which he had been living with B14. He first built a cluster of his own, shown in the 1950 diagram as inhabited by C17. This was in 1947. In 1949, he decided to move west to Simuyobe chieftaincy where he would have more opportunity to hunt. For several years he had been complaining that his true work was hunting and that in this area he had little opportunity for it. He may have been hastened in his decision when he discovered his second wife involved in an affair with C30.

7. B14 remained where he was, but in 1949 he brought to live with him his sister's son (C27), an unmarried boy, and C 27's two small brothers who worked as cattle herds.

8. C29 married and moved to another village located near his work with a government technical department. In 1950, he had quarrelled with his immediate neighbours over the depredations of their cattle in his fields and over an adultery case and had moved back to Ndaba. This time he built with B15 in the fields.

9. B2 married a second wife in 1949 and brought her to live with him.

10. B2 and B4 were joined in 1949 by C2, the mother's sister's daughter's son of B4. C2 who had been living in Bulawayo for at least ten years came home without a penny but was welcomed and subsidized by B4 who had been trying to persuade him to come home for many years.

11. B21 moved in 1950 to live near his field, not far from B15. His quarrel with B20 had grown more serious. B20 had taken back the field he had given him; B21 had sued B20 over a cattle claim. B21 said he moved out to be close to his field. Most people in the village said he moved because of his quarrel with B20. Others said he was angry because he had caught his wife in adultery with B2 and he disliked living in B2's vicinity.

12. B22 married a man in another village in 1949 and moved to join him. She decided on the step when the headman ordered her to leave the village or stop making beer. She supported herself by the sale of beer, and was not prepared to give up brewing. She now lived only a few yards from the last huts in Ndaba and continued her profession.

13. C30 ran away to work in 1949 when his adultery with the wife of C14 was discovered. Now that C14 had moved away, he visited the village in his free hours and planned to return for planting in 1950 if he could smooth over another quarrel with the wife of B20 by whose unmarried daughter he had begotten two children. He wanted to marry the girl, and her mother who disliked him wanted to prevent the match. He apparently had no quarrel with B20 though he complained that he was forced to work away from the village because B20 did not provide him with a field large enough so that he could raise maize for the market.

14. C6 moved in 1948 from his position in the headman's cluster to a spot a short distance away, slightly closer to his paternal kinsman, B19. He said he moved because he wanted a place of his own which he could fence against the village pigs and chickens so that he could have a small sweet-potato and

o

ground-nut patch near his hut and also plant fruit trees. He fenced and planted. It was generally felt, however, that he was determined to move because of strained relations with his mother's brothers, B10 and B8, who resented his presence as a reminder of the inheritance of their matrilineal relatives. They made contemptuous references in his hearing to the general failings of sisters' sons. After he moved to the new site, they claimed that he had left them and no longer helped them, and so it always went with matrilineal kin. When he came to visit them, they snorted that he had come to eye the property he expected to inherit. After he built his own homestead, he spent little time in the cluster of his mother's brothers.

15. C5, who was an askari during the 1939–45 war, spent about two years in the village after he left the army. In 1947 he took his wife and baby girl to Nkana where he found work on the mines. He said he went because the village was dull and offered no opportunities. Probably he also felt the strain of living with his mother's brothers, B10 and B8.

16. C9 married in November 1946, and brought his wife to live with him in a hut close to B8, his mother's brother. He and his wife fought constantly, largely over their failure to beget living children. After she had had a series of miscarriages, he left her in 1948 to live with other women. Late in 1948 he went off to work on the railway line. He returned to sue his wife's lover for adultery, and then remained in the area. At first he stayed with his sister, the wife of B17, but by July 1950, he had married again and gone to live in his wife's village. He never ventured near his mother's brothers, B8 and B10, with whom he was at odds. They objected to his liaisons with women which cost them cattle to settle, to his treatment of his wife for whom they had given marriage cattle, and generally to him as a bad example of a sister's son. He complained that his mother's brothers despised him and quarrelled with him.

17. C3 and C4, sons of B8, married in 1949 and 1950 and brought their wives to live with them close to their father's hut.

18. A2, the mother's mother's brother of C18 and C19, moved

into the village in 1949, complaining that his children and
other relatives neglected him. He had been living about 30
miles away in the eastern part of Chona chieftaincy. He was
senile. He was probably brought by famine conditions in his
own home, as he arrived early in the 1949-50 famine. B8
gave him an old kitchen to live in and the wife of C18 fed
him.

19. C17 moved in 1949 to occupy the abandoned huts built by
C14. He had been occupying a house belonging to the headman who now needed the additional quarters for his own
growing family. C17 also wanted the independence of his
own homestead. It was an amicable arrangement between the
two men.

20. C7 married in 1950 a matrilineal kinswoman of his father,
B10, who had been living for several years as a member of
B10's household. B10 planned to build them a new house
close to his own, and hoped that by this marriage he might
manœuvre the recognition of C7 as the heir to his homestead.

21. C8 quarrelled violently with his father, B10, and in 1947 went
off to work on a European farm. The two men quarrelled
over C8's gambling and his wasting of property given to him
by his father. Early in 1949, C8 returned to the village and the
two men were reconciled for some months. Late in 1949, B10
told C8 that he would no longer have him in the village. C8
moved to the neighbouring village where he stayed with his
wife's parents while he waited for his father to relent. C8
claimed that his father neglected him in favour of his children
by the mother of C7. He argued that it was foolish for him to
work for his father when his father's matrilineal kin would
inherit all the property, and justified the numerous paternity
and adultery suits which followed in his wake as a means of
enjoying his father's wealth. B10 said his son was lazy and
good for nothing, that he was a gambler and worse. He was
afraid that if C8 returned to the village he might use the
opportunity to poison his father or other members of the
family.

22. B1, an ex-askari, married and settled in the village when he returned from the army. In 1947 his wife died in childbirth, and he went off to join the Northern Rhodesian Police and later married a Lenje woman whom he met in Lusaka. He said he left the village because of grief over the death of his wife. He may also have found the village dull after army life, and the people of the village complained that he was too lazy to attempt to farm his fields.

23. C13 moved to a village some ten miles away in 1950. He said he needed more land and could find none close to Ndaba. He undoubtedly was short of sufficient land to raise large crops, but he was not an ambitious farmer and he moved to an area equally short of land and with poorer soil. Others said that he moved because of quarrels with B10 who objected to his drinking, his gambling, and his mistreatment of his wife. C13 was also said to have been caught in the theft of chickens from B10. B10 did not prosecute, but C13 was chagrined at the contempt displayed by B10 and disliked being in his presence. When he said he would move, B10 gave immediate consent.

24. C12, the brother of C13, married in 1949 and brought his wife to live in the village. He refused to accompany C13 when the latter moved and remained with B10, with whom he was on good terms.

25. C10 moved out of the village in November 1946, after several years of dissension with B10, who objected both to his drinking and to his independence. He moved to a village thirteen or fourteen miles away.

26. C18 moved to another chieftaincy in 1947 to start a tearoom. This failed, and C18 then moved to join his wife's relatives on the borders of Ndaba. There was no open quarrel between him and the others in the village, but there was considerable distrust; for C18 had a propensity to borrow money for dubious business enterprises which always failed, and his debts embroiled him with all and sundry.

27. C23 had only a tenuous attachment to the village by 1946. He had already started a store in another chieftaincy, perhaps 30 miles from Ndaba, and lived most of the time at his store. In

1947, he moved all of his belongings and settled permanently at his store, taking with him the two small sons of B12 to act as cooks and general assistants.

28. B12 with his wives and children moved out to build in their fields in 1950. They complained that their site was too small for them to build extra huts to accommodate their children when these came on visits, since in the rainy seasons the land about was waterlogged. They also wished to escape complaints about the depredations of their many pigs.

29. B13 moved in 1948 to a new site slightly east of his former cluster and found himself with only one wife, several young unmarried sons, and the occasional presence of D2 and C22, as other members of his old cluster now built on their own.

30. C26 moved to join his brother, C25, close to their tearoom. Their mother died in August 1946, and her death broke their attachment to B13's cluster.

31. C24, the son of B13, also moved out to build his own homestead, taking with him his old mother who was past childbearing and no longer wished to live with her husband. Two young unmarried brothers moved with them. C24 further enlarged his following by marrying a second wife.

32. B6 was joined in 1949 by his wife's brother, B5, who married and brought his wife to live in B6's homestead.

33. C16 married a second wife. He also brought his dead brother's son, D1, to live with him in 1949. D1 was an unmarried youth. With him came his younger brother. C16 also brought the small son of his sister to help with herding.

Thus frequent changes occurred among the households that made up the village, which at the same time had to cope with a shifting population of youngsters whose goings and comings frequently escaped my notice and therefore have not been included here. Their shifts do not affect the basic framework of the village at the present time, though they are important for its future development.

Other threats to the continuity of the village were smoothed over for the time being, though the potential cleavage may still remain. Such threats were fairly numerous. B17 threatened to move because of protests against the presence of his kinswoman (cf. item 3 above). B16 threatened to move with his family to Chongo chieftaincy, where he said, he would be able to hunt and also would have more room for his cattle. These were specious arguments since he did not hunt and had few cattle. Since B16 was married to a sister's daughter of B10, B10 discussed the matter with other men of his matrilineal group living in the village and they refused to consent to the move. B16 was supported by his wife and opposed by his children who threatened to remain in the village with their mother's mother's brothers (B10 and B8) or with their father's mother's sister's son (B15) if their parents moved. It was generally agreed that B16 and his wife were angry because when cattle entrusted to them by B8 and B10 died they received no further cattle to herd. B10 also refused to kill a beast for the puberty ceremony of their daughter, being annoyed by their failure to inform him of the arrangements they had made for her seclusion. B10 had sent cattle to another sister's daughter who lived in a nearby village where there was better grazing. These cattle had thrived, and he presented some of the progeny to the herders. B16's wife now complained, 'My mother's brothers care for my sister and not for me.' She was a querulous woman who brooded over the matter and stirred up her husband. B10 and others interpreted the threat to move as a way of bringing this grievance to the fore. They refused permission, however, on other grounds. They could not refuse, they said, B16 the right to take his wife to his own home where they would live with his relatives, but he wished to take her to another area to live among strangers and this they could not permit. B16's sons would soon be of an age when they would require cattle for marriage, and marriage payments are higher in the western areas where they would be likely to find wives if they went to live in Chongo chieftaincy. Moreover, they might embroil themselves in paternity suits or adultery cases, and demands for compensation would inevitably come back upon their matrilineal relatives since B16 had few cattle and no relatives to help him supply the needs of his sons. Moreover, the wife of B16 was ill, and if she should die in her new home, her matrilineal kinsmen would be required to provide cattle to cleanse the area of her death. The matter was argued at great length, but gradually blew over, and B16 agreed to stay, apparently satisfied with having brought his grievances to public attention.

C19 also threatened to move to another village where he would be closer to his fields. No one took this threat seriously since C19 was a lazy ne'er-do-well regarded with long-suffering contempt by everyone, including his wife and his thirteen-year-old daughter. Constantly he meditated moving to some other village or going away to work for the Europeans, while he moaned that he had been marked for trouble since his birth and that no one helped him or loved him. His wife refused to consider moving and pointed out that C19 was not troubled by the distance to the fields since he did little work in them anyway, and that if she were prepared to walk the distance he had no reason to complain.

More serious was a quarrel between B8 and B10, full brothers, which threatened to split B10's section of the village. C3, a son of B8, was accused of begetting children by four unmarried girls and was asked to pay compensation. B10 insisted that they must pay compensation to clear their names and maintain the respect of the community. B8 sided with his son who denied the charges and refused to pay. He held that his brother, B10, ought to help them fight the unjust accusations rather than side with the accusers.[1] The two men quarrelled. B8 threatened to move out to his fields with his sons, and they began to gather materials for the new huts. Then in 1950 B8's small son died, and the brothers were reconciled during the mourning. C3 and C4, who had not forgotten the opinion of them so freely expressed by their father's brother, still talked of moving out to the fields, leaving their father to remain with his brother. By the end of 1950, however, B8 had moved with his sons, without any further quarrel with B10. The quarrel appears to have been only the ostensible reason for the projected

---

[1] B10's position was the more difficult since one of the girls involved was his wife's sister's daughter who had been living in his house.

move, and when that was ended, the real motive still remained. B8 felt himself entitled to the dignity of his own homestead, and considered that while he remained in B10's cluster his position as the head of a numerous family with dependent households was not sufficiently recognized.

All quarrels, however, do not end in changes within the village or movement of one of the contenders from the village. One quarrel which had been maintained for a number of years had no such result. B20 had a long-standing quarrel with B10, the headman and his wife's paternal half-brother. Various incidents had added fuel to the flames. B10 disapproved of B20's fondness for beer, while B20 objected to B10's ban on brewing which prevented his wives from catering to his tastes. B20 had accused C8, B10's son, of adultery with one of his wives and had forced him, or rather B10, to pay compensation. Later when B20 again grew suspicious he broke into C8's house, and assaulted C8. This time he was made to pay compensation to C8 who was vigorously supported by his father. B10 and B20 also fought over the ownership of some cattle to which both had a claim—a quarrel which involved B21 and may have led to his move to his field—and dragged the case from court to court to the general disgust of the onlookers. At one court they were told to drop their quarrel or to live apart; for otherwise whenever misfortune befell one of them the other would inevitably be accused of having bewitched him. This had no effect on either man. They no longer visited each other or spoke or acknowledged each other's presence in any gathering, though when B20 was drunk it was not unknown for him to shout abuse as he passed the headman on the road. B10 was only too anxious to have B20 leave the village and to sever all connection with him, but felt that he could not order out a man who was the husband of his sister and the father of his sister's children. B20 refused to move, apparently finding a certain satisfaction in the knowledge that he was frustrating B10's wishes. A move would in no way have prejudiced his claim to his fields, and he could have joined either of two nearby villages and been equally near to his fields. It was therefore not possession of fields which kept him in the village. He was determined to stay and stay he did.

C24 had also quarrelled with B10 and with B3 and his supporters (B2, B4, and B6), when it was discovered that he was the lover of B3's wife, with whom he allegedly conspired to administer medicine to make B3 impotent. The disputants tried to settle the matter in the village before going to the courts. C24 was disrespectful to B10 who sided with B3. C24 finally paid compensation, but thenceforth avoided B10's section of the village. His old father, B13, who had been one of B10's close friends also ceased his visits to B10, though there was no open breach between the two men. Neither C24 nor B13, however, made any move to transfer their allegiance to another village, though they lived close to the huts of kinsmen who were attached to the next village.

Many of the quarrels which threaten to disrupt a village may thus simmer down, leaving no apparent trace or only a state of cool hostility between the disputants. In other instances, the original quarrel may not bring about a move, but some subsequent action, small in itself, may bring an upsurge of the old hostility and one of the aggrieved parties may move, either to build a separate homestead at some distance from other members of the village or to join some other village. It is possible for men to remain within the village despite covert antagonisms and open breaches because of the very loose organization of the village. Quarrels between the inhabitants of a single cluster or homestead must lead to the disruption of the cluster unless they are quickly settled, since these people are in constant daily contact and frequently depend upon each other for assistance in ordinary activities. Those who live in different clusters of the same village may be quite independent of each other, and if they quarrel and cease to speak or to have any intercourse with each other, normal life is not thereby disrupted to any extent. Even a quarrel between the headman and another member of the village does not seriously affect the ordinary activities of either man since there is no need for them to co-operate in any village activity. Quarrels which break up clusters therefore may leave the village intact, but this is only because the village rarely acts as a unit and the authority of the headman weighs but lightly on the members of the village.

If we again examine the way in which the village has been built up, other significant facts appear. Twenty-three of the men joined the village as adults, though when they came they may have been young unmarried men. Of these, one is the headman; twelve followed some matrilineal relative into the village; two followed a paternal half-brother; two followed brothers of their dead fathers; three came to live with relatives of their wives; one followed an affinal link; and two settled in the village without any obvious kinship link with its inhabitants. Maternal ties therefore appear to be of the greatest significance in determining the settlement of an adult man if he wishes to settle in a new village.[1]

Fourteen of the men came to the village as children when their parents or a grandparent joined the village. Six came with a mother or grandmother who followed a matrilineal relative into the village; eight came with their fathers or with a father's brother who had inherited their mother on the father's death. Twelve came to the village as boys to work as herd-boys for men living in the village. Of these, five came to work for matrilineal relatives; four came to work for paternal relatives; and three joined affinal relatives. The herding relationship has been almost as important as the parent-child relationship in recruiting the younger members of the village.

The history of the four years between 1946 and 1950 also indicates that today the village is no longer recruiting any adult members, save young unmarried men who come to work for relatives; for during this period no man with a family came to

---

[1] At first sight this may seem to contradict the conclusion drawn from Table VIII, that patrilineal links may have a slightly stronger pull than matrilineal links in determining residence. Table VIII, however, disregards the period of life at which the adults covered by the Table joined the village. Some of them were born in the village, others came as children, others as adults. Ndaba is a new village, nearly half of whose members joined as adults. If one ignores the age at which now adult members of the village joined it, 47·8 per cent are there because of matrilineal ties, 33·3 per cent because of patrilineal. The figures given in Table VIII for the two categories are respectively 34·5 per cent and 39·5 per cent. The numbers involved are too small to justify any certain conclusion, but it is probable that matrilineal ties are more important in new villages, patrilineal in old-established villages.

join it. This apparently is due to the shortage of land in the neighbourhood. On a number of occasions, married men asked permission to join the village, but the headman refused them on the ground that they would be unable to find land. When C13 moved away in 1950, the headman resumed the fields which he had given him. One field he gave to C12, the younger brother of C13, but he held back in his own hands another field so that he would have land to give to the next likely recruit; for he said that he was tired of refusing the applicants. However, B19 immediately begged for a field, pointing out that he was short of land and was unable to grow maize for sale. The village can now recruit new members from outside, only if men living in immediately adjacent villages and already in possession of fields in the area will transfer their allegiance to Ndaba.[1]

The land shortage, however, has been relatively unimportant in bringing about moves from the village during this period. Only C13, used insufficient land as an excuse to move from the village and as we have seen, other considerations probably determined the move. But quarrels over land and the use of equipment have led men to form their own homesteads apart from others. Other economic motives have also been important. Some have moved because they felt they could better exploit their skills in some other area (B22 who moved to a village where she could brew beer; C14 who moved to a hunting area; C18 and C23 who moved to work at stores or tearooms; C29 who moved to be nearer to his work). Of almost equal importance, however, have been quarrels

---

[1] The shortage of land is relative to the ambitions of the people in the village. The men of Ndaba desire fields on which they can produce maize for the market as well as for their own food, and consider themselves short of land if they have only enough for their immediate subsistence. Moreover, the land itself does not supply enough scope for the ambitions of all the men. Two have full-time employment on an adjacent farm, though they also have fields which they cultivate with the assistance of youngsters who work for them. Three men have trading stores or tearooms, two of them in other areas. One man regularly ships chickens to the Copper Belt markets, and others make sporadic shipments. Four men act as cattle-buyers during slack seasons in the agricultural year; and many of the younger men make occasional trips to the Kafue River to buy fish for resale in the reserves. Two are employed by government technical departments. All, however, save for C23, consider themselves primarily farmers.

about women and domestic disturbances. Quarrels about adultery offences play their part, and though they may not of themselves decide a man to move they may tip the balance if he is indicisive (the moves of B21, C14, C29, C30, and the earlier move of B6). A disastrous quarrel with a wife, followed by a divorce, will lead to a move if the man has been living with his wife's relatives (as with C22). The death of a wife may influence a man to go off to work (B1).

The most striking point that emerges from a study of the changes that have occurred in this village is the dispersal of matrilineal kinsmen. In 1946, the headman had living in his village 11 matrilineal kinsmen who were undoubted members of his own inheritance group. B13 and his close matrilineal kin were a rather dubious affiliate to this group. By July 1950, only six of these men remained in the village; two of these had left the headman's cluster to found their own homesteads, and one was threatening to move to his fields and actually did so before the end of the year. Two others had built their own homesteads prior to 1946. This highlights a major tension within the Tonga social system. We may argue that the Tonga male is eager for the co-operation of his matrilineal kinsmen while his own children are small, but as his sons mature and can assist with his work and at the same time demand more assistance from him, his relations with his matrilineal kinsmen become more and more strained. Each man desires to use his equipment, his labour, and his funds to further the interests of his own household, and resents demands made upon these by his kinsmen, and at the same time he resents the preoccupation of his kinsmen with their own interests. Moreover, in his kinsmen he sees his heirs who will replace him and enjoy his property when he is dead. The tension apparently is highest between those most closely related, but to a lesser extent it affects all since all may inherit. Younger members of the group therefore tend to move away to ease the tension, or at least they found their own homesteads. The same situation moreover is likely to repeat itself over a period of years; for as a man's sons mature, he again attempts to draw in small relatives to herd his cattle and to help with his work, and as these in turn mature and found their own families and become absorbed in their own affairs to the neglect of the interests of their old guardian, the tension mounts again.

Meantime, the sons themselves begin to assert their independence. They feel that they must found their own households, obtain their own cattle and other farming equipment, and achieve an independent status; for their father is ageing and on his death they will not inherit his property nor his place in the homestead. They must be independent of his assistance before that day arrives and their father's matrilineal heirs take possession. Sons therefore are likely to skimp their work for their father and attempt to turn his property to their own advantage. While their father may be in sympathy with their desire to obtain security and oppose the inheritance of his own matrilineal relatives, nevertheless he feels the drive of his sons towards independence as a threat to his own position as head of a strong homestead. Tension exists therefore between father and sons, and the sons tend to move out to establish their own homes (the sons of B13), or they may be driven out by their irate father (B10 and his son C8).

In this situation neither the bond between father and son nor the bonds between matrilineal relatives can have sufficient strength to hold people together as enduring units. In less progressive villages, the tensions give rise to accusations of witchcraft, or to brooding suspicion, which widens the rifts. Village instability is a reflection of these tensions and of the attempts to solve them.

It thus appears that though some of the mobility displayed by the Tonga population in the last half-century can certainly be traced to factors such as displacement from the area set aside for Europeans, to population increase and to land shortage, nevertheless Tonga social organization itself is also a major factor in producing mobility.

The examination of the data on village residence suggests a further practical point for the anthropologist, or for anyone engaged in collecting information on the structure of villages or other local groups. It is not enough to record the kinship links which exist between members of a village, especially if the area shows a high degree of mobility. The recorder should attempt to discover the approximate age at which each adult joined the village, and the reason for his coming. It was only from such data, for instance, that the importance of the recruitment of herd-boys in the formation of clusters and villages appeared. It is from this type of detailed material that we can expect to deepen our analyses of the significance of local groups.

GENEALOGY OF NDABA VILLAGE

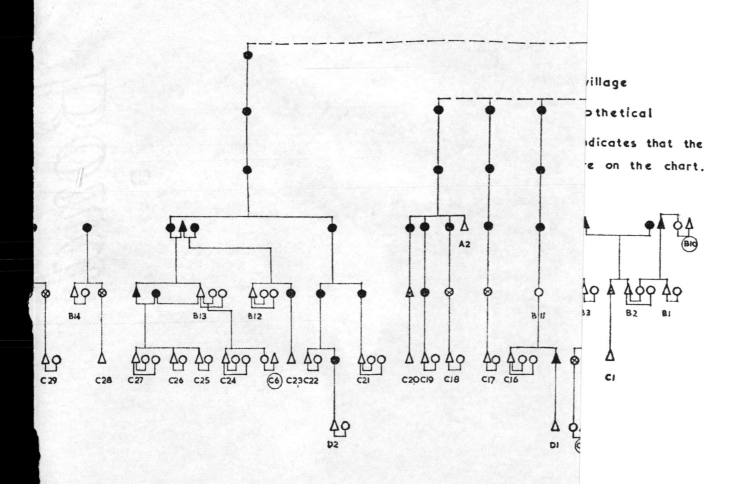

village

othetical

dicates that the

e on the chart.

A2

B14   B13   B12   B11   B3   B2   B1   B10

C29   C28   C27   C26   C25   C24   C6 C23 C22   C21   C20 C19   C18   C17 C16   C1

D2   D1

DIAGRAM 6

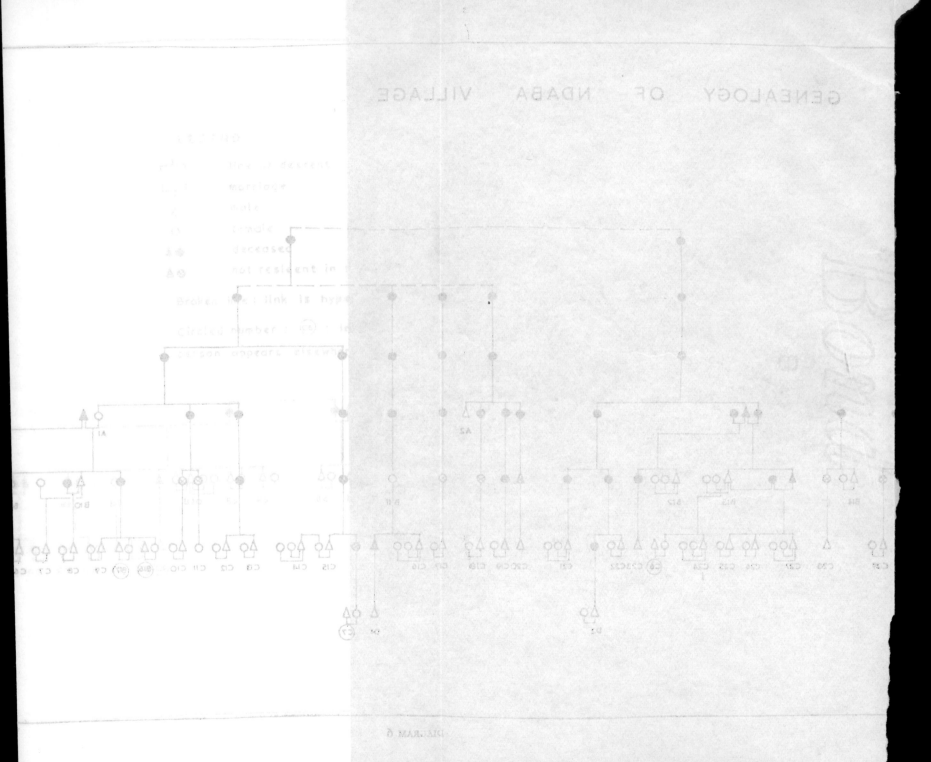

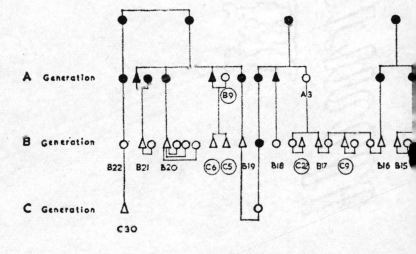

CHAPTER VII

MODERN POLITICAL ORGANIZATION OF THE PLATEAU TONGA[1]

INTRODUCTION

THE Plateau Tonga are a group of egalitarian matrilineal people living in what is now known as the Maize Belt of Northern Rhodesia. Traditionally they were cattle keepers and shifting cultivators with little trade or economic differentiation. Settlement was in small villages scattered across the countryside. These villages were but loosely bound together into larger social and political units. Political authority, if it existed, was in embryonic form and never extended over any large group or wide territory. There were no courts, chiefs, or disinterested parties with authority to judge claims and enforce decisions. The feud was the real sanction. Enforcement of claims ultimately rested on the solidarity of small groups of matrilineal kinsmen who would resort to force to protect their members' rights or to avenge their wrongs. Such kin-groups, however, did not form part of a segmentary lineage system, nor did they fit into a territorial organization.

Today this stateless society has received new political forms. I shall deal here chiefly with the position of the Native Authorities

---

[1] This chapter is based on work done among the Tonga, 1946 to 1947. It refers to the situation at that time before the reform of the Native Authority in 1949. It was originally written for a seminar at the London School of Economics and I have revised it for publication. I must thank members of that seminar for criticisms. I also wish to thank my colleagues of the Rhodes–Livingstone Institute: Mr. John Barnes and Mr. Clyde Mitchell, and Dr. M. Gluckman, former Director of the Institute. The picture given here of the working of the court system and the relationship of the authorities to the District Administration did not change greatly prior to 1950 although the staff of the District Office was increased, with the result that touring was once more possible. District boundaries were changed after 1950 and a new district created, which reduced the area to be supervised and also placed the District Office more nearly in the centre of Tonga country. Since 1950 radical changes have altered the political scene.

who have been created by government and with their courts which fill the gap left by the outlawing of self-help. However, to understand the position of the Authorities, it is necessary to sketch rather fully the indigenous forms of organization.

The Tonga

It is difficult to define what we mean when we speak of the Plateau Tonga, since they were not demarcated from their neighbours by political boundaries. In Northern Rhodesia and adjacent areas of Southern Rhodesia, there are people who speak a number of related dialects of what Doke has called the Tonga Group.[1] Within this group there are people who are commonly referred to as the Plateau Tonga. I am dealing here with the northern branch of the Plateau Tonga who live within the Mazabuka District. At the present time they number between 70,000 to 110,000, with an average population density in the neighbourhood of 50 per square mile. They inhabit an area stretching from the Escarpment hills of the Zambezi on the east to the Mutama basin on the west, with northern and southern borders roughly at the town of Mazabuka and at Muzoka stream. Today it is divided into eastern and western sections by the railway line which runs between Livingstone and the Congo border. The area includes about 7,600 square miles, and is little differentiated topographically except on the east where it runs into the Escarpment and on the north-west where it reaches the flood plains of the lower Magoye and the Kafue River. Across this area, slight changes in dialect and custom eventually accumulate to distinguish those at one end of the country from their fellow Tonga at the opposite end, while those on the borders merge into the Ila, Valley Tonga, Lenge, Sala, and other groups speaking related dialects. Nowhere is there

---

[1] C. M. Doke, *Bantu Modern Grammatical, Phonetical and Lexicographical Studies since 1860*, p. 31. The Plateau Tonga have no connection whatsoever with the people described by Junod.

Throughout this chapter I have adopted the common practice of dropping the prefixes to tribal names and thus write Tonga instead of Batonga, etc. Moreover since Tonga is now a written language I have attempted to follow standard spellings for the few native words which appear here in preference to strict phonetic renderings.

any sudden break which defines a limited unit within the whole linguistic group.

History

Practically nothing is known of the early history of the Tonga. They themselves have no legends of migration nor any historical accounts which go back beyond the middle of the last century. It is safe only to assume that they were in their present area before the end of the eighteenth century. If they met and overcame any earlier inhabitants, the descendants have been completely assimilated into the general Tonga society.

During the nineteenth century, the Tonga were badly smashed by raids in which Kololo, Ndebele, and Lozi overran the country. When Livingstone passed through the area in 1855, the Tonga told him that formerly they had lived in large towns and had owned great herds of cattle. About 1832 a raiding party under Pingola came from the north and looted much of the cattle. Before the Tonga had recovered from this raid they were beset by the Kololo who at one time established themselves in the country of the Tonga south of the Muzoka. When Livingstone visited the Tonga, they were living in tiny hamlets scattered over the countryside and had lost most of their cattle. The raids continued for another forty years. At the time the European occupation began most of the Tonga were paying tribute to the Lozi, which secured them some slight immunity from raids from that direction, though they were never incorporated into the Lozi kingdom.[1] The Ndebele were not so easily handled. By 1890, the Tonga were a harassed and beaten people hiding out in the Escarpment hills or in other slightly protected spots.

On the other hand they were away from the main slave and trade routes which brought the Portuguese and Arabs into the country. Occasionally Mambari traders passed through collecting slaves in exchange for iron hoes, but they did not attempt to strengthen local leaders or to set up their own strongholds as they did further north.

---

[1] The Tonga south of Muzoka were incorporated to some extent, and were given Lozi rulers.

P

I. INDIGENOUS ORGANIZATION

It is thus over a hundred years since the indigenous organization could operate undisturbed from foreign attack or from foreign control. The Tonga may once have had a more complex structure which perished during the period of the raids. I am not prepared therefore to argue that the system which I am now presenting was workable in the days before the European peace established a general community of law. But it is the system which the Tonga today conceive as their indigenous one and which therefore presumably conditions their response to the new system introduced by European administration. It also forms the framework of the present-day society, for it still exists, though again it adapts itself to the presence of new political institutions and new social elements fostered by European occupation.

In the indigenous system social and political structure rests on four basic elements: village, district, kin-group, and clan. The first two are local groups in which membership is largely a matter of personal choice. Kin-group and clan affiliation are determined at birth, through matrilineal inheritance,

Clan and Kin-Group

The clan (*mukowa*) is the only one of the four which includes any large number of people, or extends over any great area. Twelve clans are spread widely throughout the country: two or three more appear only in the western areas. Near the northwestern border the system of clan names changes radically, but over the rest of the country the stranger has a chance of affiliating himself to some member of any community in which he may find himself by using the common bonds of clanship. Such bonds, however, must not be strained too far. The feeling of kinship evoked by common clan membership is rather vague and is unlikely to lead to more than provision of hospitality. The only other aspect of the clan that appears today is its exogamous character. This is the aspect which the Tonga themselves stress. For the rest— the clan is a dispersed group with no corporate existence. It owns no land, has no shrines common to the entire clan, and never assembles for any purpose. Within the clan there are no recognized leaders who speak for the clan as a whole, or for any portion of it larger than the kin-group. Nor are the clans graded with respect to each other or given professional or ritual roles which they must perform in the interests of the community as a whole.

The kin-group, on the other hand, is of considerable importance. It is the group of people who share at least a fiction of common matrilineal descent, though the exact genealogical links may not be known. To it are affiliated the slaves, today the former slaves, of its members. The children of female slaves keep this affiliation and within a generation or so all distinctions between them and bona-fide members of the group disappear, save that marriage with such affiliated people is not considered a breach of exogamy though they now bear the same clan name. The Tonga commonly refer to the kin-group as *mukowa*—which is also the word for clan—but older informants in some areas say that it is more properly called *chitiba*.[1] It is this group which acts in inheritance, which owns joint property, which provides and receives bridewealth, which demands compensation for injury to its members and is held responsible for its members' actions. It is this group, and not the village, which is involved in feuds. At the present time such groups probably rarely exceed more than twenty to thirty adult members. We have no reason to assume that they were ever much larger. Internally, the group is not differentiated. That is, the children of one woman do not regard themselves as a unit in distinction to the children of their mother's sisters, and the children of sisters do not combine to form a unit in distinction to the children of their grandmother's sisters. All members of the group have equal rights within it. Therefore there is no need of exact genealogical knowledge to define one's position and rights in relation to the other members. Usually some older man is regarded as the leader of the group, but his authority depends largely on his own personality and is not institutionalized. The kin-group is thus essentially egalitarian. When

---

[1] This term literally means 'dish' or 'plate'. According to informants, it is applied to the kin-group because at the funeral of a member of the group they all gather to eat from one plate.

the leader dies the group chooses a successor from among their members, or if no suitable person is available they might even take a son of the dead man.

Such a group is not necessarily localized. The Tonga are matrilineal, but they tend to be patrilocal. The rule is that each man has the right to live where he will. In pre-European days a man tried to settle with close relatives and preferred to marry into kin-groups with which marriage ties were already established. Cross-cousin marriage was common. But if genealogies are to be believed, distant marriages and frequent shifts of residence have always been fairly common. Some children return to live with their maternal relatives; many do not. So, over a generation or so, the kin-group may become widely dispersed. A woman may marry a man who lives some distance away; her children marry into still more distant villages. Soon all memory of the original kin ties are lost. A striking feature of Tonga genealogies is the failure to remember the names of ancestors beyond the grand-parent generation. Often even these are forgotten. Kin-groups thus constantly are being reduced to small units, seldom of more than three generations depth beyond the oldest living members. Once the original kin tie is forgotten, the relationship fades into clanship. But so long as the memory of the link remains, the rights and duties involved in the kin-group do not depend on common residence. The property which is inherited through the group is largely movable property such as cattle and other goods, and not land. This was plentiful. With a growing land shortage, however, it is beginning to be regarded as property which can be inherited. This might lead eventually to a localization of the kin-group since the only right in land which can be inherited is the right to cultivate it or to place one's dwelling upon it. This right can only be vested in those who live close enough to the inheritance to undertake the cultivation. Today, therefore, land is only claimed by the kin-group if it has members who live in the immediate vicinity and who are in need of land. Otherwise it is left to the wives or children of the dead, or allowed to pass to strangers or abandoned entirely. There is still sufficient land so that a man need not cling to his kin for rights to cultivate a bit of it.

He is therefore free to wander and to establish himself in new territory or with relatives against whom he has no strictly enforceable claims.[1]

Though an individual has his primary kin affiliation through his matrilineal line, he also has an honorary life membership in his father's matrilineal group. He has a right to look to this group for assistance and protection, and they in turn have certain rights over him and his property. This twofold affiliation is recognized on all ritual occasions surrounding the life cycle of the individual—at naming, at puberty, at marriage, and at death. Both matrilineal groups contribute to the bridewealth of the men who link them, and share in the distribution of the bridewealth of the women. A man's matrilineal group will call upon his father's group to help them pay his fines or other claims which have arisen against him. Each group has claims on his property. When a man dies, his property is divided into two portions. The smaller is given to the matrilineal group of his father; the larger to his own matrilineal group. Finally, the ancestral spirits of both groups can affect the individual's welfare.

Such a share in responsibility and in interest implies an expectation of co-operation between the two groups which will end only at the final ceremony of inheritance. Since common residence in a territory soon sets up a series of intermarriages between kingroups, there is an intricate linking of the matrilineal groups represented in any neighbourhood. A general neighbourhood dispute would involve the rupture of this balance of interlocking groups. On the other hand these linkages are not permanent ones. They are dissolved at the death of the individuals who themselves form the links, while new ones come into existence with each generation.

Village and District

Village and district are made up of people whose primary allegiances are to a number of different matrilineal groups, since residence is largely a matter of personal choice. Nevertheless

---

[1] Cf. W. Allan, M. Gluckman, D. Peters, and C: G. Trapnell, *op. cit.*

village and neighbourhood loom larger in everyday life than do the dispersed kin-groups. They are the units within which ordinary co-operation in productive activities takes place, within which people live, work, and play.

At the present time a village (*muunzi*) contains about a hundred individuals and perhaps thirty huts. There are no really large villages. To the north-west and in the Escarpment country to the east fairly compact villages are common, and each village is separated from its neighbours by a stretch of country. Elsewhere the village is composed of a number of tiny clusters of huts united under a common headman, and the huts of neighbouring villages are so intermixed that it is impossible to sort out their village affiliations save by questioning. Nevertheless, even here the corporate nature of the village is recognized. It is known by the name of its headman. At most beer drinks people are seated and served according to their village affiliation. The people of a village may go in a body to attend the funerals of their neighbourhood.

Villages as such, however, do not undertake responsibility for their members. Formerly if trouble arose a stranger settled in a village might find himself handed over into slavery. Even today there is little feeling that common residence creates any bond of common responsibility. In 1947, two men from Chobana village ventured near a man to whom one owed money. An attempt was made to hold them both for payment of the debt, but the companion announced: 'We're not related. We just live in the same village.' With that he cleared off home, leaving the debtor to face the music. The same attitude is shown in the modern chief's courts. When a man has a case, he should be accompanied by members of his matrilineal group and by members of his father's group. Rarely would his headman come unless he happened to be a member of one of these two groups.

The authority of the headman, except that derived from government, is largely nominal and depends upon his personal qualities. Though most of the residents in his village have usually at least some tenuous tie of relationship to him, these ties are of a most varied pattern. His own matrilineal kin-group usually represents only a minority of the adult inhabitants. If the headman attempted to enforce his authority, he would soon find himself alone with his people departed to join other relatives or to try their luck with some stranger. In this case his village probably vanishes and he is forced to join some neighbouring village with the remnant of his followers. On the other hand, new villages are formed with almost equal ease. Any man who can persuade nine adult men to join him can found his own village and become a headman.[1] Since the village as such owns no property, the processes of dissolution and formation are simplified. In some cases a man may shift his village affiliation without shifting his huts or his fields. Part of the inhabitants of a village may decide to hive off under a new headman, and will do so, though all the time they move not a step from their previous location.

Not only do the members of a village often change their residence. Villages themselves shift as lands become exhausted, or if for some reason the area becomes uncongenial to them. Most of such shifts are within the range of a few miles, but some may take the village twenty miles or more from its old site. Thus while a village is a localized group, it is not territorially defined. Nor is it firmly integrated into a larger territorial framework. Most villages, however, do exist within a larger unit which we may call a neighbourhood. In some parts of Tonga country this merely consists of a group of villages in fairly close proximity bound loosely together by a relatively dense set of interrelationships established by intermarriages. In such cases a neighbourhood can be defined only with reference to a particular village. The next village will be within a slightly different neighbourhood. For such neighbourhoods, the Tonga seems to have no word. Elsewhere rather more organization exists, and we might be justified in speaking of a group of villages constituting a district (*chisi* or *katongo*). According to the Tonga, the first man to move into an unoccupied area to found his village is regarded as the owner of the area and the leader of those who come after him. He is known as *ulanyika* or *sikatongo*. Either term can be translated as 'owner of

---

[1] Before the days of European administration introduced the rule that each village must contain at least ten tax-payers the formation of new villages was even easier.

the country'. Those who followed him might join his village or found their own, but they recognized a tenuous alliance to the leader, and therefore to each other. The authority of the *ulanyika* was exceedingly nebulous. He was distinguished by no badge or mark of office and was treated with no special respect. Theoretically newcomers should consult him before settling near him but he had no redress save fighting if they did not. They usually did not pay him tribute in kind or in labour. He had no authority to settle their cases, nor did he have any way to enforce his judgment if they did not consult him. He was essentially a first among equals. In any event his district consisted of only a few square miles, and probably did not have any definite boundaries. In the north-west, such districts occasionally mobilized for inter-district battles. Elsewhere even such signs of cohesion are lacking.

When the *ulanyika* died, his matrilineal kin-group chose a successor—usually from among the group, but if no suitable person was available it might choose a slave, or a son, or some non-related person. When the successor died, the next heir might belong to the original kin-group, to the successor's kin-group, or to some third group. The recognized rule was that the chosen person must be someone with the ability to keep the people properly. This was the same rule which applied in the choice of a successor to the leader of the kin-group or to the headman of a village.

The Rain-Shrines

Such districts are frequently given more tangible expression in the form of a common rain cult and rain shrine.[1] The Tonga believe that certain spirits are able to intercede on their behalf to obtain rain or relief from pestilence or other general disaster which besets the whole community. These spirits are called *basangu*.[2] Shrines are built where they are invoked during the yearly ceremonies held at the beginning of the rains or in times of crisis which affect the entire community.

---

[1] See chapter III.

[2] In the north-western area they are called *baami ba imvula*, 'chiefs (or lords) of the rain'. In this area *basangu* refers to evil spirits.

A shrine may be built at the grave of the *ulanyika*, on the grounds that since he led the community during his life he is still interested in its general welfare. Here his spirit is invoked as a *basangu* and appealed to as a protector of the whole community and everyone is expected to take part in the ritual. On other occasions, his own kin-group may approach him as a *muzimo*, ancestral spirit, but in this role he had power to affect only his own kin or his own descendants—then only his own kin-group may participate in the ritual and this is never performed at the rain-shrine. Other shrines are in the hands of people whom we might call 'rain-makers' though the Tonga themselves have no special name for them. Such a person is possessed by a *basangu*, which may be that of some former member of the community or may be a foreign spirit previously unknown to the area. A few such individuals became famous and people from distant areas visited their shrines to ask for rain or for protection in times of crisis. Most shrines have only a local appeal.

During the period when the ritual was being enacted at the shrine a general community peace was imposed, and those who broke it or who failed to take part in the ritual could be punished by a fine, which went either to the shrines or to the elders of the whole community. At all times sacrilege against the shrine was a matter involving the community and was punished by the community through its elders. Thus within the context of the rain cult community you begin to find the emergence of public law in contrast to the private vengeance of the kin-groups. The custodians of the rain-shrines, whether 'rain-makers' or not, had some power over the community by virtue of their positions. They set the time for the performance of the ritual and assigned to various people their roles in the rite. Occasionally those who were possessed by *basangu* might make some pronouncement which had political implications. Ordinarily, however, their authority did not extend beyond the ritual sphere.

When the rain-maker died, the cult which he had initiated would continue. His kin-group would appoint one of its members to lead the ritual, just as at the shrine of the *ulanyika* the ritual remained in the hands of his kin-group. There was thus some integration of a rain cult community over time, though shrines and cults seem to have a high mortality. None of those which I traced seem to go back much before 1850, and many are even more recent. Since the units in Tonga society were constantly shifting, the communities symbolized by the rain-shrines were unstable. I suspect that there was a constant redrawing of community lines. New shrines came into existence which represented the new alignment better than could the old shrines, and these lost their popularity and disappeared. But so long as the shrine existed and the ritual was enacted, the district had a rallying point which served to keep the peace: for at least once a year all within the community had to co-operate in the common ritual if they wished to secure rain for their fields.

On the whole, however, the boundaries of community feeling were fluid. In a sense customary law was recognized over a larger territory than that outlined above, for a system of compensation payments was recognized and used. However, it is difficult today to learn where compensation ended and retaliation began. The Tonga say that those people who visited back and forth were likely to settle differences by compensation, but they also claim that it was against neighbouring people that you were most likely to resort to retaliation since they were within easy reach.

II. MODERN POLITICAL DEVELOPMENT

Upon this system has been imposed a superstructure created by the European administration. At the present time the Tonga are organized under the Plateau Tonga Native Authority, under the guidance of the district officers of the Mazabuka District. The territory has been divided into fourteen districts, each with its own chief, one of whom acts also as Senior Chief of the Tonga. Each chief has a Native Authority court with two assessors, a court clerk, and various court messengers. From their courts, an appeal is sent to the court of the Senior, which also functions as the local court of the Senior's own district. Or it may be sent directly to the Appeal Court which is constituted four times a year at the quarterly meetings of all Native Authorities of the area. The Native Authorities have power to make rules and orders changing native customs and instituting new customs which they think necessary for the welfare of their people. In the area is also the administrative organization of the District Officer who has his own messengers and clerks, and the right to review all court proceedings from Authority Courts. There are European police officials and their trained African police, who are not responsible to the Native Authority. There are various technical officers with their African assistants who are responsible ultimately to the heads of their departments, though to some extent they co-operate with and work through the Native Authorities. There are a number of missions, which provide most of the schools in the area and which also maintain a right to a moral supervision of their converts and attempt to interfere with the lives of the pagans.

Within the Tonga community itself, where formerly you had an egalitarian group, with almost no status differences, you now find political, religious, educational, occupational, and economic differentiation. A few Tonga have emerged as cash crop maize farmers on a large scale. They represent less than 1 per cent of the group, but another 14 per cent of the people are raising maize for the market. Some men have become hawkers, who buy eggs and chickens and bring them to the railway; others have opened tea-rooms and small trading stores. Some have become teachers, agricultural assistants or veterinary assistants, or have entered some other field of specialization. Others have gone to work as labourers on the European farms in the area, while still others work in the little settlements along the railway line. Twenty-five per cent of the able-bodied men are away as labour migrants. Even those who remain as subsistence cultivators have adopted the plough and have abandoned the old type of agriculture for a concentration on maize. Even the composition of the group is changing—men of foreign tribes have been drawn to the area by the opportunities to work on the railway line or on the European farms, and many of them marry Tonga women and settle in Tonga villages after they tire of working. On the west there is an influx of Lozi and Balovale, some of whom have set up their own villages. On the east a steady flow of immigration from the Gwembe swells the population. Down the railway line come Bemba, Lozi, Ngoni, and men from Nyasaland or Tanganyika. Men returning from Southern Rhodesia may bring with them Shona or Ndebele wives. Ndebele servants from one of the missions have founded a colony which is demanding autonomy.

This complex society has been created in approximately the last forty years. Some of the stresses and strains found here are incidental to a fairly rapid change, and could be expected in any group. Others are due to the attempt to impose an organized political structure of chieftaincies on a stateless society. Still others are due to the cleavage in interests between black and white.

The Tonga passed under European administration at the end of the nineteenth century when the Lozi signed the Barotseland Concession with the British South Africa Company. The Lozi ceded to the Company many of its tributary areas, though they stipulated that the rights of Africans to land and water supplies must not be disturbed. The legal right of the Company—and therefore ultimately of the British Crown—to administer Tonga country rests on this concession, for the Tonga were among those who paid tribute, though they were outside the limits of the Lozi kingdom. It is not a right based on conquest. The Tonga had never considered themselves a warlike group, and they seem to have accepted the announcement that they must now obey the Europeans with considerable equanimity. It is quite possible that they even conceived the presence of company officials as something which was primarily for their benefit, as an agency which protected them from the raids which had devastated their country. At least the older people will often say that they thank the Europeans for the peace they brought. One chief declared: 'There was an old trouble here, and we were very glad to see the Europeans come to help us. Before, if you had a child, it could not grow. If you had to run away before the raiders, you had to put something in its mouth so it wouldn't cry and betray you. That is the way the Europeans help us. The Europeans want only to take money from us. The Ndebele and Lozi took our cattle and killed us. Now we are becoming rich with many cattle and there are many people.' Others will say that the Government is good because it stopped the wars and now the people can have their cattle in peace.

By 1903, civil administration began. Most of the records from the early period were lost when the district office was moved about 1927, and I have been unable to discover what the administrative organization was at this period or with what it concerned itself. It did institute a system of taxation; it prohibited the local feuds which formerly had been the alternative to compensation; and it introduced the ten tax-payer rule which tended to stabilize the village. The village was then made the basis of what political organization existed. The area was toured, and village headmen were appointed. This seems to have amounted to the recognition of the most important man in the village as the responsible head. No attempt was made to interfere with his position or to set up new people in contrast to him. His authority must indeed have been strengthened by the regulations against scattering out into tiny settlements which gave him some slight power to hold his people to him. When he died, or resigned, his kin-group continued to choose a successor, who was confirmed by the District Officer as the new headman of the village. This is still the position of the headman. Gradually, however, an attempt was made to combine these headmen and their villages into larger units under chiefs. Before 1918, 116 districts under various leaders were recognized. This probably amounted to a recognition of the *ulanyika* or the ritual leader of a community, and did not run counter to the indigenous organization. But in 1918, these units were combined into twelve districts under chiefs, and Monze was regarded as having some claim to be chief of all the Tonga. When the Native Authorities Ordinance came into force in 1930, the basic political divisions were already drawn. The Administration had now only to cloak this framework with the powers authorized by the Ordinance, to institute courts with paid clerks and assessors, and later to institute the tribal treasury and the Native Authority Meetings.

Today administrative officers recognize that the Tonga had no chiefs in pre-European days; the early officials on the other hand assumed that there was a chiefly status with some territorial basis, and they went to some effort to find out who should be the proper holder of the status in a particular area. Some of the men chosen were *ulanyika*, or the descendants of *ulanyika*. Others were rain-makers or the leaders of rain cults. The successor of the most famous rain-maker was recognized as the Senior Chief. The administration assumed that such status was hereditary, not re-alizing that it had created an entirely new status. The Tonga assumed that since the kin-group had always had the rights to choose the successors to its own members, that it had the right to choose the successors to the chiefs, though this choice now in-volved a leader for an entire chieftaincy as well as for the kin-group itself. Thus small groups of matrilineal kin obtained a vested right in an office which was financed by the whole chief-taincy and which had power over all the people in the chieftaincy. It is still too early to be certain just how rigidly the group will enforce its claims, but there are indications that where formerly the kin tried to choose the best man even if they had to go outside the kin-group to find him, they now feel that the inheritance of chiefly status must remain strictly within the group itself. In 1947, the District Officer proposed to the assembled Native Authorities that in the future succession to the office should be by a modified form of election to ensure that the best man became chief. The chiefs vetoed the proposal on the grounds that the kin-group would lose its rights. Thus real authority attached to a status position with territorial jurisdiction is vested in a small kin-group. This group, because of its control of an office, is differenti-ated from the multitude of other kin-groups in the community with which it was formerly equal. Members of chiefly kin-groups have not consolidated themselves into a distinct class as yet, though it is possible that they may do so. So long as legislative powers remain in the hands of the chiefs, who are also representa-tives of their kin-groups, the method of succession is unlikely to change.

The rest of the Tonga view their chiefs not as hereditary repre-sentatives of their community but as government appointments. They often call them 'government chiefs'. They treat such men with no particular reverence. One chief with a few followers moved away from his main village because his people beat him up whenever he was drunk. The chiefs are supposed to control movements between villages, but they are not able to control even their own kin-groups. In 1947 when one chief was absent at the Native Authority Meeting, some of his immediate kin hurried their goods on to sledges and moved off to a site about a mile from his village. The chief had refused them permission to move, so they ran away when they knew he would be gone for several days. Even where the chief can enrol the support of his own kin-group, this is a numerically insignificant element in his district. To some extent he tries to gain popular support by spending his salary or using his crops to feed or give gifts to his people. His peers under the old system, the *ulanyika* or ritual leaders, are not recognized by government in any way at the present time. In one district, however, the chief is said to hand over to them a portion of his salary in an attempt to enlist their backing. Despite these measures, I know of only one chief who is really popular with his people, and this may be due to the fact that his district is so small that he can keep in personal touch with all his people, and so in a sense is only a glorified *ulanyika*.

To consolidate their positions, the chiefs then turn to other devices. Some send tribute to the Lozi to try to establish a claim as having been tribute collectors and therefore community leaders in the pre-European days. They emphasize the importance of the rain cults in the control of their kin-groups, and ignore the other rain-shrines and cults in their districts. The Senior Chief even refuses to admit that there are any rain-shrines except that of the Monze in the whole of Tonga country. But mainly, chiefs and counsellors emphasize their position to the people as representatives of government. This is stressed again and again. In 1947, the District Officer sent a request for carriers to the Senior Chief. A counsellor and several court messengers accompanied the Boma messengers to find men. One headman who had been told to assemble his people was not able to round them up. The whole village was ordered into court, where the counsellor lectured them: 'Here at the court we do the work of the government. We get the law of the government. So we don't want you to fight us and refuse to listen if we come to your villages. That is our work. If you fight with us, you don't fight only with us. You are fighting the government. We must follow only the law of the government. Long ago we ourselves had no court like this or books. We belong to the government and we had better understand its laws. Now I can't be afraid to come by myself to your village, for since I have joined the work of the government I am the government. If you fight me, you fight the government.' He made no appeal to any loyalty to chief or court, nor any suggestion that their dignity and rights were offended. In the discussion, the village headman commented: 'I always try my best when I hear the law. I myself wonder at my people. I told them: "If you do like this, you will be wrong to the government, for I am the headman of the government and I get the law from the government." ' Then men of the village agreed wholeheartedly and probably quite hypocritically that they had misunderstood the instructions and that 'We can't fight the word of the government at all.'

The chiefs and courts need this government backing, and make no mistake in emphasizing it. It is said that the people of one chieftaincy are so incensed when the court gives a judgment against them that they refuse to give chief or other court officials food or water if they chance to come through the village. Clerks and counsellors say they are liable to be cursed when they meet men who have lost cases. Court messengers are threatened with beatings when they go out to issue summons. At one of the more popular courts, they chose a new messenger who, at best could be called only a drunkard, always in trouble of some sort or another, but the court philosophized that at least he was not afraid to go out to call men to the court. Since this is so, perhaps the courts and chiefs are wise to shift responsibility to government, especially when it comes to new rules or modifications of old customs. In some cases the attitude is that if government gives them an order they will be happy to pass it on, but they refuse to take the responsibility on their own authority. When the government got a grant to supply the schools with work oxen, the agricultural officers had great difficulty in buying oxen though the area is overstocked. In one chieftaincy the people openly said that they would not sell their stock unless ordered to do so by the Native Authority. The Native Authority promptly said they would not issue such an order unless told to do so by the District Officer.

Even where the Native Authorities have taken initiative, they still stress their position as government agents. In months of listening to chief's courts, I never heard a reference made to Native Authority orders. The courts always refer to them as government rules imposed from the District Office, though theoretically at least such rules are the legislation of the Authorities themselves. At a court case referred to the Authority by the District Officer, one of the counsellors boasted: 'We have real power here! This case was sent to us by the D.O. and not by another chief.'

Obviously such reliance on the authority of the administration involves an admission that their own powers are distinctly limited. The chiefs and counsellors realize only too clearly that they sit in danger of suspension or removal if they go counter to government instructions. When a man demands a large compensation, they may even produce the court record book and show him where the D.O. has commented that the fines and compensations allowed are too large and must be brought down. Sometimes a case provokes them to considerable indignation, and they may declare that they want to give the man a large fine and would do so if only they did not fear that he would run to the District Office and the District Officer would send to say: 'I think you are tired of being a chief and that is why you gave this man such a heavy charge.' The chiefs may even use this insecurity of tenure against each other. At least one went riding off in great wrath accompanied by his clerk and counsellors to threaten a neighbouring chief, who had decided a case in favour of his own nephew, with the wrath of the District Officer and possible dismissal from office. In a sense, the District Officer sits in every court, influencing its judgments.

By what I have said above, I do not mean to imply that the Tonga completely disregard their Native Authorities or that they do not use their courts. With the outlawing of feud and self-help some other method of settling disputes became necessary. The courts handle a large number of cases and are constantly extending

Q

their influence. A good many cases are still settled outside the court, through the discussion among the elders of the kin-groups involved, or are taken for arbitration to other old people in the community, or to the headman. The court officials themselves sit on many cases outside the court. But cases of all types, including those for witchcraft, find their way into the regular court, and the courts regard it as part of their duty to educate people in more regular procedures for settling their cases. They urge their people to come to the court on any matter where the transfer of property is involved so that a proper record can be made. To some of the Native Authorities the possession of a popular court has become an established goal, and they conceive of themselves as an agency for re-establishing community peace as well as an agency for educating people in the new legal rules.

It is difficult to say how far they attain their goal, and some courts, of course, make no such efforts. It is not an easy matter to be court officials in an area where the court system is just being established, where many cases arise from new types of economic and social relationships, for which there are as yet no established rules, and where even those cases arising from an indigenous background may be without established precedent. One counsellor suggested to me that government should set up a regular course for counsellors where they could learn how to decide cases and not have to depend entirely on their own judgments. In some courts, an attempt is made to get community backing for decisions by inviting the headmen to sit with the counsellors and to advise on judgments. The headmen usually refuse. One counsellor complained that if they settled a case one way, the headmen sneered at them for attempting to follow European law, if they took the headmen's decision, then they were questioned and reprimanded by the D.O. My own impression is that the headmen see no reason to take responsibility for court decisions. When one was asked for his opinion on one case, he complained indignantly: 'Why ask me about his case? Next time we drink beer together he'll start a fight with me about this.'

The people in their turn are not convinced that the court is the final authority. They frequently attempt to by-pass their own authorities and appeal directly to the district officials. Many Tonga take their cases directly to the District Office, only to have them referred back to the local court for hearing. Others first take their cases to the local authorities but meet any adverse decision with a demand that they be sent to the District Officer. Any Tonga may do this, but it is true especially of the new class of wealthy farmers. This is a natural development since these men in any event are more likely to be concerned with problems arising from their new economic interest than they are with matters arising from native custom.

The authority of the local courts is also questioned in other ways. Some men will accept judgment in the court itself and refuse to pay once they have returned home. Others refuse to accept judgment and drag their cases from court to court, hoping always for a favourable verdict. Legally appeal is allowed from a sub-court to the superior court of the Senior Chief and thence to the Appeal Court, and at any stage to the District Officer. It is also possible to send an appeal directly from sub-court to the Appeal Court. The Tonga are much more eclectic. Any hierarchy of justice, or jurisdiction, is foreign to their own ungraded social system. They fail to grasp—or at least to respect—that laid down for them by the Government. A case may start in the Senior's court, pass to a sub-court, then to another sub-court, then to the District Officer, then to another sub-court, then to the Appeal Court, and finally appear in still another sub-court. Or a case may first be brought to a sub-court of a chieftaincy in which neither party to the case is resident and which therefore has no legal jurisdiction in the matter. The result is that in practice court jurisdiction is not on a truly territorial basis, and the personal appeal of the various Native Authorities affect their range of jurisdiction more truly than does their official status within the judicial hierarchy.[1]

---

[1] While the District Officer reviews all court cases the records are rarely sufficiently complete to enable him to discover that a particular case has in fact been judged previously in another court and that therefore the new judgment is illegal. Where he is aware of the facts, he would set aside the new judgment and reprimand the court for rehearing the case.

This failure of the Tonga—and of their courts—to accept the principle of jurisdiction sets the officials of the different sub-courts in active competition with each other and hinders the development of an *esprit de corps* or of a respect for the judicial status as such. It is not uncommon for the Native Authorities to sneer publicly at the judgments and procedures of another chief's court. There is thus a cleavage of interests between the authorities in the different chieftaincies.

Another cleavage within the ranks of the Native Authorities—which is not bridged by any system of traditional loyalty—is that between clerks and other officials. The clerks, since they must be literate, represent the younger and more educated element in the community. The chiefs are almost all old men with little or no education; counsellors are likely to represent a similar group. According to district officials the clerks regard themselves as checks upon the arbitrary powers of chiefs and counsellors and as champions of the educated element. While theoretically they have no power to influence decisions, they may dictate the policy of the court by refusing to write down judgments of which they do not approve. I have heard a clerk inform a chief: 'You have given a decision, but now tell me just what charge are we to say was involved?' There may even be open antagonism between chief and clerk. This is reflected in the attitude of the district officials who have more contact with the clerks than with other members of the Authority. Clerks are more often called in for interviews; since they speak some English, they are often the only members of the Authority with whom district officials can talk. The antagonism of the clerks is therefore passed on to district officials, who regard the chiefs as inefficient, prejudiced, and narrow-minded.

This judgment is not likely to be reversed at Native Authority Meetings, where the district officials are in a hurry to present a programme and be gone. Attempts by the chiefs to speak are hurriedly interrupted with the statement that there is no real time for discussion. My impression is that a matter is usually put to a decision long before the Authorities have had a chance to understand it. The district is a large one, complicated by European settlers and Indian traders. The district officials are overburdened to a point where even if they desire more intimate contact with the people they cannot find time or energy to make the effort. Almost no touring is done. Moreover this district has had an unusually high turn-over of district officials. Under such conditions mutual confidence on a personal basis is quite impossible. This leaves the Native Authorities in a peculiarly vulnerable position, faced as they are with the contempt of those from whom they derive their authority.

But fully to understand their position, we must turn again to the events of the last forty years. We have seen that European administration was welcomed as a deliverance from Lozi and Ndebele raids. Soon after administration began, however, the area began to be opened up economically by other Europeans. By 1906 the railway had been driven through the heart of Tonga country. In its wake came European traders and farmers. At first farmers were allowed to take up land where they would. Later on a broad belt on either side of the rail was set aside for European occupation. As the Europeans took up land, the Tonga were ordered off. Later on, all those living in the area demarcated for European occupation were ordered off, whether these lands had been taken up or not. Today you have the picture of Tonga living on overcrowded reserves, bordering on large tracts of completely unoccupied land with good soil. The Tonga constantly move back on to this land, only to be found and ordered off again. At every meeting of the Authorities the District Officer must lecture the chiefs on this subject and order them to control their people. The Tonga attitude to the administration is now largely coloured by this land policy, and by the existence of a differential price for maize which discriminates against the African. The old people still remember that the administration brought peace; but this is not an attitude which will outlast this generation, while the bitterness over land may well increase as the reserves become more and more overcrowded.

At one meeting, the agricultural officers presented a new land policy to the Authorities. The response was: 'We are very thankful that you have given us this law, but we want to say first that we know that before we were troubled by Lozi and Ndebele. Today we are all right with many cattle and many children. But now we can say that you Europeans are becoming like our enemies the Lozi and Ndebele. For today the Europeans come and when they find the people in their villages they say: "Now you must go away because I am going to put my farm here." We can see that the European comes with only a pair of shorts and a shirt, and then when he starts to work his farm he becomes rich. So we say: "These Europeans are becoming rich on our land. They have taken all of our land for themselves." So we say: "How can the Europeans help us now? Always they trouble us. Now they are becoming like our enemies." ' This attitude exists though there are friendly relations betwen some farmers and some Africans. Some of the big African growers have got their start through assistance from European neighbours, and they admit this' and are grateful. But this does not prevent a general suspicion towards the motives of the Europeans. And the administration is now identified as the champion of European interests against the African.

The Native Authorities are thus today caught between their dependence upon the administration and the necessity to stand against the administration if they are to develop into popular representatives. Moreover, they themselves as Tonga share the sentiments of their people. It is not surprising that though they are expected to be spearheads in a programme of improvement, they find it difficult to feel real enthusiasm for it. In 1947, government wished to start a programme of improved stock by distributing breeding bulls and informed the Authorities that the stock would be given to them. The chiefs said: 'We want these bulls, but we don't want you to give them to us. We want to buy them. If you give them to us, soon you will say: "The government provided the bull so all the cattle in the country belongs to the government." Then you will take all our cattle.' An agricultural officer was ready to build a dam in an area which suffers from yearly water shortages so severe that the cattle must go long distances to water. The chief was eager for the dam and sent out word to his people that men should turn up for work, which was to be paid for, incidentally. Only a few appeared. The officer threatened to put the dam elsewhere unless the people wanted it enough to work for it, and the chief excitedly swore to get the men. A few days later, he not only refused to get the men but said that neither he nor his people wanted this dam or any dam to be built. The agricultural officer said this had happened so often before he knew what was behind it—the people had decided that if the dam was built and the area improved the government would take it for European settlement.

The Authority is thus Janus-faced. To the Administration it must try to prove itself as composed of men with traditional authority and popular support, and thus it must voice the suspicions of the community. To the people it must represent itself as cloaked with the authority of the government. Yet surprisingly enough, one can say that Tonga political organization does work —partly because it rests on the ultimate sanction of administrative backing, partly because the indigenous structure still bears much of the brunt of the regulation of social life. The courts, the one aspect of the new political system which has the most popular acceptance, fill a need left by the falling away of the old sanction of the feud. The political organization has to work, for in the nature of things the Administration cannot supervise it closely. This does not mean that the administration can be accused of deliberate negligence. It does not need to keep minute check on activities within every village or every court. Channels of complaint are open and the people are aware of them. The Tonga are thus protected, if they wish, against gross invasion of their rights by their own officials or by their fellow Tonga. But it is not a situation likely to heal the breach opened between Tonga and administration by the land policy, nor is it likely to lead to a rapid education of Native Authorities or other Tonga in new political or economic developments. The district officials and the Tonga farmers are attacking the matrilineal principles underlying the kin-group; there are suggestions that the village be replaced by a parish system; the ritual integrity of rain cult communities is attacked by missions and school people. If these succeed and the indigenous structure is overthrown before the new political structure has gained popular support, the Native Authority and the Administration, which attempts to work through it, may have an exceedingly difficult time.

BIBLIOGRAPHY

ALLAN, W., GLUCKMAN, M., PETERS, D. U., and TRAPNELL, C. G., 1948. *Land Holding and Land Usage among the Plateau Tonga of Mazabuka District*, Rhodes-Livingstone Paper, No. 14. (*The Tonga Report.*)

CASSET, A., 1918. *St. Mary's Out Station, Chikuni, Zambezi Mission Record*, 6 (No. 82), pp. 101-4.

COLSON, E., 1949. *Life Among the Cattle-Owning Plateau Tonga*, Livingstone, Rhodes-Livingstone Museum.

— 1950. 'Possible Repercussions of the Right to Make Wills upon the Plateau Tonga of Northern Rhodesia', *Journal of African Administration*, 2, pp. 24-34.

— 1951. 'The Plateau Tonga of Northern Rhodesia', in E. COLSON and M. GLUCKMAN (editors), *Seven Tribes of British Central Africa*, London, Oxford University Press, for the Rhodes-Livingstone Institute. Second edition, Manchester University Press, 1960.

DOKE, C. M., 1945. *Bantu Modern Grammatical, Phonetical and Lexicographical Studies since 1860*, London, Percy Lund, Humphries & Co. Ltd., for the International African Institute.

DOKE, E. M., 1931. *The Lambas of Northern Rhodesia*, London, Harrap.

FORTES, M., 1945. *The Dynamics of Clanship*, London, Oxford University Press.

GLUCKMAN, M., MITCHELL, J. C., and BARNES, J. A., 1949. 'The Village Headman in British Central Africa', *Africa*, Vol. 19.

HOLE, H. MARSHALL, 1905. 'Notes on the Batonga and Batshukulumbwi Tribes', *Proceedings of the Rhodesia Scientific Association*, v., part II.

HOPGOOD, C. R., 1950. 'Conceptions of God among the Tonga of Northern Rhodesia', in E. W. SMITH (editor), *African Ideas of God*, pp. 61-7, London, Edinburgh House Press.

McCULLOCH, M., 1951. *The Southern Lunda and Related Peoples*, London, International African Institute.

MELLAND, F. H., 1923. *In Witch-Bound Africa*, London, Seeley, Service & Co.

MYERS, J. L., 1927. *Religious Survey of the Batonga*. Proceedings of the General Missionary Conference of Northern Rhodesia.

PERISTIANY, J. G., 1939. *The Social Institutions of the Kipsigis*, London, G. Routledge & Sons.

RADCLIFFE-BROWN, A. R., 1940. 'On Joking Relationships', *Africa*, Vol. XIII, pp. 195-210.

— 1949. 'A Further Note on Joking Relationships', *Africa*, Vol. XIX, pp. 133-40.

— 1952. *Structure and Function in Primitive Society* (Chapter VIII, originally delivered as the Henry Myers Lecture, 1945), London, Cohen & West.

READ, J. GORDON, 1935. *Report on Famine Relief: Gwembe*, 1931-32, Livingstone. Government Printer.

RICHARDS, A. I., 1934. 'Mother-Right among the Central Bantu', in E. E. EVANS-PRITCHARD, R. FIRTH, B. MALINOWSKI, and I. SCHAPERA (editors), *Essays Presented to C. G. Seligman*, London, Kegan Paul.

— 1939. *Land, Labour and Diet in Northern Rhodesia*, London, Oxford University Press, for the International African Institute.

— 1947. 'Reciprocal Clan Relationships among the Bemba of N.E. Rhodesia', *Man*, Vol. XXXVII, pp. 188–93.

SCHAPERA, I., 1937 (editor). *The Bantu-speaking Tribes of South Africa*, London, Routledge & Kegan Paul.

SMITH, E. W., and DALE, A. M., 1920. *The Ila-Speaking Peoples of Northern Rhodesia*, London, Macmillan & Co.

STEFANISZYN, B., 1950. 'Funeral Friendship in Central Africa', *Africa*, Vol. XXII, pp. 296–306.

TEW, MARY, 1951. 'A Further Note on Funeral Friendship', *Africa*, Vol. XXIII, pp. 122–4.

TONGA REPORT. See ALLAN, W., 1948.

TORREND, J., 1931. *An English-Vernacular Dictionary of the Bantu-Botatwe Dialects of Northern Rhodesia*, London, Kegan Paul.

The chapters in this book first appeared as articles in the following Journals:

Chapter

INDEX

Administration, British, 119, 124, 127, 180, 218, 220–1, 229–30
Administration, District, 96,180, 219, 223, 225, 226, 227, 228, 229, 231
Affines, duties of, 77, 80, 115, 117, 118
Agriculture Department, 125, 228–9, 230–1
Ancestral spirits, 1–65, 217; and offerings, 2–3, 4, 6, 14, 15, 17, 40, 43, 46, 48, 50, 51, 52, 53, 55, 56, 57, 62, 92–3, 109; as causal explanations, 3–5, 11, 45; nature of, 4–8, 39, 41; origin of, 5–6, 9, 14–16, 58–61; and kinship, 7, 47, 50, 179, 213; and matrilineal groups, 7–28, 41–3, 59, 86, 109; classification of, 8–20; and names, 7, 9 11, 15, 19, 54; inheritance of, 9, 15, 16–19, 31, 35–7, 43, 62; anger of, 11, 17, 40–43, 45, 54, 63, 64, 109; and crafts, 13; influence on character, 11–13; as house guardians, 17, 49–50, 53, 54–5; and polygyny, 51–2

Basangu, 4, 47, 90, 92–5, 97, 100, 113, 216–17
Beer, ritual significance, 48, 50, 52, 58, 96, 169, 192, 217
Bridewealth, 11, 21, 28, 31, 34, 41–2, 43, 48–9, 57, 59, 61, 82, 106, 108, 109, 130, 136, 142
Bujwanyina, see under joking relationships

Cattle, 122–71; number of, 122, 132; breeding, 123–4, 230; ownership of, 124–32, 170, 200; acquisition of, 129–31; use of, 139–43, 170; slaughter of, 142–3, 146; desire for, 143–4, 220–1; in agriculture, 143–144; in transport, 144; sale of, 145–147; as investment, 146–7; marketing of, 149; and herdboys, 162–4; taboos on, 167; and damage to fields, 167–8; and European farms, 168; and ritual, 169
Cattle Loans, 110–11, 131, 132–41, 170

Celo, see under Ghosts
Chiefs, 92, 99–100, 111, 149, 206, 221–225, 228; and dependence on Administration, 223–5, 230–1
Chieftaincy, 1, 21, 67, 218–19, 221, 222
Christianity, 35
Ciliyango, see under Shrines
Clan-Joking, see under Joking-relationships
Clans, 11, 24, 55, 57, 68–83, 85, 106, 111, 210–11; nature of, 68; function of, 68–9; origin of, 68; and intertribal relationships, 69; and exogamy, 70; names of, 70–1; association with animals, 70–1; in address, 71; reciprocal duties between, 77 ff; and joking, 72–83
Clerks, role in Native Authority, 228
Clients, 134, 135
Compensation, for injury, 108, 109, 114, 116, 118, 124–5, 142, 167, 198, 199, 200, 211, 218, 221
Courts, 42, 111, 118, 126, 127, 128, 200, 207, 208, 214, 218, 221, 224, 225–8, 230
Curing Dances, 4

Death, cause of, 54, 63–4, 109, 119
Disputes, 43, 63, 81, 87–90, 158, 169, 191–200, 204; settlement of, 103, 104, 111–20, 223, 225
District Office, see under Administration, District
Divination, 3, 10, 11, 15, 17, 40, 44, 45, 49, 51, 55, 61, 63, 64, 92, 119, 120
Dreams, 10

Europeans, relations with, 229–30

Famines, 81
Fields, see under Land
Folk-tales, 75–7
Foreigners, incorporation of, 69, 219–220
Funeral Friendships, 66, 83
Funerals, see under Rituals

235